365

Days of Faith and Devotional for Black Women

A Year of Strength, and Spiritual Growth, and Empowerment

© Tiffany Barker

Thank you message

Thank you for choosing this devotional and allowing it to be part of your journ ey. I wrote this with you in mind—knowing how much faith, strength, and grace you carry every day. It's a privilege to walk with you for the next 365 days, and I pray that each devotion speaks to your heart and strengthens your spirit. You are powerful, resilient, and loved, and my hope is that these pages will remind you of that on your toughest days and celebrate it on your best. From my heart to yours, thank you for letting me be a part of your walk with God.

Table of Contents

Introduction

Welcome Message

Every day is a new beginning, and this devotional is a place where you can find the strength to rise, no matter what life throws your way. Imagine starting each day with a sense of peace and purpose, knowing that you're not alone on this journey. This devotional is here to guide you, uplift you, and remind you of the incredible power that lies within you as a Black woman.

Life can be tough. Sometimes, the weight of expectations, responsibilities, and challenges can feel overwhelming. But you, my sister, are resilient. You carry within you the wisdom of generations, the courage of those who came before you, and the unshakable faith that keeps you grounded, even when the storms of life rage on. This book is crafted with you in mind, understanding the unique experiences and struggles you face. It's a companion for the days when you need a reminder of your worth, your strength, and your beauty.

This devotional isn't just about reading; it's about connecting—connecting with yourself, with your faith, and with the powerful community of women who share your journey. Each day, you'll find a scripture that speaks directly to your heart, a reflection that relates to your life, and a Prayerto carry you through the day. These words are here to lift you up, to remind you that you are seen, you are loved, and you are enough.

As you go through these pages, you'll embark on a journey of self-discovery and spiritual growth. You'll uncover truths about yourself that maybe you've forgotten, or perhaps never fully realized. You'll be encouraged to embrace your flaws, celebrate your successes, and find joy in the everyday moments that make up your life.

This year, let this devotional be a safe space for you. A place where you can come as you are, without judgment, and find solace in the words that echo the deepest parts of your soul. Whether you're seeking guidance through tough times, or simply looking to strengthen your relationship with God, this book is here to walk alongside you.

You'll find that each day's message is crafted to speak to your heart and soul. Some days, it may challenge you to see things differently or to take a step out in faith. Other days, it will offer comfort and a sense of peace, reminding you that it's okay to rest and just be. Each reflection is a small reminder that you are loved unconditionally, and that your life is a testimony to God's grace and goodness.

Remember, this is your journey. There's no rush, no pressure to be perfect. You may have days where you feel on top of the world, and others where getting out of bed feels like a victory. This devotional is here for all of those moments. It's here to encourage you, to be a source of strength, and to remind you of the beautiful truth that you are never alone.

So, as you open this book each day, know that these words are written with you in mind. You are the reason this devotional exists. Your story, your struggles, and your triumphs are woven into every page. Let this be the year where you fully embrace who you are and step boldly into the purpose God has for your life.

Your journey starts here, in these pages, where faith meets everyday life, and where you are invited to grow in grace, love, and strength. This is your time. This is your year. Let's walk this path together, one day at a time.

How To Use This Devotional

Start by finding a quiet moment each day that you can dedicate to yourself and your spiritual growth. It could be first thing in the morning, setting the tone for the day ahead, or perhaps in the evening when you can reflect on the day's events. Choose a time that works best for you, a time when you can be present, without distractions, and truly engage with the words on the page.

As you begin your daily reading, take a deep breath and allow yourself to settle into the moment. Open your heart and mind to the message that awaits you. Remember, this time is just for you—to reconnect with your faith, recharge your spirit, and refocus your thoughts.

Each day, you'll find a scripture that is thoughtfully chosen to speak directly to your experience as a Black woman. Start by reading this scripture slowly, letting each word resonate with you. Consider writing it down or repeating it out loud, allowing it to sink into your heart.

Next, move on to the reflection. These reflections are written to relate to your daily life, addressing the joys and challenges you may face. As you read, think about how the message applies to your current situation. Don't rush through it—take your time to digest the words and let them speak to your soul.

After reflecting on the message, you'll find a prayer. Use this Prayer as a way to connect with God, to seek guidance, and to express your thoughts and feelings. Prayer is a powerful tool for aligning your heart with God's will, and this is your opportunity to pour out your heart in sincerity and faith.

You may also find it helpful to incorporate the daily Affirmation into your routine. These affirmations are designed to empower you, reminding you of your strength, worth, and divine purpose. Speak them over yourself with conviction, and carry their truth with you throughout the day.

If you have a few extra minutes, consider journaling your thoughts. Reflect on what the day's reading has stirred in you. What insights did you gain? What challenges or encouragements did the message bring to light? Writing down your reflections can help solidify the lessons and allow you to track your growth over time.

Consistency is key. Try to make this devotional a non-negotiable part of your day, even if it's just for a few minutes. Over time, these small daily investments will build up, leading to significant spiritual growth and a deeper connection with God.

Remember, this devotional is a journey. There may be days when the words speak directly to your situation, and others when the message takes time to fully reveal its relevance. Trust the process and allow each day's reading to meet you whee you are.

Finally, don't be hard on yourself if you miss a day or two. Life happens, and this devotional is meant to be a source of grace, not guilt. Simply pick up where you left off, and continue moving forward.

This devotional is more than just a book; it's a companion on your spiritual journey. By making it a daily habit, you'll find that it becomes a cherished part of your routine, guiding you, uplifting you, and helping you grow into the empowered woman God created you to be.

Acknowledgment

When I set out to create this devotional, I knew it would be a journey of faith, love, and dedication. But I didn't walk this path alone. There are so many hearts and hands that have contributed to the creation of this book, and I am deeply grateful to each one.

First and foremost, I want to thank God, whose grace and guidance have been the foundation of this entire project. Without His wisdom and love, this devotional would not exist. Every word written, every Prayerspoken, and every reflection shared has been inspired by His unending love and faithfulness.

To my family, your unwavering support and encouragement have been my greatest strength. You believed in this vision from the start, and your prayers, love, and understanding have carried me through every step of this journey. Thank you for being my rock, my inspiration, and my constant source of joy.

To the countless Black women whose lives and stories have inspired this devotional, this book is for you. Your resilience, courage, and unwavering faith have been the heartbeat of these pages. Thank you for sharing your experiences, your struggles, and your victories. Your stories are a testament to the strength and beauty that resides in every Black woman, and it is an honor to uplift and celebrate you through this devotional.

A special thank you to my friends and mentors who offered their wisdom, insight, and feedback throughout the writing process. Your honest words and loving guidance helped shape this book into something truly special. You pushed me to dig deeper, to write with authenticity, and to create something that would genuinely touch the hearts of others. I am forever grateful for your input and your belief in this project.

To the church community that has been a home and a haven, thank you for your prayers and encouragement. Your fellowship and faith have been a source of inspiration, reminding me of the power of community and the strength we find in one another.

And finally, to every reader who picks up this devotional, thank you for trusting me to be a part of your spiritual journey. I pray that these pages bring you comfort, strength, and renewal. May you find in these words the encouragement you need to continue walking in faith, knowing that you are never alone.

This book is a labor of love, created with the hope that it will uplift, inspire, and empower Black women everywhere. It is my deepest Prayerthat through these daily readings, you will grow closer to God, discover the depth of your strength, and walk boldly in the purpose He has for your life.

Thank you, from the bottom of my heart, for being a part of this journey.

January
New Beginnings and Purpose

January 1
A Fresh Start: Embracing New Beginnings

"Therefore, if anyone is in Christ, the new creation has come: The old has gone, the new is here!" (2 Corinthians 5:17, NIV)

Devotional Reflection

As the new year begins, we reflect on the past and look ahead with hope. Today's scripture reminds us that in Christ, we are made new. No matter what happened in the past, today marks a fresh start. Imagine a blank canvas, ready for new experiences and growth. God offers you this, especially at the start of a new year. It's a chance to leave behind regrets and mistakes. Embrace this new beginning with faith, trusting that God is doing something new in your life.

Starting fresh doesn't mean forgetting the past but refusing to let it define your future. Through Christ, you are not bound by past failures. God's mercies are new each day, and He is eager to help you grow and become who He created you to be.

As you step into this new season, consider where God is calling you to change or grow. Trust in His timing and plan for your life. There may be challenges, but with God by your side, you can overcome anything.

Today is your fresh start. Embrace it with hope and faith, ready to receive God's blessings this year.

Prayer

Heavenly Father, guide me in this new year. Help me embrace Your plans and grow in faith. In Jesus' name, Amen.

Affirmation

I am a new creation in Christ. I embrace this new beginning with faith and trust in God's plan for my life. Today, I choose to walk in purpose, strength, and renewal.

January 2
The Power of Setting Intentions

"Commit to the Lord whatever you do, and He will establish your plans." (Proverbs 16:3, NIV)

Devotional Reflection

Setting intentions shapes your life. It's not just wishing; it's committing your energy and efforts toward a goal. As scripture reminds us, our intentions should align with God's will.

Think about the difference between drifting and living with purpose. Drifting takes you wherever the current leads, but living with purpose sets a clear course. Intentions anchor you, even when life pushes you off track.

As you begin this year, reflect on the power of intentions aligned with God's plan. What changes do you want to see? How do these intentions reflect your purpose? When you commit them to God, He will guide your steps.

Intentions go deeper than fleeting resolutions. They're rooted in spiritual growth. Be mindful and deliberate, making choices that reflect who God has called you to be. Wake up each day focused, trusting that your actions lead you toward His purpose.

Take time to reflect on your intentions, pray over them, and let them be a reflection of your faith. God will establish your plans.

Prayer

Lord, thank You for a new day. Guide my steps and align my intentions with Your will. Strengthen me to pursue my goals in faith. Amen.

Affirmation

I commit my intentions to the Lord, trusting that He will establish my plans and guide me in the path of purpose and fulfillment.

January 3

God's Purpose for Your Life

"For I know the plans I have for you," declares the Lord, "plans to prosper you and not to harm you, plans to give you hope and a future."

(Jeremiah 29:11, NIV)

Devotional Reflection

One comforting truth in our journey is knowing that God has a purpose for each of us. Jeremiah 29:11 reminds us that God's plans are filled with hope and a future.

God's purpose is a journey, not a destination. It's about trusting that God is guiding you, even when the road is unclear. Life's challenges may leave you wondering, but God's plan is woven into your daily life, passions, and gifts.

God's purpose isn't just about grand achievements; it's about living with intention and faith. It's in acts of kindness, encouragement, and moments of prayer. Each part of your life plays a role in His plan.

The challenge is discerning this purpose amidst distractions. Staying connected to God through Prayerand scripture reveals His unfolding plan. His purpose evolves as you grow, but it is always rooted in His love for you to flourish.

Take comfort today in knowing God has a purpose for you, filled with hope and love. Trust His plans, even when you can't see the full picture. He's working all things for your good.

Prayer

Father, thank You for Your plans for me. Help me trust Your purpose, guide my steps, and strengthen my faith. In Jesus' name, Amen.

Affirmation

I trust in God's purpose for my life. His plans for me are filled with hope, love, and a future. Today, I walk in faith, knowing that God is guiding my every step.

January 4
Renewing Your Mind for a New Season

"Do not conform to the pattern of this world, but be transformed by the renewing of your mind. Then you will be able to test and approve what God's will is—His good, pleasing, and perfect will."

(Romans 12:2, NIV)

Devotional Reflection

Renewing your mind is key to stepping into a new season with clarity and purpose. Romans 12:2 reminds us that transformation begins in the mind. The thoughts, beliefs, and attitudes we hold shape our reality. To embrace this new season, let go of old patterns and align your mindset with God's truth.

The world pressures us to conform, but as a woman of faith, your call is to rise above. This transformation is daily—letting go of negative thoughts and filling your mind with God's love, promises, and wisdom.

Be intentional about what you feed your mind. Are you nourishing it with God's Word or letting the world dictate your thinking? Focus on His faithfulness, and your faith will flourish.

This season of renewal also means surrounding yourself with positivity and people who encourage you in your walk with God. Meditate on scripture, speak affirmations, and pray for a mind renewed by His Spirit.

Let go of past mistakes and regrets. God's mercy is new each day, offering a fresh start. Commit to renewing your mind daily, and God will reveal His will, guiding you step by step.

Prayer

Lord, thank You for a new season. Help me focus on Your truth, transform my mind, and guide my thoughts in Your love, wisdom, and peace. Amen.

Affirmation

Today, I renew my mind with God's Word. I release all negative thoughts and embrace a mindset of faith, love, and purpose.

January 5

Letting Go of the Past

"Forget the former things; do not dwell on the past. See, I am doing a new thing! Now it springs up; do you not perceive it? I am making a way in the wilderness and streams in the wasteland."

(Isaiah 43:18-19, NIV)

Devotional Reflection

Letting go of the past is one of the most challenging yet liberating things you can do for yourself. The Bible encourages us not to dwell on former things, but to open our eyes to the new work that God is doing in our lives. Holding onto past mistakes, regrets, or hurts can hinder the new blessings that God wants to bring into your life. By clinging to the past, you might miss out on the opportunities for growth, healing, and renewal that God is offering you in this season.

The past can be a heavy burden, weighing you down with guilt, shame, or sorrow. But God's message through Isaiah is clear: He is doing a new thing in your life. This new thing is full of hope, purpose, and promise. To fully embrace this new season, you must be willing to release the past and trust in God's plan for your future.

As you let go, imagine God making a way for you through the wilderness, creating streams in the wasteland of your past. These streams represent the new life, joy, and possibilities that await you. Trust that God's plan for you is good and that He is leading you into a future filled with hope and abundance. Embrace the new thing God is doing, and allow yourself to move forward with confidence and faith.

Prayer

Dear Lord, help me to let go of the past and embrace the new things You are doing in my life. Give me the strength to trust in Your plan and to walk forward in faith, knowing that You are making a way for me. In Jesus' name, Amen.

Affirmation

I release the past and embrace the new life that God is creating for me. I trust in His plan and move forward with hope and confidence.

January 6
Trusting God's Plan for Your Life

"For I know the plans I have for you," declares the Lord, "plans to prosper you and not to harm you, plans to give you hope and a future."

(*Jeremiah 29:11, NIV*)

Devotional Reflection

Trusting God's plan for your life can sometimes feel challenging, especially when the path ahead seems unclear or filled with obstacles. Yet, God's promise through Jeremiah reminds us that His plans for us are good—plans to prosper us, give us hope, and secure our future. It's easy to become anxious or frustrated when things don't go as we've planned, but God's perspective is far greater than our own.

When we trust God's plan, we acknowledge that He knows what's best for us, even when we can't see the full picture. This trust doesn't mean that life will always be easy, but it does mean that we are never alone. God is with us every step of the way, guiding, protecting, and leading us towards His divine purpose for our lives.

Take comfort in knowing that God's plan is tailor-made for you. It's a plan that considers your strengths, your struggles, and your unique gifts. As you move forward, place your trust in God's hands, knowing that He is working all things together for your good. Lean into His wisdom, and let go of the need to control every detail. By doing so, you open yourself up to the beautiful, unexpected blessings that God has in store for you.

Prayer

Dear Lord, help me to trust in Your plan for my life, even when the path seems uncertain. Guide my steps and give me the courage to follow Your lead, knowing that Your plans for me are good. In Jesus' name, Amen.

Affirmation

I trust in God's plan for my life, knowing that He is guiding me towards a future filled with hope and purpose.

January 7
Starting the Year with Faith

"Now faith is confidence in what we hope for and assurance about what we do not see." (Hebrews 11:1, NIV)

Devotional Reflection

As the new year begins, it's important to start with a foundation of faith. Faith isn't just about believing in what you can see or what you already know; it's about trusting in God's promises even when the future is uncertain. Hebrews 11:1 reminds us that faith is confidence in what we hope for and assurance in the unseen. This kind of faith is crucial as we step into a new season, full of unknowns but also full of potential and promise.

Starting the year with faith means choosing to believe that God is at work in your life, even when you can't see the whole picture. It's about trusting that He has a plan and that His plan is good. Faith is what keeps us grounded in hope, especially when challenges arise. It encourages us to move forward, knowing that God is with us every step of the way.

As you embark on this new year, let faith be your guide. Let it be the lens through which you view your goals, your dreams, and even your setbacks. When you start with faith, you open yourself up to the limitless possibilities that God has in store for you. Trust that He will provide, that He will lead, and that He will fulfill the promises He has made to you.

Prayer

Lord, as I begin this new year, help me to start with faith. Strengthen my trust in Your promises, and guide me through every step I take. In Jesus' name, Amen.

Affirmation

I begin this year with faith, trusting that God is guiding my every step and fulfilling His promises in my life.

January 8
Aligning Your Goals with God's Will

"Commit to the Lord whatever you do, and He will establish your plans." (Proverbs 16:3, NIV)

Devotional Reflection

When we set goals, it's easy to get caught up in what we want to achieve and how we plan to get there. But as believers, it's essential to align our goals with God's will. Proverbs 16:3 reminds us that when we commit our plans to the Lord, He will establish them. This means that our ambitions, desires, and objectives should be rooted in seeking God's guidance and direction.

Aligning your goals with God's will doesn't mean you have to give up your dreams; rather, it's about inviting God into your planning process. It's asking Him to show you the path He wants you to take and being open to His leading, even if it's different from what you envisioned. When your goals align with God's will, they carry a purpose beyond personal success—they become a part of His greater plan for your life.

As you set your goals for this year, take time to pray over them. Ask God to reveal His desires for you and to help you let go of anything that doesn't align with His plan. Trust that when you put God first, He will guide you toward what's best, and you'll find fulfillment not just in achieving your goals but in knowing you're walking in His will.

Prayer

Heavenly Father, help me to align my goals with Your will. Guide my steps and lead me in the direction that brings glory to Your name. In Jesus' name, Amen.

Affirmation

I commit my goals to the Lord, trusting that He will guide and establish my plans according to His will.

January 9
Walking in Your Divine Purpose

"For we are God's handiwork, created in Christ Jesus to do good works, which God prepared in advance for us to do." (Ephesians 2:10, NIV)

Devotional Reflection

Walking in your divine purpose means understanding that you were created for a reason beyond just existing. Ephesians 2:10 reveals that you are God's handiwork, made with intentionality and love. Your life is not random; it is part of a grand design crafted by God Himself.

To walk in your divine purpose, start by recognizing your unique gifts and passions. These are not just random talents but clues to what God has designed for you. Think about the things you are naturally drawn to and the ways you find fulfillment. God uses these clues to guide you toward your purpose.

Walking in your divine purpose also involves trust. It means believing that God has a plan for you, even when the path isn't clear. It's about stepping out in faith, knowing that each step you take in obedience brings you closer to fulfilling the work He has prepared for you. Embrace the journey with confidence, and let God guide you. Trust that your purpose is unfolding as you live each day with intention and faith.

Prayer

Lord, thank You for creating me with a purpose. Help me to discover and walk in the path You have set for me. Guide my steps and strengthen my faith. In Jesus' name, Amen.

Affirmation

I am God's handiwork, created with purpose. I trust in His plan for my life and step forward in faith.

January 10
Overcoming Fear of the Unknown

"So we say with confidence, 'The Lord is my helper; I will not be afraid. What can mere mortals do to me?'" (Hebrews 13:6, NIV)

Devotional Reflection

Facing the unknown can be daunting. It's natural to feel anxious about what lies ahead, especially when the future is uncertain. But Hebrews 13:6 reminds us that we have a constant source of strength and security in God. When we trust in His presence and support, our fears diminish.

To overcome the fear of the unknown, start by anchoring your confidence in God's promises. Remember that He is always with you, guiding and protecting you. When you focus on His faithfulness, your fears are replaced with courage.

Think about the last time you faced a challenge and how God helped you through it. Reflect on those moments to build your trust in His ability to handle what's ahead. Instead of letting fear control you, let your faith in God's help be your guide. Take each step forward with the assurance that He is walking with you.

Prayer

Dear Lord, I am anxious about the unknowns in my life. Help me to trust in Your guidance and find courage in Your promises. I rely on Your strength and peace. In Jesus' name, Amen.

Affirmation

I am confident in the Lord's help. I am not afraid, for God is with me in every unknown.

January 11
Discovering Your Unique Gifts

"Each of you should use whatever gift you have received to serve others, as faithful stewards of God's grace in its various forms."

(1 Peter 4:10, NIV)

Devotional Reflection

Everyone has unique gifts given by God, and discovering them can be an exciting journey. 1 Peter 4:10 reminds us that these gifts are not just for our benefit but are meant to serve others and honor God. Your talents and abilities are special and have a purpose beyond yourself.

To uncover your unique gifts, start by reflecting on what you enjoy and what you're good at. Think about times when you felt fulfilled and energized. These moments often highlight your strengths and passions.

Consider how you can use these gifts to help others and make a positive impact. Whether it's through creativity, compassion, leadership, or another talent, your gifts are valuable and needed. By focusing on how you can serve others, you'll find joy and fulfillment in using your gifts for God's purpose.

Prayer

Dear God, thank You for the unique gifts You have given me. Help me to discover and use these talents to serve others and bring glory to You. Guide me in finding ways to use my gifts for Your kingdom. Amen.

Affirmation

I am grateful for my unique gifts. I will use them to serve others and fulfill God's purpose in my life.

January 12
The Importance of Vision and Clarity

"Where there is no revelation, people cast off restraint; but blessed is the one who heeds wisdom's instruction." (Proverbs 29:18, NIV).

Devotional Reflection

Vision and clarity are like a map guiding us through life's journey. Proverbs 29:18 highlights how crucial vision is. Without it, we might lose direction and purpose. A clear vision helps us see where we are going and keeps us focused on what truly matters.

Having vision means understanding what God wants for us and where He is leading us. It's more than just setting goals; it's about aligning our dreams and actions with God's plans. When we lack clarity, we may feel lost or uncertain. But when we seek God's guidance and embrace His vision for our lives, we gain a sense of purpose and direction.

Take time to pray and seek God's will for your life. Ask Him to reveal His plans and give you the clarity you need. With vision, you'll navigate life's challenges with confidence, knowing you're on the path God has set for you.

Prayer

Lord, grant me clarity and vision for my life. Help me to see Your plans and guide me in fulfilling them. Give me the wisdom to follow Your path and stay focused on Your purpose. Amen.

Affirmation

I am guided by God's vision for my life. I trust in His plans and seek clarity in all that I do.

January 13
Pursuing Purpose with Passion

"Serve the Lord with enthusiasm, knowing that you are serving Christ." (Ephesians 6:7, NIV)

Devotional Reflection

Pursuing purpose with passion is about more than just doing something well—it's about doing it with heart and soul. Ephesians 6:7 encourages us to serve the Lord with enthusiasm. This means that when we follow our purpose, we should do it with energy and joy, fully aware that we are serving God.

Passion drives us to give our best, even when the path gets tough. When you're passionate about your purpose, you'll find motivation in the smallest tasks and perseverance through challenges. It's this passion that transforms ordinary actions into acts of worship.

Think about what fuels your enthusiasm. Whether it's a dream, a cause, or a mission, pursuing it with passion means you're not just going through the motions—you're investing your whole self into it. This dedication honors God and aligns your work with His greater plan for your life.

Prayer

Lord, fill me with passion and enthusiasm as I pursue my purpose. Help me to serve You with all my heart and stay motivated, even when the journey gets hard. Amen.

Affirmation

I am passionate about my purpose, and I serve with enthusiasm. My dedication honors God and fuels my journey.

January 14
Breaking Free from Limiting Beliefs

"Do not conform to the pattern of this world, but be transformed by the renewing of your mind." (Romans 12:2, NIV)

Devotional Reflection

Breaking free from limiting beliefs requires a change in mindset. Romans 12:2 reminds us not to follow the world's standards but to let God transform our thinking. Our beliefs can hold us back more than any external obstacle. They shape how we see ourselves and our possibilities.

Often, we may believe things like, "I'm not good enough" or "I can't change." These thoughts limit us and stop us from reaching our full potential. But God wants us to see ourselves as He sees us— capable and worthy of His blessings. Transforming your mind means replacing these negative beliefs with God's truth.

Start by identifying one limiting belief you hold. Then, find a scripture that speaks to your worth and potential. Let this truth replace the old belief. Remember, God's view of you is full of hope and possibilities, not limitations.

Prayer

Lord, help me to break free from limiting beliefs and embrace the truth of who I am in You. Transform my mind and fill me with Your truth, so I can live fully and freely. Amen.

Affirmation

I am not defined by my past or limitations. I am transformed by God's truth and live in the fullness of His promise.

January 15
Trusting God in Uncertain Times

"Trust in the Lord with all your heart and lean not on your own understanding; in all your ways submit to Him, and He will make your paths straight." (Proverbs 3:5-6, NIV)

Devotional Reflection
When life is uncertain, trusting God can be incredibly challenging. Proverbs 3:5-6 teaches us to trust God completely and not rely on our own limited understanding. During times of uncertainty, we may feel overwhelmed and unsure of what steps to take. It's easy to let fear and doubt cloud our vision.

Trusting God means believing that He knows what is best for us, even when we can't see the path ahead. It involves surrendering our worries and choosing to rely on His wisdom rather than our own. This trust brings peace and clarity, allowing us to move forward with confidence, knowing that God is guiding our way.

Consider a recent situation where you felt uncertain. How can you apply this verse to that situation? Remember, God is always with you, even in the most confusing times. Lean on Him and trust that He will lead you through.

Prayer
Dear God, in times of uncertainty, help me to trust You fully and not rely on my own understanding. Guide me through the unknown with Your wisdom and peace. Amen.

Affirmation
I trust God with my whole heart, and I know He will guide me through any uncertainty.

January 16
Embracing Change with Courage

"Be strong and courageous. Do not be afraid; do not be discouraged, for the Lord your God will be with you wherever you go."

(Joshua 1:9, NIV)

Devotional Reflection

Change is a constant part of life, but it can be daunting. Joshua 1:9 reminds us to be strong and courageous as we face new challenges. Embracing change often means stepping out of our comfort zones and facing the unknown with faith. This can be intimidating, but God promises that He will be with us through every transition.

Consider a recent or upcoming change in your life. It might be a new job, a move, or a shift in personal relationships. While these changes can be scary, they also offer opportunities for growth and new experiences. Embracing change with courage involves trusting that God has a plan and will guide us through it. When we face change with faith, we are not alone; God's presence gives us strength and reassurance.

Reflect on a time when embracing change led to a positive outcome. How did God support you through that process? Remember, change is a part of God's plan for our lives, and He is always with us, ready to help us navigate through it.

Prayer

Lord, give me the courage to embrace change with faith. Help me trust in Your guidance and find strength in Your presence. Amen.

Affirmation

I am strong and courageous because God is with me in every change and challenge.

January 17

Living with Intentionality

"Teach us to number our days, that we may gain a heart of wisdom."
(Psalm 90:12, NIV)

Devotional Reflection

Living with intentionality means being purposeful in everything we do. Psalm 90:12 invites us to be mindful of how we spend our time. When we live intentionally, we make choices that align with our values and goals, focusing on what truly matters.

Consider how you approach each day. Are your actions aligned with your faith and values? Living with intentionality involves setting clear priorities and making decisions that reflect your beliefs. It's about being present and making the most of every opportunity.

Reflect on areas in your life where you might need more focus. Are there routines or habits that are not helping you grow spiritually or personally? Being intentional helps us live a more fulfilling and meaningful life by ensuring that our daily actions are in harmony with our deeper values and purposes.

Prayer

Lord, guide me to live each day with purpose and intention. Help me to make choices that align with Your will and bring me closer to my goals. Amen.

Affirmation

I live with purpose and intentionality, making choices that align with my faith and values.

January 18
Seeking God's Guidance in Every Step

"Trust in the Lord with all your heart and lean not on your own understanding; in all your ways submit to him, and he will make your paths straight." (Proverbs 3:5-6, NIV)

Devotional Reflection

Seeking God's guidance in every step of life means trusting Him completely, even when the path isn't clear. Proverbs 3:5-6 reminds us that we should not rely solely on our own wisdom or judgment. Instead, we are invited to trust God with our whole heart.

Imagine making decisions without a map or directions. It can be confusing and stressful. Similarly, navigating life without God's guidance can leave us feeling lost. When we seek His direction in every aspect of our lives—whether it's big decisions or small daily choices—we align ourselves with His will and purpose. This trust doesn't mean everything will be perfect, but it assures us that we are on the right path.

Think about areas in your life where you might be leaning on your own understanding. Are there decisions or challenges where you haven't fully sought God's guidance? Trusting Him in these moments means letting go of control and believing that He will lead you where you need to go.

Prayer

Dear Lord, help me to trust You in every decision and step I take. Guide me with Your wisdom and keep me aligned with Your will. Amen.

Affirmation

I trust in the Lord with all my heart and seek His guidance in every step of my life.

January 19
The Role of Prayerin Finding Purpose

"Devote yourselves to prayer, being watchful and thankful."
(Colossians 4:2, NIV)

Devotional Reflection

Prayeris like a compass for finding our purpose. In Colossians 4:2, we're encouraged to devote ourselves to prayer, which means making it a central part of our lives. Through prayer, we can connect with God, seek His wisdom, and understand the direction He wants us to take.

When we pray regularly, we're not just talking to God; we're opening our hearts and minds to His guidance. It's during these moments of Prayerthat we often receive clarity and insight about our life's purpose. It's easy to get caught up in daily activities and lose sight of our goals, but Prayerhelps us refocus and stay aligned with what truly matters.

Think of Prayeras a conversation where you share your thoughts and listen for God's responses. When we ask Him for direction, He can reveal steps to take and changes to make, helping us move toward fulfilling our purpose. Trust that God listens to your prayers and is guiding you, even if the answers come gradually.

Prayer

Lord, guide me through my prayers and reveal the purpose You have for me. Help me stay focused on Your plan and trust in Your timing. Amen.

Affirmation

Through prayer, I find clarity and direction for my purpose, trusting in God's guidance every step of the way.

January 20
Stepping Out in Faith

"Now faith is confidence in what we hope for and assurance about what we do not see." (Hebrews 11:1, NIV)

Devotional Reflection

Stepping out in faith means trusting God even when the path ahead is unclear. Hebrews 11:1 tells us that faith is being sure of what we hope for and confident about things we cannot see. This can be challenging, especially when you're faced with uncertainty or fear about the future.

Imagine standing on the edge of a cliff. You can't see the ground below, but you believe that if you jump, you'll be safe. This is what stepping out in faith feels like. It's about taking that leap, knowing that God is with you even when you can't see the outcome.

Faith requires action. It's not just about believing in God's promises but also acting on them. When you step out in faith, you're showing trust in God's plan for your life. This might mean making a career change, starting a new project, or pursuing a dream that seems risky. God calls us to move forward with courage, even when the future feels uncertain.

Remember, faith isn't about having everything figured out; it's about trusting God to guide you. By stepping out in faith, you show that you believe in His power to lead and support you.

Prayer

God, give me the courage to step out in faith and trust in Your plan. Help me to act on my beliefs, even when the path is unclear. Amen.

Affirmation

I trust God to guide me as I step out in faith, believing in His promises and His plan for my life.

January 21
Celebrating Small Beginnings

"Do not despise these small beginnings, for the Lord rejoices to see the work begin." (Zechariah 4:10, NIV)

Devotional Reflection

Celebrating small beginnings is essential for growth and progress. Zechariah 4:10 reminds us not to overlook the small starts in our lives. These small steps are the foundation for larger achievements and are just as important as the final outcome.

Think about the early stages of any journey. A seed planted in the soil doesn't instantly become a tree; it starts as a tiny seed, gradually growing and strengthening. Similarly, when we start something new, it often begins with small, seemingly insignificant actions. These initial steps might feel minor, but they are crucial in laying the groundwork for something greater.

In our lives, we might set big goals or dreams, but the progress often happens in small, manageable steps. Celebrating these small beginnings helps us stay motivated and grateful. Each small step forward is a victory worth acknowledging.

When you recognize and celebrate these small achievements, you build confidence and resilience. It reminds you that even small progress is still progress. By focusing on the journey and valuing each step, you stay connected to the process and to God's work in your life.

Prayer

Thank You, Lord, for every small step I take toward my goals. Help me to see the value in these beginnings and to celebrate each small victory with joy. Amen.

Affirmation

I celebrate and value every small beginning, knowing that each step is part of God's greater plan for my life.

January 22
The Power of Positive Affirmations

"Finally, brothers and sisters, whatever is true, whatever is noble, whatever is right, whatever is pure, whatever is lovely, whatever is admirable—if anything is excellent or praiseworthy—think about such things." (Philippians 4:8, NIV)

Devotional Reflection

Positive affirmations are a powerful tool for shaping our thoughts and actions. Philippians 4:8 encourages us to focus on what is true, noble, and praiseworthy. This verse highlights how important it is to keep our minds on positive and uplifting thoughts.

Think of your mind as a garden. Just as you wouldn't want weeds taking over your garden, you don't want negative thoughts crowding your mind. Positive affirmations help to plant seeds of encouragement and faith in your mind, which can grow into positive attitudes and actions.

When you repeat affirmations like **"I am capable"** or **"I am worthy of love and success,"** you are training your mind to believe these truths. Over time, these affirmations can change how you see yourself and your situation. They can build your confidence and help you face challenges with a stronger, more positive outlook.

Using positive affirmations daily aligns your thoughts with God's truth about you. It reminds you of your worth and strengthens your faith in His plans for your life. By focusing on what is noble and praiseworthy, you invite God's peace and strength into your daily experience.

Prayer

Lord, help me to embrace the power of positive affirmations. Guide my thoughts to focus on what is good and true. Strengthen my faith in Your promises. Amen.

Affirmation

I am worthy of God's love and equipped for His purpose. My thoughts are aligned with His truth and strength.

January 23
Living with Purpose and Direction

"Many are the plans in a person's heart, but it is the Lord's purpose that prevails." (Proverbs 19:21, NIV)

Devotional Reflection

Living with purpose means aligning your life with God's plans. Proverbs 19:21 reminds us that while we have many ideas, it is God's purpose that shapes our lives. This verse encourages us to seek God's will and trust that His plans are better than our own.

Imagine planning a journey. You might choose a destination, map your route, and prepare. But what if unexpected changes occur along the way? Similarly, our lives are full of plans, but God's purpose often leads us in directions we didn't expect. This doesn't mean our plans are useless; it means God's plans are supreme.

When we live according to God's purpose, we find deeper direction. We begin to see that our true purpose is not just about achieving personal goals but about fulfilling God's greater plan. It's about using our gifts to serve others and glorify God. Embracing this helps us live with clarity, knowing our lives are part of a bigger story.

Living with purpose means praying for guidance and being open to God's leading. Trusting God's purpose gives peace, knowing He is directing our steps toward a meaningful life.

Prayer

Lord, help me to align my life with Your purpose. Guide my steps and direct my plans according to Your will. Give me clarity and trust in Your divine plan for my life. Amen.

Affirmation

I am guided by God's purpose and trust that His plans for me are good. I embrace each day with clarity and direction.

January 24
Surrendering to God's Timing

"But as for you, be strong and do not give up, for your work will be rewarded." (2 Chronicles 15:7, NIV)

Devotional Reflection

Surrendering to God's timing is one of the most challenging aspects of faith. We often want things to happen on our schedule, believing our timing is best. However, God's timing is perfect, and He knows when things should unfold.

2 Chronicles 15:7 encourages us to remain strong and not give up, even when waiting for prayers to be answered or goals to be reached. This verse reminds us that while our efforts may seem slow at times, God is working behind the scenes to bring about His plan. His timing is not only precise but filled with wisdom.

We often rush through life, pushing for quick results. Yet, when we surrender to God's timing, we allow Him to work out details in ways we might not expect. Trusting His timing means accepting that He knows what's best for us.

Surrendering to God's timing requires patience and trust. God's delays aren't denials but preparation for something greater. By focusing on the journey and trusting His plan, we find peace knowing He's guiding us toward our purpose in His perfect time.

Prayer

Lord, help me to trust in Your perfect timing. Teach me patience and strengthen my faith as I wait for Your plan to unfold. Guide me to remain hopeful and steadfast in my journey. Amen.

Affirmation

I trust in God's perfect timing and believe that His plan for me is unfolding just as it should. I am patient and confident in His guidance.

January 25
The Joy of New Opportunities

"See, I am doing a new thing! Now it springs up; do you not perceive it? I am making a way in the wilderness and streams in the wasteland."

(Isaiah 43:19, NIV)

Devotional Reflection

New opportunities can be both exciting and daunting. Isaiah 43:19 speaks to this experience of encountering fresh starts with a hopeful promise. This verse is a reminder that God is always at work, creating new paths even in the most unexpected places.

Sometimes, we may feel stuck in routines or situations that seem unchangeable. Yet, God assures us that He is constantly making new ways for us. This might mean a new job, a new relationship, or even a new perspective on life. Embracing these new opportunities requires faith and openness to change.

The joy of new opportunities lies in the growth and possibilities they bring. God's promise to make a way in the wilderness and streams in the wasteland highlights His ability to transform our circumstances. When we open ourselves to these new experiences, we also open ourselves to new forms of joy and fulfillment.

It's important to recognize these opportunities as gifts from God. They can lead us to new places, both physically and spiritually, helping us grow and discover new aspects of ourselves. Each new opportunity is a chance to step into a future that God has prepared for us, full of potential and promise.

Prayer

Lord, thank You for the new opportunities You provide. Help me to see and embrace the paths You are making for me. Grant me the courage to step into these new beginnings with joy and trust in Your plan. Amen.

Affirmation

I am open to the new opportunities God brings into my life. I embrace change with joy and trust in the paths He creates for me.

January 26
Building a Strong Foundation of Faith

"Therefore everyone who hears these words of mine and puts them into practice is like a wise man who built his house on the rock." (Matthew 7:24, NIV)

Devotional Reflection

Building a strong foundation of faith is like constructing a house on solid rock. In Matthew 7:24, Jesus compares those who follow His teachings to a wise builder who creates a stable and secure home. This shows how essential it is to build our lives on the solid ground of faith.

Just as a house needs a strong foundation to withstand storms, our faith must be grounded in God's Word. When challenges come, having a solid foundation helps us stay steadfast and resilient. It's not just about hearing God's words but applying them to our daily lives.

Strengthening our faith foundation involves prayer, studying Scripture, and trusting in God's plan. It means making choices that reflect our beliefs and relying on God in uncertain times. This keeps our faith steady through life's trials.

Consider how you can build a stronger foundation of faith today. Reflect on whether your actions align with God's teachings. The more we invest in spiritual growth, the better equipped we are to face challenges with confidence and hope.

Prayer

Heavenly Father, help me build my life on the strong foundation of Your Word. Guide me to practice Your teachings daily and trust in Your promises. Strengthen my faith and keep me steady through all life's challenges. Amen.

Affirmation

I am building my life on the strong foundation of faith in God. I trust in His Word and find strength in His promises.

January 27
Overcoming Obstacles on the Path to Purpose

"I can do all this through him who gives me strength."

(Philippians 4:13, NIV)

Devotional Reflection

Overcoming obstacles is a crucial part of walking in purpose. In Philippians 4:13, Paul reminds us that our strength comes from Christ. This verse is a powerful Affirmationthat no matter what challenges we face, we are not alone. God provides the strength we need to overcome any obstacles that come our way.

Obstacles can take many forms—unexpected setbacks, personal doubts, or external difficulties. They can make our journey seem overwhelming, but they are also opportunities for growth. When we face these challenges with faith, we allow ourselves to experience God's strength in action.

Imagine you are climbing a steep hill. Each step can be tiring, but each step brings you closer to the top. Similarly, each obstacle you overcome brings you closer to fulfilling your purpose. By leaning on God and relying on His strength, you can push through difficulties and continue moving forward.

Think about a recent challenge you've faced. How did relying on God's strength help you overcome it? Reflect on how you can continue to trust in His power as you face future obstacles. With God's help, even the biggest hurdles become stepping stones to your purpose.

Prayer

Dear Lord, thank You for being my source of strength in every challenge I face. Help me to trust in Your power and lean on Your guidance as I navigate obstacles on my path to purpose. Grant me the courage to persevere and the faith to believe in Your support. Amen.

Affirmation

With God's strength, I overcome every obstacle in my path. I trust in His power and grace to guide me toward my purpose.

January 28
The Strength to Start Over

"Forget the former things; do not dwell on the past. See, I am doing a new thing! Now it springs up; do you not perceive it?"

(Isaiah 43:18-19, NIV)

Devotional Reflection

Starting over can feel daunting, but Isaiah 43:18-19 encourages us to embrace new beginnings with hope. This verse reminds us that God is constantly working to bring new opportunities into our lives. No matter what has happened in the past, God is ready to do something new and wonderful.

When faced with the need to start over, it's natural to feel overwhelmed or discouraged. You might think about past mistakes or missed opportunities, but this verse assures us that dwelling on the past won't help us move forward. Instead, we are called to see the new things God is bringing into our lives.

Think of it like a fresh start each day. Just as a new day begins with the sun rising, your life can begin anew with God's grace. Every morning offers a chance to begin again, to set new goals, and to embrace new opportunities with a positive outlook.

Reflect on a recent situation where you felt like you needed a fresh start. How can you view this as an opportunity for growth rather than a setback? Embrace the new possibilities that God is offering you, and trust that He is guiding you toward something good.

Prayer

Heavenly Father, thank You for the chance to start over and for the new opportunities You bring into my life. Help me release the past and welcome the new things You are bringing into my life. Give me the strength and faith to move forward with hope and confidence. Amen.

Affirmation

I let go of the past and embrace the new opportunities God is bringing into my life. I trust in His plan for a fresh start and new beginnings.

January 29
Finding Peace in God's Purpose

"Peace I leave with you; my peace I give you. I do not give to you as the world gives. Do not let your hearts be troubled and do not be afraid."

(John 14:27, NIV)

Devotional Reflection

Finding peace in God's purpose is comforting, especially during times of uncertainty. In John 14:27, Jesus offers us peace that's different from what the world gives. His peace is deeper, enduring, and rooted in His love and promises.

When life feels chaotic, it's easy to feel lost. But Jesus's promise of peace reminds us that even in difficulties, we can find calm in His purpose for our lives. His peace is not just a temporary feeling but a steady foundation that helps us navigate through storms.

Reflect on how God's purpose may be guiding you through your current situation. Even when you don't understand why things are happening a certain way, trust that God's purpose is at work, and His peace is available to you. This peace keeps our hearts from being troubled and helps us stay focused on what truly matters.

Consider how you can invite this peace into your life. Maybe it's through prayer, meditation, or taking a moment to remind yourself of God's promises. Allow His peace to fill and guide your steps.

Prayer

Dear Lord, thank You for the peace that You give, which is beyond understanding. Help me to trust in Your purpose and find comfort in Your presence. When I feel troubled, remind me of Your peace and guide me through the challenges I face. Amen.

Affirmation

I trust in God's purpose for my life and embrace the peace He provides. His peace fills my heart and guides me through every challenge.

January 30
Trusting the Process of Growth

"But the fruit of the Spirit is love, joy, peace, forbearance, kindness, goodness, faithfulness, gentleness, and self-control."

(Galatians 5:22-23, NIV)

Devotional Reflection

Growth is a journey, and it's often not a straight path. The Bible shows us that spiritual growth, much like personal growth, takes time and patience. Galatians 5:22-23 lists the fruits of the Spirit—qualities that develop in us as we walk with God. These qualities don't appear overnight; they grow slowly, much like a fruit ripening on a tree.

Sometimes, we might feel discouraged when we don't see immediate changes or progress in our lives. But just as a seed needs time to grow into a strong tree, our spiritual growth requires patience. Trusting the process means believing that God is working in us even when we can't see it.

Reflect on the areas of your life where you're seeking growth. Maybe it's patience, kindness, or self-control. Instead of focusing on how far you still need to go, celebrate the small victories and trust that God is nurturing you every step of the way. Growth is a continuous process, and each day is a chance to cultivate the fruits of the Spirit in your life.

Prayer

Dear God, help me trust in Your timing and process of growth. Give me patience as I work on developing the fruits of the Spirit in my life. Guide me and strengthen me as I continue to grow in faith and character. Amen.

Affirmation

I trust in God's process of growth in my life. I am patient and grateful for the progress I make each day.

January 31
Looking Ahead with Hope and Determination

"For I know the plans I have for you," declares the Lord, "plans to prosper you and not to harm you, plans to give you hope and a future."
(Jeremiah 29:11, NIV)

Devotional Reflection

As we close one chapter and look ahead to the next, it's important to embrace the future with hope and determination. Jeremiah 29:11 reminds us that God has a plan for our lives, filled with promise and hope. This verse assures us that no matter what challenges we face, God's plans for us are always for our good.

Looking ahead can sometimes feel daunting. We might worry about the uncertainties and obstacles that lie ahead. But this scripture encourages us to replace fear with hope. God's plans are designed to lead us toward a future where we can thrive.

To approach the future with determination, start by setting small, achievable goals. Each step forward, no matter how small, is a victory. Trust that God is guiding you through every challenge and that He is with you every step of the way. Embrace each new day with confidence, knowing that God's plans for you are filled with hope and possibilities.

Prayer

Lord, thank You for the hope and future You have promised me. Help me face each new day with confidence and determination, trusting in Your plans. Guide my steps and strengthen me as I move forward. Amen.

Affirmation

I embrace the future with hope and determination, trusting in God's good plans for my life.

February
Self-Love and Worth

February 1
Embracing Your Unique Self

"I praise you because I am fearfully and wonderfully made; your works are wonderful, I know that full well." (Psalm 139:14, NIV)

Devotional Reflection

You are a unique creation, designed with purpose and care. Psalm 139:14 reminds us of this powerful truth: you are made in a way that reflects God's greatness. Embracing your unique self means recognizing the qualities, strengths, and even the imperfections that make you who you are. It's easy to get caught up in comparing ourselves to others or wishing we were different, but remember, you are exactly as you should be.

God crafted you with a special blend of talents, personality, and experiences. Each of these aspects contributes to your unique place in the world. Embracing who you are involves acknowledging and celebrating these attributes rather than focusing on what you might lack. When you accept yourself fully, you open the door to live out your purpose with confidence and joy. Celebrate the person God made you to be and let your unique light shine.

Prayer

Lord, thank You for making me so wonderfully unique. Help me to embrace who I am with confidence and gratitude. May I see myself through Your eyes, and use the gifts You've given me to make a difference in the world. Guide me as I celebrate my uniqueness and trust in Your perfect design. Amen.

Affirmation

I am wonderfully made by God. I embrace my unique qualities and celebrate who I am.

February 2
The Beauty of Self-Acceptance

"For we are God's handiwork, created in Christ Jesus to do good works, which God prepared in advance for us to do." (Ephesians 2:10, NIV)

Devotional Reflection

Self-acceptance is a beautiful act of faith. When you embrace who you are, with all your strengths and weaknesses, you honor the work God has done in creating you. Ephesians 2:10 reminds us that we are God's handiwork—lovingly shaped and prepared for a purpose. Self-acceptance isn't about settling for less or ignoring your need for growth; it's about recognizing that you are a work in progress, and God is not done with you yet.

Too often, we focus on what we think is missing or broken in ourselves. But when we pause and see ourselves through God's eyes, we begin to appreciate the beauty and uniqueness within us. Accepting yourself as you are today allows you to fully embrace the journey ahead. You are enough because God says you are, and He's already prepared the good works you're called to do. Let go of the pressure to be perfect and walk confidently in the truth that God's love is enough to sustain you.

Prayer

Heavenly Father, thank You for making me in Your image. Help me to see myself as You do, with love and grace. Teach me to accept my flaws and imperfections as part of Your divine work in me. Amen.

Affirmation

I am God's handiwork, beautifully created with purpose and intention. I accept myself fully, knowing I am loved and valued.

February 3
Recognizing Your Worth in Christ

"You are not your own; you were bought at a price. Therefore honor God with your bodies." (1 Corinthians 6:19-20, NIV)

Devotional Reflection

Recognizing your worth in Christ is a powerful realization. The world may often define value based on appearance, success, or status, but God defines your worth in a completely different way. In 1 Corinthians 6:19-20, Paul reminds us that we are not our own; we were bought with a price—the ultimate sacrifice of Jesus Christ. This means your worth is not tied to anything you do, but rather to what has been done for you.

When you embrace this truth, you can stand confidently in the knowledge that you are precious to God. No matter your past mistakes or what others may say, your worth remains unchanged in His eyes. He paid the highest price for you, which speaks volumes about your value. Today, let go of any feelings of inadequacy or insecurity. Your worth is not up for debate—it is secure in Christ, and nothing can take that away.

Prayer

Dear Lord, thank You for reminding me that my worth is found in You. Help me to reject the lies that make me feel less than and embrace the truth that I am loved, chosen, and valuable in Your sight. Amen.

Affirmation

I am priceless in God's eyes, loved, and redeemed by the sacrifice of Jesus Christ. I embrace my worth and walk confidently in His love.

February 4
The Power of Self-Care

"Come to me, all you who are weary and burdened, and I will give you rest." (Matthew 11:28, NIV)

Devotional Reflection

Self-care is more than a trend; it's a biblical principle rooted in caring for the temple of God—your body, mind, and spirit. In Matthew 11:28, Jesus invites those who are weary to come to Him for rest. This is an important reminder that caring for yourself is not selfish but necessary. As Black women, there are so many responsibilities to juggle, from family and career to ministry and community. It's easy to put yourself last, but the truth is, when you don't take time to recharge, you risk burnout.

Self-care involves not just physical rest but spiritual renewal. Taking time to read Scripture, pray, and nurture your soul helps you stay aligned with God's purpose for your life. By resting in His presence and caring for yourself, you are better equipped to care for others. Today, embrace self-care as an act of love—both for yourself and for those around you.

Prayer

Lord, help me to see the importance of caring for myself. Teach me to rest in You and find the peace and renewal that only You can provide. Amen.

Affirmation

I deserve to rest, recharge, and care for myself, knowing that God values my well-being.

February 5

Overcoming Self-Doubt

"I can do all this through Him who gives me strength."

(Philippians 4:13, NIV)

Devotional Reflection

Doubt has a sneaky way of creeping into our hearts, even when we know better. Picture this: you've just been offered an incredible opportunity—one that aligns with your gifts and dreams—and instead of celebrating, you start questioning yourself. "Am I really capable?" "What if I fail?" Sound familiar? This is the voice of self-doubt, and it's one of the enemy's most effective tools to keep you from walking in the fullness of what God has called you to do.

Philippians 4:13 tells us that we can do all things through Christ, who strengthens us. This isn't just a motivational quote; it's a spiritual truth. The same God who called you has already equipped you with the strength, wisdom, and grace you need to succeed. So the next time self-doubt whispers in your ear, remind yourself of God's promises. You don't have to do it alone—His strength is with you every step of the way.

Prayer

Lord, when doubt begins to cloud my mind, remind me of Your promises. Help me to trust in Your strength, knowing that I can overcome anything with You by my side. Amen.

Affirmation

I am confident, capable, and equipped for everything God has called me to do.

February 6
Cultivating Positive Self-Talk

"The tongue has the power of life and death, and those who love it will eat its fruit." (Proverbs 18:21, NIV)

Devotional Reflection

How often do you find yourself saying things like, "I'm not good enough" or "I'll never get this right"? It's easy to be your own harshest critic, but the words you speak to yourself matter. Proverbs 18:21 reminds us that our words have incredible power—they can bring life or death. This isn't just about what we say to others; it's also about how we speak to ourselves.

Negative self-talk is like planting seeds of doubt and insecurity in your heart. Over time, those seeds grow, affecting how you see yourself and even how you live your life. But positive self-talk can have the opposite effect. When you begin to speak life over yourself, you nurture a sense of self-worth and confidence that reflects God's truth. So, the next time a negative thought crosses your mind, replace it with God's promises. You are His masterpiece, fearfully and wonderfully made. Let your words reflect that truth.

Prayer

Father, help me to speak life over myself. When negative thoughts arise, remind me of Your truth and help me to align my words with Your promises. Amen.

Affirmation

I speak words of life, love, and encouragement over myself, knowing that I am fearfully and wonderfully made.

February 7

Letting Go of Perfectionism

"But he said to me, 'My grace is sufficient for you, for my power is made perfect in weakness.' Therefore I will boast all the more gladly about my weaknesses, so that Christ's power may rest on me."

(2 Corinthians 12:9, NIV)

Devotional Reflection

Have you ever felt like you had to get everything just right, only to be overwhelmed by the constant pressure of perfection? Maybe it's the need to excel at work, to be the perfect mom, or to always have it together. Perfectionism can trap us in a cycle of stress and disappointment, making us feel like we're never enough. But here's the truth: God doesn't call us to be perfect. He calls us to rely on His grace.

2 Corinthians 12:9 teaches us that God's power is made perfect in our weaknesses, not our perfection. That means we don't have to strive for flawless performance. Instead, we can lean on God's strength, knowing that His grace is enough for every flaw and shortcoming we face. Letting go of perfectionism allows us to experience the freedom that comes from trusting in God's sufficiency rather than our own abilities. Embrace your imperfections, for they are the very place where God's power shines through.

Prayer

Lord, I release my need to be perfect and trust in Your grace. Help me to accept my weaknesses and lean on Your strength in all things. Amen.

Affirmation

I am enough, just as I am, because God's grace covers my imperfections and makes me whole.

February 8
The Gift of Forgiveness to Yourself

"Therefore, there is now no condemnation for those who are in Christ Jesus." (Romans 8:1, NIV)

Devotional Reflection

Have you ever found it hard to forgive yourself for past mistakes? Maybe it's something you did years ago or even just yesterday, and it keeps replaying in your mind. Self-forgiveness is often harder than forgiving others. We tend to hold ourselves to impossible standards, and when we fail, we carry guilt and shame long after God has forgiven us.

Romans 8:1 reminds us that if we are in Christ, there is no condemnation. God has already wiped the slate clean through His grace and mercy. Holding onto self-condemnation keeps us trapped in a cycle of regret and guilt. But today, you have the power to release yourself from that burden. The gift of self-forgiveness allows you to heal and grow, accepting that God's grace is greater than your mistakes. Embrace the freedom of knowing you are fully forgiven, and start seeing yourself as God sees you—loved, redeemed, and worthy.

Prayer

Lord, help me to release the guilt I carry and embrace Your forgiveness. Let me see myself through Your eyes, free from condemnation. Amen.

Affirmation

I forgive myself because God has forgiven me. I am free from guilt and shame, and I embrace God's love for me.

February 9
Celebrating Your Achievements

"Let another praise you, and not your own mouth; a stranger, and not your own lips." (Proverbs 27:2, NIV)

Devotional Reflection

Do you struggle with celebrating your achievements? Many of us have been taught to be humble and modest, to the point that we downplay our accomplishments. But there is a difference between pride and self-acknowledgment. Sometimes, we need to pause and recognize how far we've come. It's not about boasting; it's about giving thanks to God for the journey and the strength He's given us to succeed.

Think about all you've achieved—whether it's big or small—and realize that these are not accidents. God has equipped you with gifts and abilities, and He delights in seeing you use them. When you celebrate your wins, you're also celebrating His goodness. Today, give yourself permission to honor your hard work and the milestones you've reached. Celebrate with gratitude, knowing that God's hand is in every achievement.

Prayer

Lord, thank You for guiding me through every challenge and victory. Help me to celebrate my achievements with gratitude and give You the glory for all I have accomplished. Amen.

Affirmation

I celebrate my achievements with joy, knowing that God has been my guide and strength through it all.

February 10
Setting Healthy Boundaries

"Above all else, guard your heart, for everything you do flows from it."

(Proverbs 4:23,NIV)

Devotional Reflection

Setting healthy boundaries is essential for a balanced and fulfilling life, yet it can be one of the hardest things to do. Many of us struggle with saying "no" or creating limits, fearing that it might upset others or lead to conflict. But boundaries are not about pushing people away; they're about protecting your heart and well-being. When you establish clear boundaries, you honor your own needs and make space for growth and peace.

Imagine a garden where plants need space to grow. If they're crowded, they can't thrive. Similarly, when you set boundaries, you're creating room for yourself to flourish. By respecting your limits and expressing them clearly, you're not only protecting your time and energy but also showing respect for yourself and others. Today, reflect on areas where you might need to set or reinforce boundaries. It's a step towards self-care and healthy relationships.

Prayer

Lord, help me to set and maintain healthy boundaries with grace and clarity. Give me the strength to honor myself while being kind to others. Guide me in protecting my heart and well-being. Amen.

Affirmation

I set healthy boundaries with confidence, knowing that it is an act of self-respect and care.

February 11
Nurturing Your Inner Strength

"I can do all this through him who gives me strength."

(Philippians 4:13, NIV)

Devotional Reflection

Nurturing your inner strength is vital for living a life of resilience and purpose. Many of us face daily challenges that test our limits. It can be easy to feel overwhelmed, but remember, your inner strength is a powerful resource that you can cultivate and draw upon. Think of it like a muscle that needs exercise to grow.

Imagine a time when you faced a tough situation but managed to get through it. That experience is a testament to your inner strength. It wasn't just about getting through the challenge but also about growing stronger in the process. Nurturing this strength involves leaning into God's support, practicing self-care, and acknowledging your achievements. Each step you take towards caring for yourself and trusting in God builds your resilience and fortitude.

Take time today to reflect on your sources of strength. What practices or beliefs help you stay grounded and empowered? Recognizing and nurturing these can help you face future challenges with greater confidence and grace.

Prayer

Dear God, thank You for the strength You provide me each day. Help me to nurture this inner strength and rely on You in times of need. Guide me to recognize and embrace the power You have given me. Amen.

Affirmation

I nurture my inner strength with faith and confidence, trusting that I am empowered to overcome any challenge.

February 12
Valuing Your Time and Energy

"Be very careful, then, how you live—not as unwise but as wise, making the most of every opportunity, because the days are evil."

(Ephesians 5:15-16, NIV)

Devotional Reflection

Time and energy are two of our most valuable resources, yet they are often taken for granted. Think about how many times you've felt stretched thin, trying to juggle multiple tasks and responsibilities. This can lead to burnout and diminish the quality of everything you do. By valuing your time and energy, you're not only taking better care of yourself but also honoring the life God has given you.

Consider a story where someone learned to set boundaries and prioritize their well-being. Maybe they started saying "no" to extra commitments, found time for rest, or dedicated moments for personal growth. This shift didn't just improve their productivity; it also made them feel more fulfilled and focused. When you consciously choose how to spend your time and energy, you're more effective and less stressed.

Start by assessing where your time and energy are going. Are there areas where you can make changes? Small adjustments can lead to significant improvements in your overall well-being and effectiveness. By making these changes, you show that you value yourself and the gifts God has given you.

Prayer

Lord, help me to value my time and energy wisely. Guide me in making choices that reflect my priorities and well-being. Thank You for giving me the strength and wisdom to manage my life effectively. Amen.

Affirmation

I value my time and energy, making choices that honor my well-being and purpose.

February 13
Finding Joy in Self-Compassion

"But the fruit of the Spirit is love, joy, peace, forbearance, kindness, goodness, faithfulness, gentleness and self-control."

(Galatians 5:22-23, NIV)

Devotional Reflection

Self-compassion might seem like a luxury, but it's actually a necessity for a joyful life. Imagine a friend who always supports and uplifts you, no matter what. That's the kind of support we need to give ourselves. When we're kind to ourselves, we open the door to true joy and inner peace.

Think about a time when you were hard on yourself. Maybe you didn't meet a goal or made a mistake. Instead of being your own biggest critic, what if you spoke to yourself with the same kindness you'd offer a loved one? Self-compassion isn't about ignoring mistakes; it's about understanding and forgiving yourself, just as God forgives us.

When we practice self-compassion, we not only feel better about ourselves but also become more resilient. It allows us to bounce back from challenges with a renewed spirit. So, take a moment today to be kind to yourself. Recognize your efforts, celebrate your progress, and remember that you are worthy of love and joy.

Prayer

Dear God, help me to practice self-compassion and find joy in Your love. Teach me to be kind to myself as You are kind to me. Grant me peace and understanding in times of struggle. Amen.

Affirmation

I embrace self-compassion, knowing that I am worthy of love and joy.

February 14
Loving Yourself Through Challenges

"He gives strength to the weary and increases the power of the weak."

(Isaiah 40:29, NIV)

Devotional Reflection

Loving yourself during tough times can be incredibly challenging, yet it's essential for maintaining your well-being. Picture this: You've hit a rough patch. Life seems overwhelming, and your self-doubt is creeping in. It's easy to be hard on yourself when things aren't going well. But remember, even in these moments, you deserve kindness and support.

When we face difficulties, it's tempting to focus solely on the problem and forget about ourselves. However, self-love means acknowledging our struggles without letting them define us. Just as God promises strength and support in our weakest moments, we can draw on this promise to show ourselves love and compassion.

Think about what you would say to a friend in a similar situation. You would offer encouragement and understanding, not criticism. Apply that same grace to yourself. Loving yourself through challenges means embracing your imperfections and recognizing that your worth is not tied to your circumstances. You are valuable and loved, no matter what you're going through.

Prayer

Dear God, in my challenges, help me to see Your strength and love. Guide me to offer myself compassion and support, just as You do. Fill me with Your peace and remind me of my worth. Amen.

Affirmation

I am worthy of love and strength, even through life's challenges.

February 15
Appreciating Your Journey

"The Lord has done great things for us, and we are filled with joy."

(Psalm 126:3, NIV)

Devotional Reflection

Appreciating your journey is about recognizing the value in every step you've taken. Life can feel like a series of hurdles and obstacles, and it's easy to focus only on the destination. But every moment of your journey, including the challenges, contributes to the story of your life.

Think of your life as a beautiful quilt, each patch representing a different experience, whether joyful or difficult. It's tempting to only appreciate the bright and easy patches, but every piece is essential to the whole. Each struggle you've faced and every triumph you've achieved has helped shape who you are today.

Remember, God walks with you through every part of your journey. He sees the effort you put into overcoming obstacles and celebrates each victory with you. Reflecting on how far you've come can bring a renewed sense of joy and gratitude. Embrace your journey with all its ups and downs, knowing that each step is a part of your unique and valuable story.

Prayer

Lord, thank You for guiding me through every part of my journey. Help me to see the value in each step I've taken and to appreciate the path You have set before me. Fill my heart with gratitude and joy as I reflect on how far I've come. Amen.

Affirmation

I appreciate and celebrate every step of my journey, knowing each one is a part of my growth.

February 16
Building Confidence in Your Abilities

"I can do all this through him who gives me strength."

(Philippians 4:13, NIV)

Devotional Reflection

Building confidence in your abilities starts with recognizing the power you already have within. It's easy to doubt yourself when faced with new challenges or when you compare yourself to others. Yet, the Bible reminds us that through Christ, we are empowered to tackle any task before us.

Imagine a time when you accomplished something you thought was impossible. Maybe it was a job task, a personal goal, or a challenge you faced. That moment of success wasn't just luck; it was a result of your hard work and God's strength working through you.

Building confidence isn't about being perfect or never feeling afraid. It's about trusting that God has given you the skills and strength needed to succeed. When you feel uncertain, remind yourself of past victories and the strength that got you through them. Embrace your abilities with the confidence that comes from knowing you are supported by God.

Prayer

Heavenly Father, thank You for the strength You provide in every situation. Help me to build confidence in my abilities and to trust that I can do all things through Your power. Guide me to use my skills for Your glory and to grow in self-belief. Amen.

Affirmation

I am confident in my abilities, knowing that through God's strength, I can achieve great things.

February 17
Embracing Your Imperfections

"But he said to me, 'My grace is sufficient for you, for my power is made perfect in weakness.' Therefore I will boast all the more gladly about my weaknesses, so that Christ's power may rest on me."

(2 Corinthians 12:9, NIV)

Devotional Reflection

Embracing your imperfections can be challenging. It's easy to feel pressure to be perfect or to hide our flaws. Yet, the Bible tells us that God's grace is enough for us, even in our weaknesses. We don't have to be perfect to be loved or to be effective in our roles.

Think about a time when you felt you fell short of expectations. Maybe you made a mistake at work, or you struggled with a personal goal. In those moments, it's tempting to feel defeated or inadequate. But what if, instead of focusing on those flaws, you saw them as opportunities for God's strength to shine through?

Your imperfections are not failures but chances for growth and for God's grace to be visible. By embracing your flaws, you allow God's power to work through you, transforming your weaknesses into sources of strength and authenticity. This approach not only helps you grow but also shows others that they can embrace their imperfections too.

Prayer

Lord, thank You for Your grace that covers all my imperfections. Help me to embrace my weaknesses and trust that Your power can work through them. Teach me to see my flaws as opportunities for growth and to celebrate Your strength in my life. Amen.

Affirmation

I embrace my imperfections as opportunities for God's grace and strength to shine through.

February 18
The Importance of Self-Respect

"Do to others as you would have them do to you." (Luke 6:31, NIV)

Devotional Reflection

Self-respect is not just about how we see ourselves but also how we let others see us. When we respect ourselves, we set boundaries that honor who we are and what we value. For Black women, embracing self-respect is especially vital, given the historical and cultural pressures that often seek to undermine our worth.

Consider a time when you felt disrespected or overlooked. It could have been in a professional setting, a social situation, or even within your own family. Such experiences can shake your confidence and make you question your value. But remember, self-respect begins with you. It's about recognizing your own worth and standing firm in that truth, even when faced with challenges.

Imagine how much stronger and more confident you would feel if you stood up for yourself and honored your own needs and values. When you respect yourself, you teach others to do the same. Your actions and choices reflect the respect you have for yourself, and this, in turn, influences how others interact with you.

In your daily life, practice self-respect by setting healthy boundaries, speaking up for yourself, and making choices that align with your values. Your self-respect will shine through, inspiring others and reinforcing your own sense of worth.

Prayer

Lord, help me to honor and respect myself as You do. Give me the strength to set boundaries and make choices that reflect my true worth. May my actions show the respect I have for myself and inspire others to do the same. Amen.

Affirmation

I honor myself by setting boundaries and making choices that reflect my true worth.

February 19
Rediscovering Your Passions

"Delight yourself in the Lord and he will give you the desires of your heart."
(Psalm 37:4, NIV)

Devotional Reflection

Rediscovering your passions can be like finding a hidden treasure. Sometimes, life's demands and responsibilities overshadow what once brought you joy. For many Black women, cultural and societal expectations can often push personal interests to the background. Yet, these passions are a vital part of who you are and contribute to your overall well-being.

Imagine a time when you felt truly alive and excited. Maybe it was when you were painting, writing, or helping others. Over time, as life got busier, you may have set those passions aside. However, God created each of us with unique gifts and interests. Rediscovering these passions is not just about personal enjoyment; it's a way to connect with the deeper desires God has placed in your heart.

Think about a hobby or interest you once loved but haven't pursued in a while. It might be time to revisit it. Engaging in activities that light up your spirit can rejuvenate you and help you feel more connected to yourself and to God. Your passions are a reflection of God's gifts to you, and embracing them can lead to a more fulfilled and joyful life.

By reconnecting with what makes you happy, you honor the gifts God has given you and enrich your life. Take small steps today to explore and nurture these passions, knowing that they are an important part of your journey.

Prayer

Lord, help me rediscover the passions and interests You've placed in my heart. Guide me as I explore these gifts and bring them back into my life. May I find joy and fulfillment in using them to glorify You.

Amen.

Affirmation

I embrace my passions and allow them to bring joy and fulfillment into my life.

February 20
The Role of Gratitude in Self-Love

"Give thanks to the Lord, for he is good; his love endures forever."

(Psalm 107:1, NIV)

Devotional Reflection

Gratitude is more than just a polite response; it's a powerful tool for nurturing self-love and a positive self-image. For many Black women, life's demands and struggles can sometimes overshadow the things we're thankful for. Yet, recognizing and appreciating even the smallest blessings can profoundly impact our self-perception and overall happiness.

Imagine you've had a challenging day, filled with obstacles and disappointments. In such times, it's easy to focus on the negatives and forget the good things. But what if you took a moment to list a few things you're grateful for, no matter how small? Maybe it's a supportive friend, a moment of peace, or even just the strength to get through the day.

When we practice gratitude, we shift our focus from what's lacking to what's abundant. This shift not only uplifts our spirit but also helps us see ourselves in a more positive light. It's a way of acknowledging that despite challenges, there's always something worth celebrating.

For Black women who face unique societal pressures and personal battles, embracing gratitude can be a transformative practice. It allows us to appreciate our journey, recognize our strength, and affirm our worth. By fostering a habit of gratitude, we reinforce a loving and compassionate view of ourselves.

Prayer

Lord, teach me to see the blessings in my life, even when things are tough. Help me cultivate a heart of gratitude and let it shape my view of myself and my journey. Amen.

Affirmation

I am grateful for the blessings in my life, and I recognize my worth through God's love and goodness.

February 21
Developing a Positive Body Image

"I praise you because I am fearfully and wonderfully made; your works are wonderful, I know that full well." (Psalm 139:14, NIV)

Devotional Reflection

Developing a positive body image can be challenging, especially in a world that often promotes unrealistic standards of beauty. For many Black women, these standards can feel even more distant. We see images and messages that don't always reflect our unique beauty or our cultural heritage, leading to self-doubt and a negative view of our bodies.

But today's scripture reminds us that we are wonderfully made by God. Every part of us is a deliberate and beautiful creation. Your body, with all its features, is a testament to God's amazing work. It's easy to forget this truth when faced with societal pressures or personal insecurities.

Think about the last time you looked in the mirror and saw only flaws. Now, consider how God sees you. He doesn't see imperfections; He sees a masterpiece. Embracing this perspective can help you appreciate your body, not just for how it looks, but for what it does. It allows you to focus on its strength, its health, and its beauty, rather than comparing it to others.

You don't have to meet anyone's standards but God's. He created you with purpose and love. By recognizing this, you can shift from self-criticism to self-acceptance and love. Celebrate your body as a reflection of God's love and creativity.

Prayer

Dear God, help me see myself through Your eyes. Teach me to embrace and love my body as a gift from You. Amen.

Affirmation

I am beautifully and wonderfully made by God, and I embrace and love my body as a reflection of His perfect creation.

February 22
The Freedom of Self-Acceptance

"So if the Son sets you free, you will be free indeed." (John 8:36, NIV)

Devotional Reflection

Self-acceptance can be a challenging journey, especially for Black women who often face societal pressures and unrealistic expectations. The freedom that comes from accepting yourself as you are, with all your strengths and imperfections, is a profound gift.

Imagine feeling trapped by the constant need to conform to others' expectations. This struggle can lead to self-doubt and a lack of joy in your life. Yet, John 8:36 offers a powerful promise: through Christ, we can experience true freedom. This freedom is not just from external pressures but from the internal struggles of self-rejection and insecurity.

When you embrace self-acceptance, you let go of the unrealistic standards imposed by society. You start to see yourself through God's eyes, recognizing your inherent worth and unique beauty. This perspective shift is liberating. It means you no longer need to fit into someone else's mold but can live freely as the person God created you to be.

As you grow in self-acceptance, remember that this freedom is a gift from God. It allows you to live authentically and confidently, knowing that your value comes from being loved by Him, not from meeting societal standards.

Prayer

Lord, thank You for the freedom You offer through Your Son. Help me to accept myself as You see me, letting go of the need to conform to others' expectations. Fill me with the peace and joy that come from true self-acceptance. Amen.

Affirmation

I am free to embrace and love myself as God made me. I am valuable and worthy, and I live in the freedom of His love and acceptance.

February 23
Creating a Self-Love Ritual

"You shall love your neighbor as yourself." (Mark 12:31, NIV)

Devotional Reflection

Creating a self-love ritual might seem like a luxury, but it's actually an essential practice for nurturing your soul. In Mark 12:31, Jesus highlights the importance of loving others as we love ourselves. This means that self-love isn't just about feeling good; it's about recognizing our worth and treating ourselves with kindness and respect.

Consider a time when you felt drained and overwhelmed by daily responsibilities. Often, we forget to take care of ourselves in the rush of life. Establishing a self-love ritual can be a transformative way to counteract this. It could be something simple, like setting aside a few minutes each day for a calming activity or writing down affirmations that uplift you.

For Black women, who often juggle multiple roles and face unique challenges, a self-love ritual can be a powerful act of rebellion against societal pressures. It's a statement that you are worthy of love and care, just as much as anyone else. By regularly engaging in this practice, you not only honor yourself but also align with God's command to love yourself deeply.

Incorporating a self-love ritual into your daily routine can rejuvenate your spirit and help you face challenges with renewed strength and grace.

Prayer

Dear God, thank You for reminding me to love myself as You love me. Help me to create and stick to a self-love ritual that nurtures my soul and honors my worth. Amen.

Affirmation

I honor and care for myself with the same love and respect that God shows me. I am deserving of self-love and create daily rituals that nurture my well-being.

February 24
Finding Balance in Your Life

"For everything there is a season, a time for every activity under heaven." (Ecclesiastes 3:1, NIV)

Devotional Reflection

Finding balance in your life is more than just managing your time; it's about aligning your priorities with your values and well-being. Ecclesiastes 3:1 reminds us that everything has its time, and this includes balancing different aspects of our lives.

Imagine juggling work, family, and personal goals. It can feel overwhelming, especially when societal expectations often add extra pressure. For many Black women, balancing these demands can seem like a constant challenge. Yet, God's word assures us that there is a time for everything, and finding balance doesn't mean doing it all at once.

One way to start finding balance is to identify what truly matters to you. Reflect on your daily activities and see if they align with your core values. Perhaps you realize that you need more time for rest or personal growth. Balancing your life might mean setting boundaries at work, carving out time for self-care, or nurturing relationships that uplift you.

Remember, finding balance is an ongoing process. It's about making choices that reflect your values and give you space to grow. Trust that God is guiding you through each season, helping you find harmony in the midst of life's demands.

Prayer

Lord, help me to find balance in my life. Guide me to manage my time and responsibilities in a way that honors You and aligns with my values. Give me the wisdom to set boundaries and the strength to prioritize what truly matters. Amen.

Affirmation

I trust God to guide me in finding balance in my life. I make choices that align with my values and allow space for rest and growth.

February 25
The Impact of Self-Worth on Relationships

"Above all else, guard your heart, for everything you do flows from it."
(Proverbs 4:23, NIV)

Devotional Reflection

Self-worth is the foundation of how we interact with others. Proverbs 4:23 highlights the importance of guarding our hearts because our self-perception affects everything we do, including our relationships. When we see ourselves through God's eyes, as valuable and loved, it transforms how we relate to others.

Consider a woman who feels insecure and unworthy. This inner turmoil can lead her to tolerate unhealthy relationships or struggle with setting boundaries. When she doesn't recognize her own worth, she might find herself seeking validation from others, which can lead to disappointment and strained relationships.

On the other hand, when you embrace your inherent value, you bring a healthier, more confident version of yourself into your relationships. Understanding your worth helps you set boundaries, communicate openly, and make choices that reflect your true self. This self-respect naturally encourages others to treat you with the respect you deserve.

Remember, recognizing your self-worth doesn't mean you're perfect. It means you acknowledge your value and allow that understanding to shape your interactions. By doing so, you create stronger, more authentic relationships that are built on mutual respect and love.

Prayer

Lord, help me to see my worth through Your eyes. Guide me to value myself and let that understanding shape my relationships. Grant me the strength to set boundaries and seek relationships that reflect my true value. Amen.

Affirmation

I am valuable and worthy of love and respect. My self-worth guides me to build healthy and respectful relationships.

February 26
Prioritizing Your Mental Health
"Cast all your anxiety on him because he cares for you."

(1 Peter 5:7, NIV)

Devotional Reflection

Mental health is crucial to our overall well-being, yet it's often overlooked in our busy lives. 1 Peter 5:7 reminds us to cast our anxieties on God, acknowledging that He cares deeply for us. This verse is not just a comforting thought but a call to actively manage our mental health by leaning on God's support.

Imagine a woman juggling multiple responsibilities and personal life—feeling overwhelmed and stressed. She might think she needs to handle everything alone, leading to burnout and neglect of her mental health. By failing to prioritize herself, she risks her well-being and her ability to be present for others.

Prioritizing mental health means recognizing when you need help and taking steps to care for your mind. It involves setting boundaries, taking breaks, and seeking support when needed. Embracing this self-care allows you to handle stress better and remain strong for yourself and those you love.

Remember, acknowledging your mental health needs is not a sign of weakness but an act of strength. By entrusting your worries to God, you invite His peace and support into your life, helping you manage stress and maintain balance.

Prayer

Dear God, help me to recognize the importance of my mental health. Guide me to cast my anxieties on You and find strength in Your care. Teach me to prioritize self-care and seek support when needed. Amen.

Affirmation

I am worthy of peace and balance. By prioritizing my mental health, I honor myself and trust in God's care.

February 27
The Journey to Inner Peace

"You will keep in perfect peace those whose minds are steadfast, because they trust in you." (Isaiah 26:3, NIV)

Devotional Reflection

Finding inner peace is a journey, not a destination. Isaiah 26:3 offers a promise: perfect peace comes from trusting God with our hearts and minds. This verse is a reminder that peace isn't just about external calm but an inner assurance rooted in faith.

Consider the story of a woman who felt constantly unsettled due to daily pressures and challenges. From work stress to family obligations, her mind was always racing. She sought peace in various ways—meditation, exercise, and even vacations—but the relief was only temporary. It was when she turned her focus inward and leaned on her faith, trusting God with her worries, that she found lasting peace.

The journey to inner peace involves more than just quiet moments; it's about cultivating a deep trust in God. By keeping our minds steadfast on Him, we align ourselves with His peace, which surpasses all understanding. This peace helps us handle stress and challenges with grace and calm, knowing that God is in control.

In your journey to inner peace, remember that it's a process. It requires patience, prayer, and trust. Each step you take towards surrendering your anxieties to God brings you closer to the tranquility you seek.

Prayer

Lord, help me to trust You fully with my worries and fears. Guide me to find inner peace through steadfast faith in You. Let Your peace guard my heart and mind today. Amen.

Affirmation

I am at peace because I trust God with my heart and mind. His perfect peace guards me and guides me through life's challenges.

February 28
Embracing the Power of Self-Love

"Love your neighbor as yourself." (Mark 12:31, NIV)

Devotional Reflection

Embracing the power of self-love is not just about feeling good; it's about recognizing our worth through God's eyes. Mark 12:31 instructs us to love our neighbors as ourselves, highlighting the importance of self-love. If we are to love others, we first need to love ourselves.

Imagine a woman who always gave her best to everyone around her but neglected her own needs and feelings. She constantly felt drained and unappreciated. It wasn't until she started practicing self-love—by setting boundaries, nurturing her interests, and affirming her worth—that she felt renewed and more effective in her relationships.

Self-love means understanding that you are valuable and worthy of care. It involves acknowledging your strengths and weaknesses and treating yourself with kindness. By doing this, you honor God's creation—yourself. When you embrace self-love, you align with God's plan for you to live a fulfilling and empowered life. This love fuels your ability to love others more deeply and genuinely.

As you embrace self-love, remember that it's a divine command. It's not selfish; it's essential. By loving yourself, you embrace the truth of your worth and God's plan for your life.

Prayer

Lord, help me to embrace and practice self-love. Show me how to value myself as You do and to extend that love to others. Fill my heart with Your truth and peace. Amen.

Affirmation

I am worthy of love and care. I embrace my worth and let it guide my actions and relationships.

March
Resilience and Strength

March 1
Embracing Your Strengths

"I can do all this through him who gives me strength."
(Philippians 4:13, NIV)

Devotional Reflection

God has given you the ability to accomplish anything He places before you. No matter how difficult the situation, you are equipped to overcome it with His help. You are not lacking; you are filled with divine strength, ready to conquer any challenge. This verse reminds us that we don't rely solely on our abilities—God's strength empowers us, and through Him, all things are possible.

Maybe you've doubted your ability, told you aren't strong or smart enough. But God has already equipped you with everything needed to face challenges.

Black women often face unique pressures from societal expectations to balancing work and personal growth. It can feel overwhelming, but your strength comes from knowing you are enough. You are not defined by others' perceptions but by how God designed you.

As you go through life, your inner strengths guide you—whether resilience from past experiences, wisdom gained, or unshakable faith. Trust in these gifts, and you'll see no challenge is too great. You have everything you need to rise above.

Prayer

Lord, thank You for the strength You've placed inside me. Help me to recognize and embrace the gifts You've given me, knowing that with You, I can overcome any challenge. Let me trust in Your strength and use it to fulfill my purpose. Amen.

Affirmation

Today, I embrace the strength that God has placed within me. I am capable, resilient, and ready to conquer anything that comes my way.

March 2
Overcoming Obstacles with Faith

"For we live by faith, not by sight." (2 Corinthians 5:7, NIV)

Devotional Reflection

Faith isn't just for when things are going well; it's a deep trust in God, even when life doesn't make sense. The biggest obstacles often seem impossible to overcome on our own. But when we live by faith, we trust God is working for us, even when the path is unclear.

Think of a time when life threw you a curveball—maybe a setback or a relationship issue. In moments like these, it's easy to feel powerless. But this is where faith steps in. Faith allows you to trust in God's power, not your own strength.

As Black women, there are often extra layers to the struggles we face. But faith gives us the ability to rise above what we see in the physical world. You trust that God has already paved the way for your victory.

Faith doesn't make obstacles disappear. It means you face them knowing you're not alone. Whether it's systemic challenges or personal struggles, God has given you what you need to press through. Trusting Him unlocks resilience and allows you to walk through life's hurdles with grace and strength, knowing God is with you every step of the way.

Prayer

Lord, give me the strength to face the challenges before me. Help me trust in You, even when I can't see the way forward. I place my faith in Your hands, knowing that You are my guide and protector. Amen.

Affirmation

Today, I choose to walk by faith and not by sight. I trust that God is guiding me through every obstacle, and I am stronger because of His presence in my life.

March 3
The Power of Community Support

"Carry each other's burdens, and in this way, you will fulfill the law of Christ." (Galatians 6:2, NIV)

Devotional Reflection

Life can be overwhelming, and trying to carry everything alone leads to burnout. God never intended for us to navigate this journey by ourselves. We are reminded through scripture of the importance of community and how we should lift each other up, providing strength and comfort to one another.

Community support is a powerful tool for resilience. Think about the times you've leaned on others or provided a shoulder for someone else. As Black women, our communities—whether family, friends, or church—are often the cornerstone of our strength. In a world that can feel isolating, we find comfort in knowing we're not alone.

When someone steps in with encouragement, prayer, or even just their presence during tough times, that's the power of community. Relying on others doesn't mean you're weak; it means you value collective strength.

When Black women unite, we create a bond that's hard to break. Whether navigating systemic challenges or personal struggles, there's power in numbers. Through faith, we lift each other up, knowing that as we help others, we strengthen ourselves. Together, we rise and overcome.

Prayer

Lord, help me to be a source of strength for those around me, and remind me that I do not have to carry my burdens alone. Teach me to lean on my community and to support others as we walk this journey together. Amen.

Affirmation

I am surrounded by love and support. My community strengthens me, and together, we carry each other's burdens with grace and resilience.

March 4
Finding Courage in Adversity

"Have I not commanded you? Be strong and courageous. Do not be afraid; do not be discouraged, for the Lord your God will be with you wherever you go." (Joshua 1:9, NIV)

Devotional Reflection

God's call to be strong and courageous isn't a suggestion; it's a command. He knows we'll face difficulties, but He also knows we can overcome them. God's presence gives us the courage to keep going. He stands beside us, providing strength when we feel weak or afraid. This verse reminds us that no matter the challenges, we are never alone, and fear doesn't have the final say.

Courage isn't the absence of fear but the ability to push forward despite it. Life often presents hardships that seem overwhelming. Whether it's a financial struggle, health challenge, or personal crisis, the weight can feel too much to bear. As Black women, the world places heavy burdens on us, yet we stand tall.

In the storm, you can find courage knowing God is with you. Reflect on times when you thought you couldn't go on, yet you did. You felt fear but also God's pull to take one more step. That's courage in adversity.

Trust that God is in control, and courage will follow. Facing challenges is inevitable, but facing them with God's guidance makes all the difference.

Prayer

Dear Lord, in times of adversity, help me to find courage. Remind me that You are always with me, guiding me through every challenge. Strengthen my heart and give me the bravery to face anything that comes my way. Amen.

Affirmation

I am strong and courageous. God walks with me through every storm, and with His help, I can face any challenge with faith.

March 5
Turning Setbacks into Comebacks

"And we know that in all things God works for the good of those who love him, who have been called according to his purpose."

(Romans 8:28, NIV)

Devotional Reflection

This verse reminds us that no matter what life throws our way, God is working behind the scenes for our good. Even in failure or setbacks, God uses those moments to mold us and prepare us for something greater. Nothing is wasted in His hands, and every setback can lead to a stronger, more faithful version of ourselves.

Have you ever felt knocked down, wondering how to get back up? Maybe it was a failure, broken relationship, or a loss. For many Black women, society adds extra challenges, making setbacks feel like permanent barriers. But setbacks are not the end—they're just a chapter.

When adversity strikes, it can feel overwhelming. But God is still working. Setbacks often come before breakthroughs, where God turns what seems like failure into growth. Reflect on past setbacks that later led to something better, like a closed door leading to a greater opportunity or a painful experience building resilience.

Setbacks aren't signs of defeat but stepping stones toward something greater. With God's guidance, each setback can become a story of resilience and growth.

Prayer

Lord, help me to see the setbacks in my life as opportunities for growth and development. Give me the strength to trust in Your plan, even when things don't go as expected. I believe You are turning my setbacks into comebacks. Amen.

Affirmation

I embrace every setback as a chance to grow and become stronger. I am confident that God is working for my good and turning my obstacles into opportunities.

March 6
The Role of Self-Care in Building Resilience

"Do you not know that your bodies are temples of the Holy Spirit, who is in you, whom you have received from God? You are not your own."

(1 Corinthians 6:19, NIV)

Devotional Reflection

This verse reminds us of the importance of treating our bodies with care. Our health is a gift from God, and taking care of it is stewardship. Nurturing ourselves builds resilience, allowing us to fulfill God's purpose. Self-care isn't selfish; it's a spiritual practice that values the life God has given us.

Black women are often expected to be the backbone of families and communities. The pressure to be strong can lead to burnout when we don't take time for ourselves. Many are taught to see self-care as a luxury, but it's a necessity.

Think about a woman always giving to her job, family, or community. Without caring for herself, she risks exhaustion. Self-care protects her inner strength so when adversity strikes, she has the capacity to face it.

Self-care doesn't have to be extravagant. Simple practices like quiet Prayeror saying "no" to draining obligations build resilience. Caring for yourself ensures you're better equipped to care for others. You can't pour from an empty cup, so fill yourself first and see how much more you can give.

God wants you to thrive. Self-care isn't indulgence; it's preserving the body, mind, and spirit God entrusted to you. Every act of care builds your resilience and prepares you to handle life's challenges with peace and strength.

Prayer

Lord, help me to honor the body, mind, and spirit You have given me. Teach me to care for myself as an act of worship and allow me to see that self-care is part of building resilience. Amen.

Affirmation

I care for myself with love and respect, knowing that self-care strengthens me and prepares me for whatever life brings.

March 7
Balancing Strength with Vulnerability

"But he said to me, 'My grace is sufficient for you, for my power is made perfect in weakness.' Therefore I will boast all the more gladly about my weaknesses, so that Christ's power may rest on me."

(2 Corinthians 12:9, NIV)

Devotional Reflection

This verse reminds us that strength grows through vulnerability. When we admit our limits, we allow God's power to work in us. In weakness, God's grace carries us. Vulnerability isn't failure; it's a doorway to divine strength.

In a world that celebrates independence, vulnerability can seem negative. Black women are often seen as resilient, but there's strength in admitting when you're not okay. The "Strong Black Woman" image can create pressure to hide weakness, but vulnerability doesn't make you weak; it makes you real.

Consider a woman carrying the weight of family and work without admitting she needs a break. The burden becomes too much, and she feels lost. By avoiding vulnerability, she misses the support that could help her heal.

Vulnerability opens the door to deeper connections. Showing your true self invites authenticity. You don't have to hold everything together. It's okay to trust that God and loved ones will help.
God doesn't expect you to carry all burdens alone. Admitting your need for help allows His power to work. Vulnerability is courage, and in it, you discover new resilience.

Prayer

Lord, help me to embrace my vulnerability and see it as a source of strength. Guide me to open my heart to You and others, trusting that You will provide the support and grace I need in every season. Amen.

Affirmation

I am strong enough to be vulnerable, knowing that God's grace fills my weaknesses with His strength.

March 8
Lessons from Resilient Black Women in History

"Therefore, since we are surrounded by such a great cloud of witnesses, let us throw off everything that hinders and the sin that so easily entangles. And let us run with perseverance the race marked out for us." (Hebrews 12:1, NIV)

Devotional Reflection

This verse reminds us we are not alone in our struggles. Many before us ran their race with perseverance, leaving examples of faith and strength. Their stories encourage us to press forward, knowing we can overcome obstacles, just as they did. As Black women, we stand on the shoulders of those who paved the way with resilience.

Throughout history, Black women have shown resilience in the face of impossible odds. Harriet Tubman freed herself and risked her life to help others find freedom. Her bravery shows that even in dark times, we can be a light.

Maya Angelou inspired women to rise above struggles with grace. She turned her challenges into wisdom that continues to inspire.

The pain and hardship they faced may feel familiar to you. Whether it's daily life, racism, or personal battles, you, too, walk a path of strength. These women remind us we don't carry the weight alone. Their stories reveal the power of faith and perseverance.

The resilience of Black women shows the strength within you. You don't need to have it all figured out or be fearless at every moment. But you have the power to keep going. Take inspiration from these women, knowing the same spirit lives in you.

Prayer

Dear Lord, thank You for the powerful examples of resilience from the Black women who came before me. Help me draw strength from their stories, and give me the courage to keep moving forward, no matter the challenges I face. Amen.

Affirmation

I stand on the shoulders of resilient women, and their strength flows through me today.

March 9
The Impact of Positive Self-Talk

"Finally, brothers and sisters, whatever is true, whatever is noble, whatever is right, whatever is pure, whatever is lovely, whatever is admirable—if anything is excellent or praiseworthy—think about such things." (Philippians 4:8, NIV)

Devotional Reflection

This verse reminds us of the power of our thoughts. What we dwell on shapes our emotions and outlook. In hardship, focusing on positive, praiseworthy things builds resilience and strength.

Have you ever been stuck in negative self-talk? After a mistake, your mind might tell you, "I'm not good enough," or, "I can't do this." Society often expects Black women to be strong and perfect, which can reinforce those doubts. But your words, whether spoken or thought, hold immense power.

Negative thoughts weaken resilience, but choosing to speak positively shifts your mindset. Think of positive self-talk as a personal coach cheering you on. Instead of saying, "I can't handle this," say, "This is tough, but I'm stronger than I think." This simple shift changes how you approach problems.

Serena Williams faced doubt and criticism but focused on her inner dialogue, reminding herself of her strength. Her resilience came from refusing to let negativity win.

Changing your inner dialogue can help you stay grounded. Speak words that lift you up, not tear you down. You have the power to rewrite your narrative each day.

Prayer

Lord, help me to change the way I speak to myself. Give me the strength to replace negative thoughts with positive truths, and remind me that with You, I have the power to overcome any challenge. Amen.

Affirmation

I speak words of life and strength over myself, and I am resilient in the face of challenges.

March 10
Navigating Change with Grace

"There is a time for everything, and a season for every activity under the heavens." (Ecclesiastes 3:1, NIV)

Devotional Reflection

This verse reminds us life is full of seasons, each bringing changes and challenges. Transitions are natural, and God has a purpose for every moment. Embracing change with grace means trusting every season contributes to your growth and walk with God.

Change brings uncertainty. Whether it's a new job, a move, or shifting relationships, transitions can feel overwhelming. For Black women, the weight of expectations can make navigating change feel like walking a tightrope.

Imagine moving to a new city for a job, excited but leaving behind your support system. In these moments, God asks us to lean on Him and navigate transitions with grace.

Grace doesn't mean you won't feel fear or anxiety. It's about trusting God in uncertainty and letting Him guide you. Grace is giving yourself permission to feel while knowing you're equipped to handle it.

Think of Michelle Obama, who transitioned from working mother to First Lady with grace, grounded in faith. We can learn from her to rise to the occasion, trusting God is shaping us.

When life brings change, turn to God. With grace, step into the unknown, trusting each transition is for growth.

Prayer

Lord, help me to embrace the changes in my life with grace. Remind me that You are in control of every season, and give me the strength to trust Your plan even when I feel uncertain. Amen.

Affirmation

I navigate life's transitions with grace, trusting that God is leading me through every change.

March 11
The Strength in Forgiveness

"Be kind and compassionate to one another, forgiving each other, just as in Christ God forgave you." (Ephesians 4:32, NIV)

Devotional Reflection

This verse reminds us of the power of forgiveness. It's not just a command but a path to healing and freedom. When we forgive, we release bitterness and make room for peace and strength.

Forgiveness can be hard, especially when the pain is deep. Whether it's betrayal, disappointment, or regret, holding onto hurt can weigh you down. As Black women, we face challenges and pressure to be strong. But holding grudges doesn't make us stronger—it drains us.

Imagine carrying a heavy backpack on a journey. Every grudge or hurt is another stone in the bag, making life harder. Forgiveness is taking off that weight—a gift to yourself.

Sometimes, the hardest person to forgive is yourself. Mistakes lead to guilt, but strength lies in releasing that burden. When you forgive, you choose freedom and allow God's grace to build resilience.

Maya Angelou, despite struggles, found strength in forgiveness. She forgave others and herself, rising above her circumstances. Like her, you can find freedom by letting go and embracing forgiveness.

Forgiveness doesn't mean what happened was okay—it means you're no longer letting it control you. It's a strength that heals.

Prayer

Lord, grant me the strength to forgive. Amen

Affirmation

I am strong enough to forgive, and in doing so, I find peace and freedom.

March 12
Building Resilience Through Education and Knowledge

"The heart of the discerning acquires knowledge, for the ears of the wise seek it out." (Proverbs 18:15, NIV)

Devotional Reflection

This scripture highlights the value of seeking wisdom. Growth stems from learning, which fosters resilience. By nourishing our minds, we become more prepared for life's challenges. Knowledge truly is power, especially for Black women facing unique hurdles. It's not just about formal education; it's about being curious—learning about ourselves, our faith, and the world.

Think of Sojourner Truth and Mary McLeod Bethune, who used knowledge to overcome adversity. Their strength came from their wisdom, allowing them to rise above their circumstances. Learning can also be personal, like managing stress or understanding financial literacy. Every piece of knowledge enhances your strength.

As Black women, we continue to evolve, strengthening our foundation with each new insight. God has gifted you a brilliant mind, and filling it with wisdom creates resilience to face life's storms. Growth is a lifelong journey of seeking wisdom and personal development, building strength with every challenge faced.

Prayer

Lord, help me to be a lifelong learner, always seeking wisdom and knowledge to strengthen my faith and my life. Guide me as I grow in understanding and use it to better myself and serve others. Amen.

Affirmation

I am constantly growing and learning. Each piece of knowledge makes me stronger and more resilient.

March 13
Setting Boundaries for Emotional Health

"Above all else, guard your heart, for everything you do flows from it."
(Proverbs 4:23, NIV)

Devotional Reflection

This verse reminds us to protect our hearts and minds, which are key to emotional and spiritual well-being. Setting boundaries helps us guard our hearts, focusing on what nourishes us and keeps us strong in faith. As Black women, we often give so much to others, but we must also care for our emotional health. Boundaries aren't selfish—they are wise.

Imagine your heart as a garden. Without boundaries, it can be trampled, but with healthy limits, you can protect what you've nurtured. Setting boundaries allows us to preserve emotional energy and face challenges with grace. Saying "no" when overwhelmed or stepping back from draining relationships is a way to protect your heart and mind.

God wants you to thrive, and part of thriving is knowing when to draw the line. Boundaries invite others to respect your needs, and they allow you to nurture yourself spiritually and emotionally. Just as Jesus took time to pray and recharge, you too deserve time to protect your emotional health.

Prayer

Lord, help me to set healthy boundaries that protect my heart and emotional health. Give me the wisdom to know when to say no and the strength to enforce my limits with love and grace. Amen.

Affirmation

I am worthy of setting boundaries that protect my emotional health and well-being.

March 14
Finding Strength in Creativity

"For we are God's handiwork, created in Christ Jesus to do good works, which God prepared in advance for us to do."

(Ephesians 2:10, NIV)

Devotional Reflection

This verse reminds us that we are God's masterpiece, uniquely designed with purpose. Our creative gifts are part of His plan, offering strength during challenging times. Creativity allows us to express ourselves and build resilience, especially as Black women facing life's pressures. Whether balancing family, career, or navigating society, creativity becomes an outlet for healing and strength.

Creativity is more than art or music—it's any form of self-expression, like writing, cooking, or even styling hair. These outlets give space to process emotions and regain a sense of self. A woman painting, for example, finds peace in each brushstroke, pouring out her fears and hopes. Her creation reflects her resilience.

Creative expression doesn't need perfection; it's about the process. Whether through poetry, gardening, or journaling, these acts tell your story. God gave you creativity to help you grow and heal, making it a source of strength when life becomes overwhelming.

Prayer

Heavenly Father, thank You for the gift of creativity. Help me to use my creative talents to build my resilience and express the beautiful person You created me to be. In moments of challenge, guide me to find strength in the work of my hands and the joy of creating. Amen.

Affirmation

I am a creative being, designed by God to express myself and build resilience through my unique gifts.

March 15
The Role of Mentorship in Developing Strength

"As iron sharpens iron, so one person sharpens another."
(Proverbs 27:17, NIV)

Devotional Reflection

Mentorship is a powerful tool for building resilience. Whether seeking guidance or sharing wisdom, mentorship impacts growth. For Black women, it can be especially meaningful as it offers support from those who understand similar life experiences.

Picture a young woman starting her career, feeling unsure but finding a mentor who has faced similar challenges. This mentor offers advice and encouragement, helping her realize her potential. On the other hand, being a mentor allows you to share your experiences, reinforcing your knowledge and building confidence. It's an opportunity to give back and support others on their journey.

Mentorship creates a cycle of learning and support, helping everyone involved grow stronger. Through these relationships, we gain new perspectives and resilience to face life's challenges. Think about the mentors in your life and how these relationships have shaped your path. The strength gained from mentorship helps you tackle challenges and reach your goals with confidence.

Prayer

Lord, thank You for the mentors in my life and the opportunity to mentor others. Help me to be a source of encouragement and strength, both as a mentee and a mentor. Guide me to build meaningful relationships that foster growth and resilience. Amen.

Affirmation

I am grateful for the guidance and support I receive and give. Through mentorship, I grow stronger and help others do the same.

March 16
Celebrating Small Victories

"Do not despise these small beginnings, for the Lord rejoices to see the work begin." (Zechariah 4:10, NIV)

Devotional Reflection

Celebrating small victories is key to building confidence and resilience. Often, we focus on big goals and overlook the progress we've made. For Black women, acknowledging these small wins can be a powerful way to stay motivated.

Think of working hard towards a personal goal—whether starting a business or improving your health. Every step forward, no matter how small, is worth celebrating. Maybe you made a sale or stuck to a healthy habit for a week. These are victories!

It's easy to focus only on the bigger picture, but celebrating each small win boosts confidence and keeps you going. It's like giving yourself encouragement, recognizing that every step counts. For example, if you managed stress today or made a new friend, those are small victories worth acknowledging.

Recognizing these achievements helps you stay positive and focused. Progress is happening, even if slow. Celebrate these moments, share them, or take a moment to appreciate your efforts. Each small win leads to bigger goals and strengthens resilience.

Prayer

Lord, thank You for the small victories in my life. Help me to see and celebrate each step forward as a sign of Your guidance and blessing. Give me the strength to continue moving forward and the joy to appreciate the progress I make each day. Amen.

Affirmation

I celebrate each small victory as a step towards my greater goals. Each achievement, no matter how small, builds my confidence and strength.

March 17
Resilience in the Face of Discrimination

"Blessed is the one who perseveres under trial because, having stood the test, that person will receive the crown of life that the Lord has promised to those who love him." (James 1:12, NIV)

Devotional Reflection

Facing racial discrimination is tough, but resilience in such trials is both necessary and possible. It takes strength to keep going when treated unfairly. Imagine a Black woman applying for a job and facing discrimination due to her race. She could feel discouraged, but instead, she stays focused on her strengths and abilities, using her experiences to fuel her success.

Resilience means holding onto your self-worth, despite negativity. It involves trusting that God is with you in every trial. Your value isn't based on others' opinions but on your faith and God's promises.

Develop strategies to stay resilient, like finding supportive communities and practicing self-care. These remind you that you're not alone and your strength is greater than any discrimination you face. Your resilience can serve as hope and inspiration, showing others how to rise above adversity with grace and faith.

Prayer

Lord, give me strength to remain resilient in the face of discrimination. Help me to see my worth through Your eyes and to trust in Your guidance. Support me with Your grace and surround me with encouragement as I navigate these challenges. Amen.

Affirmation

I am strong and resilient. My worth is not determined by others, but by God's love and promise. I rise above challenges with grace and faith.

March 18
The Healing Power of Reflection

"But Jesus often withdrew to lonely places and prayed."

(Luke 5:16, NIV)

Devotional Reflection

In this verse, Jesus shows us the value of taking time alone to reflect and pray. Just as He sought solitude, we can use quiet moments to heal and find strength.

Self-reflection is a powerful tool for healing and growth, especially for Black women facing daily challenges. Amidst life's demands, reflection offers a way to process emotions and regain strength. Imagine a tough week at work—taking time to sit quietly and reflect can bring healing. You might recognize patterns in your emotions or identify the sources of your stress, helping you understand yourself better.

Reflection not only helps with the past but also prepares you for the future. It reveals what brings you joy and what drains you, offering insights for handling situations better next time. Ask yourself: What's causing my stress? How have I managed similar situations before? What can I do differently? Through reflection, you equip yourself to move forward with strength and clarity.

Prayer

Dear Lord, guide me in my moments of reflection. Help me to understand my emotions and learn from my experiences. Grant me the peace and insight I need to grow stronger and heal through Your wisdom. Amen.

Affirmation

I am strong and resilient. Through reflection and prayer, I gain clarity and strength. My past experiences guide me toward a brighter, more empowered future.

March 19
Cultivating Patience and Perseverance

"But the fruit of the Spirit is love, joy, peace, forbearance, kindness, goodness, faithfulness, gentleness and self-control. Against such things there is no law." (Galatians 5:22-23, NIV)

Devotional Reflection
This verse highlights patience as a fruit of the Spirit. It reminds us that patience and perseverance are key qualities that help us align with God's will.

Patience and perseverance are like the roots of a tree, keeping us grounded when life's storms arise. For Black women balancing work, family, and goals, it's easy to lose patience when things don't go as planned. Progress can seem slow, but just like a tree grows steadily, your efforts and patience are guiding you toward success.

Cultivating patience means accepting that growth is gradual, while perseverance is about pushing forward despite challenges. When obstacles appear, view them as opportunities to grow stronger. Each small step brings you closer to your goals.

Think of a time when patience paid off for you, perhaps during a tough period at work or while overcoming a personal challenge. Reflecting on these moments can remind you of the value in staying the course and trusting the process.

Prayer
Lord, grant me the patience to endure and the strength to persevere. Help me to remain steadfast in my journey and to trust in Your timing. Fill me with Your Spirit to guide my efforts and to keep me encouraged. Amen.

Affirmation
I am patient and resilient. I trust in the process and stay determined in the face of challenges. Each day, I grow stronger and closer to achieving my goals.

March 20
The Influence of Faith and Spirituality

"The LORD is my strength and my shield; my heart trusts in him, and he helps me. My heart leaps for joy, and with my song I praise him."

(Psalm 28:7, NIV)

Devotional Reflection

Faith and spirituality are like a steady anchor in a stormy sea, keeping us grounded when life gets challenging. For many Black women, navigating daily struggles and overcoming obstacles can be tough. It's easy to feel overwhelmed when facing personal or professional challenges. But faith can offer a different perspective.

Imagine a time when you faced a tough situation, like a challenging work project or a personal struggle. Reflect on how your faith helped you through. Maybe you turned to Prayeror sought comfort from your spiritual community. That connection with God provided strength and resilience you might not have found on your own.

Faith reminds us that we are not alone. It offers hope and a sense of purpose, even in the darkest times. Spiritual practices, like Prayeror meditation, help us stay focused and centered. They give us the inner strength to face difficulties with grace and confidence.

Drawing on your spirituality can make a big difference. When you face challenges, remember that your faith is a source of support. It can help you stay calm and find joy even when things are tough. By trusting in God, you strengthen your ability to handle life's ups and downs.

Prayer

Dear Lord, thank You for being my strength and support. Help me rely on my faith to face challenges and find peace. Guide me through difficult times and fill me with Your strength. Amen.

Affirmation

My faith gives me strength and resilience. I trust in God's guidance and find joy in His support. Every challenge I face strengthens my spirit and brings me closer to my goals.

March 21
Embracing Change as a Path to Growth

"Jesus Christ is the same yesterday and today and forever."
(Hebrews 13:8, NIV)

Devotional Reflection

Change is often viewed with uncertainty and fear, but it can also be a powerful opportunity for growth. Many Black women face changes in their lives, whether it's a new job, a move, or shifts in personal relationships. It's natural to feel apprehensive about these changes, but embracing them can lead to profound personal and spiritual growth.

Think about a time when you faced a big change. Perhaps you started a new job or moved to a new city. At first, the change might have seemed daunting. But looking back, you might see how it helped you grow and become stronger. Change can push us out of our comfort zones and force us to adapt and learn new things.

God often uses change to help us grow. When we trust Him during these times, we open ourselves up to new possibilities. Change allows us to develop new skills, meet new people, and discover more about ourselves and our purpose. It's through these experiences that we can build resilience and deepen our faith.

Embrace change as a chance to grow. Each change in your life can be a step toward becoming a better, stronger version of yourself. Trust in God's plan and allow change to guide you toward new opportunities and deeper spiritual understanding.

Prayer

Dear Lord, help me to embrace the changes in my life with faith and courage. Guide me through transitions and let them be a path to growth and renewal. Strengthen my spirit and help me see Your purpose in every change. Amen.

Affirmation

I embrace change as a path to growth. I trust that every transition brings new opportunities for personal and spiritual development. With God's guidance, I am strong and resilient in the face of change.

March 22
The Power of Positive Role Models

"The righteous man will flourish like the palm tree: he will grow like a cedar in Lebanon." (Psalm 92:12, NIV)

Devotional Reflection

Positive role models play a crucial role in our lives. They offer us examples of how to handle difficulties with grace and strength. Consider the powerful women around you who uplift and guide you. Their stories of overcoming struggles can give you the courage to face your own challenges.

For example, think of a mentor or a community leader who has faced hardships but remained strong. Their experiences can teach you how to manage your own trials. Seeing how they handle obstacles can inspire you to adopt their resilience and determination.

In your own life, these role models might be someone who shows you how to keep faith alive through tough times or someone whose wisdom helps you navigate your journey. By looking at their lives, you can draw strength and hope, knowing that their path can light your way.

Prayer

Dear Lord, thank You for the positive role models in my life. Help me learn from their strength and apply their lessons to my own journey. May their example inspire me to face my challenges with faith and courage. Amen.

Affirmation

I am inspired by the strength and wisdom of those who guide me. Their example empowers me to face my challenges with confidence. I am resilient and capable, just like the role models in my life.

March 23
Overcoming Fear with Faith

"For God has not given us a spirit of fear, but of power and of love and of a sound mind." (2 Timothy 1:7, NIV)

Devotional Reflection

This verse reminds us that fear is not from God. Instead, He gives us strength, love, and a clear mind to overcome the worries that try to hold us back.

Fear can creep into your life in unexpected ways, whether it's through uncertainty about the future, doubt in your abilities, or feeling overwhelmed by your responsibilities. As a Black woman, you may face unique challenges that can sometimes make fear seem like a constant companion. But faith provides the strength to overcome it.

Imagine walking into a new situation. Fear might tell you that you're not capable, that you won't succeed, or that things won't work out. But faith quiets that voice. Faith reminds you of all the times God has brought you through before.

By trusting in God's power, you can face the unknown with confidence. The same power that raised Jesus from the dead lives in you. Fear loses its grip when you stand on this truth. Faith becomes the light that guides you through the darkest moments, reminding you that you are not alone, and that God's love and strength are always with you.

Prayer

Dear God, help me to remember that You have not given me a spirit of fear, but of power and love. Strengthen my faith so that I can overcome fear with confidence in You. Amen.

Affirmation

I will not let fear control my life. I am filled with God's power, love, and peace. Through faith, I can conquer anything that comes my way.

March 24
The Strength of Forging New Paths

"Trust in the Lord with all your heart and lean not on your own understanding; in all your ways submit to him, and he will make your paths straight." (Proverbs 3:5-6, NIV)

Devotional Reflection
This verse reminds us that when we rely on God's guidance, even when forging new paths, He clears the way.

In life, there comes a time when you must step into uncharted territory—whether it's starting a business, pursuing a dream, or breaking free from expectations. For Black women, this often means overcoming societal barriers or personal fears. Yet, this is where your strength truly shines.

Think about the pioneers before you—women who dared to go where others said they couldn't. They didn't let obstacles stop them, and neither should you. Though creating your path may feel lonely, you're never walking it alone. God is with you, guiding and strengthening you. Knowing this allows you to face challenges with confidence, trusting that the path you're forging is part of His plan.

When you step out in faith, trusting God's direction, new opportunities arise. The obstacles along the way are not meant to stop you but to build your strength. Keep moving forward, knowing God is lighting your way.

Prayer
Dear Lord, give me the courage to step out in faith, even when the path is unclear. Help me trust that You are guiding me every step of the way. Amen.

Affirmation
I am brave, and I embrace new paths with faith and strength. God is guiding me, and I will not be afraid to walk where He leads.

March 25
The Importance of Rest and Rejuvenation

"Come to me, all you who are weary and burdened, and I will give you rest." (Matthew 11:28, NIV)

Devotional Reflection

This verse calls us to find rest in God, reminding us that true rejuvenation comes when we lay our burdens down and trust Him to refresh our souls.

In today's fast-paced world, it's easy to get caught in constant movement—work, family, commitments—leaving little room for rest. As Black women, we often feel the need to push harder and take on more, but true resilience isn't just about endurance. It also comes from knowing when to pause and recharge.

Rest is a form of strength, not weakness. Just as our bodies need sleep, our spirits need peace to stay strong. Without rest, we risk burnout. Jesus himself took time away to rest and pray. If He valued rest, how much more should we?

Self-care—whether through reflection, prayer, or taking a day off—isn't selfish. It's essential for resilience. When you rest, you allow God to restore you, so you can continue your journey with fresh energy. Take time to rest, knowing it prepares you for the next phase with strength and clarity.

Prayer

Lord, help me remember the importance of rest. Teach me to find peace in You and trust that in my moments of rest, You are restoring my soul. Amen.

Affirmation

I embrace rest as a gift from God. By taking time to care for myself, I grow stronger, more resilient, and ready for the challenges ahead.

March 26
Resilience Through Empowerment and Advocacy

"Speak up for those who cannot speak for themselves, for the rights of all who are destitute." (Proverbs 31:8, NIV)

Devotional Reflection

This verse highlights the importance of advocacy and standing up for those who are marginalized. It calls us to be a voice for ourselves and our communities.

Empowerment is an act of resilience. As Black women, advocating for ourselves and our communities has always been a source of strength. The challenges we face may be heavy, but through self-advocacy, we find the courage to push back, to speak our truths, and to demand fairness in a world that often tries to silence us.

Sometimes, the greatest display of resilience is in the moments when we refuse to back down. It could be advocating for yourself at work, ensuring that your voice is heard in spaces where it matters, or standing in the gap for others who may not have the strength to speak up. Advocacy isn't just about standing up for others—it's about knowing your worth, recognizing your power, and using that strength to break barriers.

True resilience means being empowered to confront systems of injustice and inequality, knowing that you carry God's strength within you. Your voice is valuable. Your presence is necessary. When you speak up for yourself and others, you are embodying the very essence of resilience and making an impact in your community.

Prayer

Lord, give me the strength to advocate for myself and others. Help me to use my voice to bring justice, fairness, and love into the world. Amen.

Affirmation

I am empowered by God to stand up for myself and my community. My voice matters, and I will use it to bring about positive change.

March 27
The Impact of Gratitude on Resilience

"Give thanks in all circumstances; for this is God's will for you in Christ Jesus." (1 Thessalonians 5:18, NIV)

Devotional Reflection

Gratitude is a powerful tool that transforms our hearts and minds. As Black women, we often face unique challenges that can leave us feeling drained or overwhelmed. But when we pause to give thanks for what we have, no matter how small, we begin to see strength emerge from places we once thought were empty. Gratitude doesn't mean ignoring hardship. Instead, it allows us to acknowledge the difficulties while also recognizing the blessings that surround us.

Imagine waking up each morning and focusing on what you're grateful for. It could be the love of family, the breath in your lungs, or the lessons learned from your struggles. This shift in perspective creates resilience. When we choose gratitude, we train ourselves to find light in the darkest moments. We grow emotionally stronger, and our outlook on life brightens. Practicing gratitude builds resilience by reminding us that, even in the face of adversity, God's goodness is still present.

By focusing on the positive aspects of your life, you're strengthening your ability to bounce back from challenges. Gratitude opens the door to a mindset of hope, making it easier to push through difficulties with grace and perseverance.

Prayer

Lord, help me to find gratitude in all things, even in my struggles. Give me a heart that sees the blessings You've given and the strength to face each day with thankfulness. Amen.

Affirmation

I choose gratitude today, knowing that it will strengthen my resilience and brighten my path. I am grateful for God's goodness in my life.

March 28
Nurturing Relationships as a Source of Strength

"Two are better than one, because they have a good return for their labor: If either of them falls down, one can help the other up."

(Ecclesiastes 4:9-10, NIV)

Devotional Reflection

Building resilience doesn't happen in isolation. For Black women, our communities, friends, and family often serve as vital sources of strength. When life gets tough, having supportive people around us can make all the difference. Whether it's a close friend who listens without judgment, a family member who encourages you, or a mentor who offers wise counsel, these relationships fortify us in ways we sometimes take for granted.

Think about a time when you felt overwhelmed. Who was there to lift you up? It might have been your mother, a sister, or a trusted friend. Healthy relationships serve as a foundation upon which we can stand tall, especially during life's storms. They provide emotional and spiritual nourishment, reminding us that we don't have to carry our burdens alone. The love and care from others are like God's embrace, giving us the courage to keep moving forward.

Nurturing these relationships, however, takes intention. It's important to give as much as we receive. Just as we rely on others for support, we must also be there to uplift them in their times of need. When we invest in building these bonds, we create a network of strength that helps us grow resilient together.

Prayer

Lord, thank You for the people in my life who strengthen and support me. Help me to nurture these relationships and be a source of encouragement to those I love. Amen.

Affirmation

I am surrounded by love and support. I invest in relationships that strengthen me and help me grow.

March 29
Reflecting on Your Journey of Strength

"Consider it pure joy, my brothers and sisters, whenever you face trials of many kinds, because you know that the testing of your faith produces perseverance." (James 1:2-3, NIV)

Devotional Reflection
Take a moment to reflect on your personal journey of strength. There have been moments when life tested your resolve, and though you may have doubted at times, you came through it with greater resilience. Often, we don't recognize our own strength until we look back at the challenges we've overcome.

For many Black women, the journey of resilience is deeply tied to both personal and collective experiences. Whether it was fighting against societal barriers, managing the pressures of family, or navigating moments of uncertainty, each experience shaped you. You have built a strength that is not easily shaken. Every trial you faced tested your perseverance, but it also refined you into the strong woman you are today.

As you reflect on your journey, recognize how far you've come. Celebrate your growth. Each step forward, each victory over adversity, is a testament to God's faithfulness in your life. Remember, the struggles weren't in vain; they were the foundation of the resilience you carry now.

Prayer
Heavenly Father, thank You for walking with me through every trial and challenge. Help me to continue growing in strength and resilience, trusting in Your plan for my life. Amen.

Affirmation
I am resilient, strong, and growing with each challenge I face. My journey is filled with purpose and strength.

March 30
The Power of Hope in Difficult Times

"But those who hope in the Lord will renew their strength. They will soar on wings like eagles; they will run and not grow weary, they will walk and not be faint." (Isaiah 40:31, NIV)

Devotional Reflection

Hope is a lifeline in difficult times. When everything feels overwhelming and it seems like there's no way out, hope shines a light on the path forward. It's like a small flame that keeps burning, even when the winds of adversity try to blow it out.

For many Black women, the journey is often marked by unique and intense challenges. In those moments of struggle, finding hope can be especially hard, yet it is crucial. Reflect on the times when hope seemed distant, but you found strength in it anyway. It might have been a supportive friend, a Prayeranswered, or a quiet moment of clarity that gave you the strength to keep going.

Remember that hope is not just wishful thinking but a deep-rooted trust in God's plan. It allows you to see beyond your current circumstances and believe in a better future. Let this hope fuel your resilience, giving you the strength to face each day with renewed energy and courage.

Prayer

Dear Lord, grant me the strength to hold onto hope during the toughest times. Help me trust in Your promises and find renewal in Your presence. Amen.

Affirmation

I am filled with hope and strength. Each challenge I face is an opportunity to grow stronger in my faith and resilience.

March 31
Preparing for Future Challenges with Resilience

"The righteous man will flourish like the palm tree: he will grow like a cedar in Lebanon." (Psalm 92:12, NIV)

Devotional Reflection
This verse speaks about the strength and resilience of the righteous, comparing them to sturdy, thriving trees. Just as these trees stand strong, we can find strength through positive influences in our lives.

Positive role models can greatly impact our lives. They are like guiding lights, showing us how to navigate our own paths with grace and strength. Think about the women in your life who inspire you – maybe it's a mentor, a family member, or a friend. Their strength and positivity can be a source of great encouragement.

Imagine you're facing a challenge, and then remember the story of a role model who overcame something similar. Their success can inspire you to keep pushing forward. By observing their actions and learning from their experiences, you can gain valuable insights into handling your own struggles.

For Black women, role models often embody resilience and perseverance, showing how to rise above obstacles and succeed. They teach us that challenges can be met with grace and determination. Reflecting on their journeys can help you see your own potential and motivate you to stay strong.

Prayer
Dear God, thank You for the positive role models in my life. Help me to learn from their strength and apply their lessons to my own journey. Guide me to be a source of inspiration for others as they are for me. Amen.

Affirmation
I am inspired by the strength and grace of positive role models in my life. Their example empowers me to overcome challenges and grow stronger. I am capable and resilient, just like those who have guided me.

April
Faith and Spiritual Growth

April 1
Finding Faith Amidst Everyday Stress

"Cast all your anxiety on him because he cares for you."
(1 Peter 5:7, NIV)

Devotional Reflection

Life can feel overwhelming, especially when juggling work, family, and personal responsibilities. Daily stresses can build up, and it's easy to feel like you're carrying everything on your own. But God invites you to give all your worries to Him. This verse from 1 Peter reminds us that we don't have to bear our burdens alone. God cares deeply for you, and He wants to relieve you of the weight you're carrying. No matter how stressful life becomes, your faith in God gives you the strength to trust Him with your challenges.

Imagine the countless moments in your day when stress tries to take over. Whether it's balancing a busy job or managing the demands of family life, it can be easy to let stress consume you. As a Black woman, society often places expectations on you to be strong and resilient in all situations. But even the strongest individuals need a place to rest. Faith provides that place. When the world is spinning fast and things seem out of control, your faith in God is your anchor. It's in those quiet moments of prayer, reflection, and trust that you find peace, even amid chaos. Take a deep breath and remember that God's love for you is constant. You don't have to have it all together all the time. Release your worries into His hands and find comfort in knowing that He's guiding you through each day.

Prayer

Heavenly Father, today I bring all my worries and stresses to You. Help me to trust in Your care and know that I am never alone in my struggles. Guide me to lean on You when life feels overwhelming. Amen.

Affirmation

I release my worries into God's hands and trust in His constant care.

April 2
Balancing Spiritual Life with Career Demands

"But seek first his kingdom and his righteousness, and all these things will be given to you as well." (Matthew 6:33, NIV)

Devotional Reflection

In the busyness of balancing a career and personal life, it's easy to let spiritual practices slip. But this verse from Matthew reminds us to prioritize our relationship with God. When you put God first, He promises to take care of your needs. Even with career pressures, seeking Him through prayer, His Word, and guidance will bring balance and peace.

As a Black woman, hard work and perseverance in a demanding career are familiar. But sometimes, the hustle can feel overwhelming, leaving little room for your spiritual life. God doesn't ask for perfection—just a heart that seeks Him. Even in busy moments, take time to pray or reflect. Whether a quiet morning moment or a short Prayerduring lunch, these times remind you that your strength comes from God, not from doing it all alone.

Balancing work and faith is about maintaining your connection to God, even in the busiest seasons. Let Him guide you, and He will provide the wisdom and strength you need to thrive in your career while nurturing your spiritual growth.

Prayer

Lord, as I navigate my career and daily responsibilities, help me to keep You at the center of my life. Give me the wisdom to balance work with my spiritual journey, trusting that You will guide me through every challenge. Amen.

Affirmation

I make time for God, trusting that He will give me the strength and guidance to balance my career and faith.

April 3
Overcoming Doubts About Your Spiritual Journey

"Immediately the boy's father exclaimed, 'I do believe; help me overcome my unbelief!'" (Mark 9:24, NIV)

Devotional Reflection

Even those with strong faith sometimes face moments of doubt. This verse shows that it's okay to admit when your faith feels shaky. What matters is that you bring those doubts to God, asking Him to strengthen you in times of uncertainty. Faith isn't the absence of doubt, but the willingness to trust God despite your questions.

There are times in your spiritual journey when you may wonder if you're on the right path or question whether God hears your prayers. As a Black woman, facing societal pressures and personal challenges can add to those doubts. It's easy to feel disconnected from your faith when life gets overwhelming, or when you face situations that make you question, "Why me?" Know that you are not alone in these feelings. Many strong believers have had moments where they cried out to God, not sure if He was there or if their faith was enough.

Doubts are not a sign of weakness; they are an opportunity for growth. When you bring your doubts to God, like the father in Mark 9:24, you open the door for Him to strengthen your belief. Your doubts can lead to a deeper understanding of God's presence in your life. Don't be afraid to ask God to help you overcome unbelief. In those vulnerable moments, His grace can fill the gaps in your faith, giving you the strength to move forward on your spiritual journey.

Prayer

Lord, I confess my doubts to You. Help me overcome them and trust You more deeply. Strengthen my faith, even when I cannot see the full picture of Your plan for my life. Amen.

Affirmation

I trust God to strengthen my faith, even in moments of doubt. My spiritual journey is guided by His love and grace.

April 4
Healing from Past Wounds Through Faith

"He heals the brokenhearted and binds up their wounds."
(Psalm 147:3, NIV)

Devotional Reflection

God is the ultimate healer. This verse reminds us that no matter how deep our wounds are, emotional or spiritual, He is always ready to bring healing and restoration. Trusting in God's power to heal can help you move beyond the pain of your past, toward a future filled with peace and wholeness.

As a Black woman, you may carry the weight of past hurts—whether from relationships, experiences of racism, or personal struggles. These wounds can be deep, leaving scars that feel hard to heal. But healing doesn't mean pretending the pain never existed. Instead, it's about allowing God to enter those broken places in your life and restore what was lost.

Faith is a powerful tool for healing. Through prayer, scripture, and spending time with God, you can find the strength to release the pain and begin the process of restoration. When you bring your wounds to Him, God not only heals but transforms your hurt into something beautiful—a testimony of resilience and strength. Trust that your faith can guide you through the darkest moments of your healing journey. Little by little, God will mend the broken pieces, giving you the courage to move forward, free from the weight of the past.

Prayer

Lord, I give You my hurts and wounds. Heal my heart and help me trust in Your process of restoration. Bring peace to the areas of my life that need Your touch. Amen.

Affirmation

I am healing through my faith. God is restoring my heart and giving me the strength to move forward with peace and hope.

April 5
Embracing Your Spiritual Identity in a Diverse World

"But you are a chosen people, a royal priesthood, a holy nation, God's special possession, that you may declare the praises of him who called you out of darkness into his wonderful light." (1 Peter 2:9, NIV)

Devotional Reflection

Living in a diverse world can sometimes make it difficult to embrace your spiritual identity. As a Black woman, you may face cultural, social, and even spiritual pressures that try to shape how you should think, feel, or express your faith. It's easy to feel like you need to fit into specific molds or hide parts of who you are, especially when the world doesn't always understand or celebrate your journey. But God has uniquely called you to stand out in His light, to embrace every part of your identity—cultural, personal, and spiritual.

Your faith is not something to be molded by the world but by God's truth. He has created you with purpose and given you a spiritual identity that is beautiful and powerful. Embrace the richness of who you are, rooted in your faith. In a world that celebrates diversity, you are a reflection of God's creation, and your spiritual walk is part of that vibrant tapestry. Stand tall in your faith, knowing that your identity is secure in Him, no matter what the world says.

Prayer

Lord, help me embrace the spiritual identity You've given me. Let me stand strong in my faith and proudly walk in the calling You have placed on my life. Amen.

Affirmation

I am fearfully and wonderfully made. My spiritual identity is rooted in God, and I embrace all that He has created me to be.

April 6
The Role of Prayerin Managing Anxiety

"Do not be anxious about anything, but in every situation, by Prayerand petition, with thanksgiving, present your requests to God." (Philippians 4:6, NIV)

Devotional Reflection

Anxiety can creep in at any moment—whether it's about your job, your family, or simply the challenges of everyday life. As a Black woman, the weight of expectations and societal pressures can sometimes feel overwhelming, adding to the stress you may already carry. In these moments, turning to Prayercan be the most powerful tool you have.

Prayeris more than just words; it's a deep connection with God, where you can lay your fears and worries at His feet. It allows you to release what you cannot control and trust that He is working things out for your good. When anxiety rises, Prayerbecomes a way to center yourself, to remind you that God is present, and that you don't have to carry the burden alone.

By inviting God into your anxious moments, you create space for peace to replace fear. Each time you pray, you are actively choosing to trust in His power and goodness, knowing that He will give you the strength to manage the challenges you face.

Prayer

Father, I come to You with my anxieties and fears. Help me to trust in Your peace and strength. Calm my heart and remind me that You are in control. Amen.

Affirmation

I am at peace because I trust in God. Prayercalms my spirit and helps me overcome anxiety and stress.

April 7
Building a Supportive Faith Community

Let us consider how we may spur one another on toward love and good deeds, not giving up meeting together, as some are in the habit of doing, but encouraging one another—and all the more as you see the Day approaching. (Hebrews 10:24-25, NIV)

Devotional Reflection

For many Black women, life can sometimes feel isolating, especially when facing unique challenges that others may not understand. Having a strong, faith-filled community around you can make all the difference. It's more than just going to church or meeting for Bible study—it's about building a circle of people who lift you up spiritually and emotionally. Think about the times when you've felt lost or overwhelmed. Now imagine having a group of women who pray with you, support you, and remind you of God's promises. This kind of community provides strength when you're weak and wisdom when you need guidance. Nurturing these relationships takes effort, but the spiritual rewards are immeasurable. When you surround yourself with people who share your faith, it becomes easier to stay encouraged, grow spiritually, and spread love to others.

Prayer

Lord, help me to build and nurture relationships that bring me closer to You. Guide me to a faith community where I can give and receive support, love, and encouragement. Amen.

Affirmation

I am surrounded by a community of love, faith, and strength that encourages me to grow spiritually and share my light with others.

April 8
Strengthening Faith During Times of Uncertainty

Trust in the Lord with all your heart and lean not on your own understanding; in all your ways submit to Him, and He will make your paths straight. (Proverbs 3:5-6, NIV)

Devotional Reflection
Uncertainty is something we all experience at different points in life. As Black women, you might face doubts about your future, career, or even relationships, which can be overwhelming. During these times, it's easy to feel like everything is out of control. But even when you don't know what's ahead, you can be sure that God does. Trusting Him when things are unclear is how faith truly grows. Picture walking through a foggy morning where you can barely see the next step. You don't stop walking—you trust that the road will continue. Faith works the same way. God doesn't expect you to have all the answers; He simply wants you to trust that He does. Even when you can't see what's next, you can rely on Him to guide you and give you strength to keep moving forward.

Prayer
Heavenly Father, during times of doubt and uncertainty, help me to trust in You fully. Strengthen my faith and guide me through the unknown, knowing that You are always in control. Amen.

Affirmation
I trust in God's plan, even when I cannot see the future. My faith gives me the strength to face each day with confidence and peace.

April 9
The Power of Gratitude in Spiritual Growth

Give thanks in all circumstances; for this is God's will for you in Christ Jesus. (1 Thessalonians 5:18, NIV)

Devotional Reflection
Gratitude has a unique power to shift your mindset and strengthen your faith. As a Black woman, life can sometimes feel overwhelming—balancing work, family, and personal responsibilities may seem like too much. Yet, in the midst of these challenges, there's a hidden opportunity to grow spiritually. When you choose to focus on what you're thankful for, even on tough days, something amazing happens. Gratitude opens your heart to see God's blessings, big or small, that might otherwise go unnoticed. Maybe it's the encouraging words of a friend, or the fact that you made it through a hard day. These moments of thankfulness bring you closer to God, reminding you of His presence and care. Practicing gratitude every day can help you grow spiritually, deepening your trust in God's faithfulness.

Prayer
Lord, help me to find gratitude in every situation. Teach me to see Your blessings even in the challenges, and let my thankfulness bring me closer to You. Amen.

Affirmation
I am grateful for God's blessings in my life, and I trust that through gratitude, my faith will grow stronger every day.

April 10
Navigating Spiritual Burnout

Come to me, all you who are weary and burdened, and I will give you rest. (Matthew 11:28, NIV)

Devotional Reflection
Spiritual burnout can sneak up on you when you least expect it. It happens when you're giving and pouring out so much in your walk with God, but suddenly, you feel drained, disconnected, and unsure of how to keep going. As a Black woman, juggling various responsibilities—work, family, ministry—can add to that exhaustion. You may feel like you're constantly trying to stay strong and keep your faith alive, but inside, you're running on empty. Recognizing burnout is the first step. It's not a sign of weakness but a reminder to pause, rest, and reconnect with God. Just like in your day-to-day life, you need moments of rest to recharge; the same applies to your spiritual journey. Take time to slow down, reflect, and ask God to refresh your spirit. Let go of the pressure to always be "on" and allow yourself to be filled with His peace.

Prayer
Lord, I am feeling weary and tired. Please give me the strength to rest in You and to find renewal in Your presence. Help me release the weight I carry. Amen.

Affirmation
I am allowed to rest and renew my spirit. God is my source of strength, and I trust Him to refresh me.

April 11
Cultivating a Daily Spiritual Routine

But seek first his kingdom and his righteousness, and all these things will be given to you as well. (Matthew 6:33, NIV)

Devotional Reflection
Life can feel like a whirlwind of responsibilities and tasks, and it's easy to let your spiritual routine fall to the bottom of the list. As a Black woman, your days might be packed with work, family duties, and taking care of everyone else. But nurturing your faith shouldn't be an afterthought. It's the anchor that keeps you grounded when life gets hectic. Cultivating a daily spiritual routine doesn't mean adding more to your plate, but rather making time to connect with God in ways that fit your life. Whether it's a quiet moment of Prayerin the morning or reading a short scripture before bed, these small but consistent practices build your faith over time. It's not about perfection—it's about persistence. By putting God first, you will feel a deeper sense of peace and purpose as you go through your day.

Prayer
Dear Lord, help me make time for You every day. Guide me in creating a routine that keeps me close to You, even in my busiest moments. Amen.

Affirmation
I am committed to growing in my faith daily. My spiritual routine is a source of strength and peace.

April 12
The Impact of Self-Care on Spiritual Well-being

Do you not know that your bodies are temples of the Holy Spirit, who is in you, whom you have received from God? You are not your own. (1 Corinthians 6:19, NIV)

Devotional Reflection

As Black women, we often carry the weight of the world on our shoulders, taking care of others while neglecting our own needs. But self-care isn't selfish—it's necessary. When you don't make time to rest, nourish your body, and care for your mental health, it's easy to feel worn out, both physically and spiritually. Self-care helps restore your energy, and when you care for yourself, you're better able to connect with God. Just like a car can't run without fuel, your spirit needs the right care to thrive. When you make time for self-care, whether through rest, relaxation, or simply breathing deeply, you allow space for God to refresh your soul. Don't feel guilty for taking a moment to step away and recharge—it's part of maintaining your spiritual well-being.

Prayer

Lord, remind me that caring for myself is not selfish but necessary. Help me prioritize my health so I can better serve You and others. Amen.

Affirmation

I deserve time for self-care, and by taking care of myself, I strengthen my relationship with God.

April 13
Overcoming Isolation in Your Faith Journey

For where two or three gather in my name, there am I with them.
(Matthew 18:20, NIV)

Devotional Reflection

Isolation can creep in, especially when life gets overwhelming. You may feel like you're walking alone in your faith journey, separated from the support of others. This is a common struggle, but you don't have to carry the burden on your own. Faith is meant to be shared, and finding connection with others can help lift you up. Whether it's through Prayerpartners, church gatherings, or even a phone call to a trusted friend, seeking fellowship can strengthen your spirit. Remember that God's presence is not limited to solitude. He moves through people, through community, and through shared faith. In moments of isolation, reach out and let others support you—God often works through the people around you.

Prayer

Father, help me find comfort and connection in community when I feel isolated. Surround me with people who will lift me up and remind me of Your love. Amen.

Affirmation

I am never truly alone; God places people in my life to walk alongside me on this faith journey.

April 14
The Influence of Cultural Heritage on Your Faith

"I praise you because I am fearfully and wonderfully made; your works are wonderful, I know that full well." (Psalm 139:14, NIV)

Devotional Reflection
Your cultural background is an important part of who you are, and it has a deep influence on your faith journey. Whether it's the way you were raised in the church or traditions passed down from generations, your heritage is woven into how you worship and connect with God. Maybe you grew up hearing your grandmother's prayers, or maybe the music at church reminds you of family gatherings. These experiences are not just memories; they are spiritual roots that ground you in faith.

As a Black woman, your heritage carries both struggle and resilience, and this is reflected in your walk with God. From the rich history of faith in the Black community to the strength passed down through generations, your culture shapes how you persevere, worship, and trust God in tough times. Embrace the beauty of your cultural heritage as a gift from God—it adds depth and richness to your relationship with Him. He crafted you with purpose, and part of that purpose is found in the unique blend of faith and culture that defines who you are. Let your heritage strengthen and empower your faith.

Prayer
Lord, thank You for the beauty of my cultural heritage and how it shapes my faith. Help me honor the traditions that draw me closer to You and guide me in using my background to inspire others. Amen.

Affirmation
I am fearfully and wonderfully made, and my cultural heritage enriches my faith and strengthens my walk with God.

April 15
Navigating Faith Challenges in Relationships

"If it is possible, as far as it depends on you, live at peace with everyone." (Romans 12:18, NIV)

Devotional Reflection

Relationships can be one of the most challenging aspects of life, especially when faith is involved. Whether it's with family members, friends, or a significant other, differing views on faith can sometimes create tension. You may find yourself navigating difficult conversations about beliefs or even questioning how to stay close to those who don't share your spiritual perspective. These situations can leave you feeling torn between holding onto your faith and maintaining important connections.

In times like these, it's important to rely on God's wisdom. Instead of seeing differences as obstacles, view them as opportunities for growth—both in your faith and your relationships. Staying grounded in your beliefs while showing grace to others can open doors to meaningful discussions and deeper understanding. This doesn't mean you have to compromise your faith, but it does call for patience, kindness, and love. Faith-based challenges in relationships are opportunities to lean into God's guidance, trusting that He will provide the right words and actions to maintain peace and strengthen your bonds.

Prayer

Lord, help me navigate challenges in my relationships with grace and understanding. Guide me to approach conflicts with love and strengthen my faith as I seek peace in all my connections. Amen.

Affirmation

I am equipped with the wisdom and grace to navigate faith challenges in my relationships, building peace and understanding wherever I go.

April 16
Finding Hope in Spiritual Practices

"Let us hold unswervingly to the hope we profess, for he who promised is faithful." (Hebrews 10:23, NIV)

Devotional Reflection

Spiritual practices like prayer, meditation, and worship are not just routines—they are lifelines that connect you to hope and renewal. When life feels heavy and you're struggling to see the light, these practices can help you re-center and find strength. Imagine Prayeras a direct line to God, where you can voice your fears and dreams, and listen for His guidance. Meditation offers a peaceful space to reflect and recharge, allowing you to feel God's presence and love in a profound way. Worship can lift your spirit, reminding you of the joy and peace found in His grace.

Incorporating these practices into your daily life nurtures hope by keeping your focus on God's promises and His plan for you. They offer comfort and clarity, reminding you that even in difficult times, you are not alone. Embrace these spiritual habits as tools to strengthen your faith and cultivate a deep, unwavering hope that sustains you through every season of life.

Prayer

Heavenly Father, thank You for the spiritual practices that bring me closer to You. Help me to use them to find and nurture hope, trusting in Your promises and Your loving presence in all aspects of my life. Amen.

Affirmation

Through my spiritual practices, I nurture hope and strengthen my connection with God, finding peace and renewal in His promises.

April 17
Trusting God's Plan in Uncertain Times

"For I know the plans I have for you," declares the Lord, "plans to prosper you and not to harm you, plans to give you hope and a future."
(Jeremiah 29:11, NIV)

Devotional Reflection

Facing uncertainty can be challenging, especially when the future seems unpredictable. During these times, trusting God's plan can feel difficult, but it's essential. Think about how a parent guides a child through unknown paths, always with their best interests at heart. Similarly, God's plan for you is filled with wisdom and love, even if you can't see it clearly right now.

When you are unsure about the future, take comfort in knowing that God's plans are always for your good. Reflect on past experiences where His guidance led you through challenging times. By trusting in His plan, you release the burden of trying to control everything and open yourself to receive His peace and direction. Let Prayerand reflection be your anchors during these times, reinforcing your trust in His faithful plan.

Prayer

Lord, in times of uncertainty, help me to trust in Your plans and Your promises. Strengthen my faith and guide me through every challenge, knowing that Your plan for me is filled with hope and a bright future. Amen.

Affirmation

I trust in God's plan for my life, knowing that He guides me with wisdom and love through every uncertain moment.

April 18
The Role of Forgiveness in Spiritual Growth

"Be kind and compassionate to one another, forgiving each other, just as in Christ God forgave you." (Ephesians 4:32, NIV)

Devotional Reflection

Forgiveness can be one of the most challenging aspects of spiritual growth, yet it is vital for nurturing your faith. Imagine carrying a heavy backpack filled with rocks—each rock representing a grudge or hurt. Forgiveness is like setting that backpack down, allowing you to walk more freely and lightly.

Forgiving others, as well as yourself, can be difficult, especially when wounds run deep. However, practicing forgiveness allows you to release the burden of anger and resentment that weighs down your spirit. It aligns you with the heart of God, who forgives us despite our imperfections. By letting go of past hurts, you open yourself to healing and growth. Embrace forgiveness not just as a command but as a gift to yourself and a way to deepen your connection with God.

Prayer

Heavenly Father, help me to embrace the power of forgiveness. Guide me to let go of anger and hurt, and to extend grace to others as You have extended grace to me. May this act of forgiveness bring me closer to You and help me grow spiritually. Amen.

Affirmation

I embrace forgiveness as a path to spiritual growth, letting go of past hurts and opening my heart to God's love and grace.

April 19
Spiritual Growth Through Acts of Service

"Serve one another humbly in love." (Galatians 5:13, NIV)

Devotional Reflection

Acts of service can profoundly enhance your spiritual journey, as they embody the love and compassion Christ teaches us. Think about a time you helped someone in need, whether it was a small act like sharing a meal or a larger gesture like volunteering. These moments often leave you feeling more connected to God and fulfilled.

Serving others not only meets their needs but also fosters your own spiritual growth. It transforms your focus from self to others, aligning your actions with Christ's teachings. When you serve with a humble heart, you reflect God's love and grace. Each act of kindness strengthens your faith and deepens your understanding of God's call to love our neighbors. Embrace opportunities to serve, and watch how these acts of love enrich your spiritual life.

Prayer

Lord, guide me to serve others with a heart full of love and humility. Help me to see opportunities to help and to act with compassion. May my acts of service reflect Your grace and bring me closer to You. Amen.

Affirmation

I grow spiritually by serving others with love and humility, reflecting God's grace through my actions and enriching my faith journey.

April 20
The Power of Scripture in Daily Life

"Your word is a lamp for my feet, a light on my path."
(Psalm 119:105, NIV)

Devotional Reflection

For you to have reached today in this devotional book, it shows that you have made scripture a part of your daily habits. This commitment is like having a personal guide to help you navigate through each day. Imagine walking through a dark forest with only a lantern; you would carefully follow the light to avoid stumbling. Similarly, incorporating scripture into your daily routine acts as that guiding light. It not only illuminates your path but also strengthens your spirit. Reflecting on this, think about how the scriptures you've read have guided you through challenges and provided clarity. For instance, when faced with a tough decision, recalling a comforting verse might have offered the reassurance you needed. Embracing scripture daily fosters a deeper connection with God and helps you see His hand in every aspect of your life.

Prayer

Lord, help me to integrate Your word into my daily life. Let scripture guide my thoughts, decisions, and actions. May Your truth be a constant light, leading me closer to You and strengthening my faith. Amen.

Affirmation

Scripture guides my daily life, illuminating my path and deepening my spiritual growth. I embrace God's word as a constant source of strength and wisdom.

April 21
Finding Peace Through Meditation and Reflection

"Be still, and know that I am God." (Psalm 46:10, NIV)

Devotional Reflection
Finding peace often feels elusive, especially in the hustle of daily life. For many Black women juggling multiple roles and responsibilities, carving out moments of stillness can be a challenge. Yet, this is where meditation and reflection come into play. Consider a time when you felt overwhelmed and took a moment to pause and breathe deeply. That brief silence allowed you to reconnect with yourself and God, offering a sense of calm and clarity. Similarly, by setting aside intentional time each day for meditation and reflection, you invite God's presence into your life, bringing peace and spiritual renewal. Whether it's through a quiet morning ritual or a brief pause during a busy day, these practices help ground you and deepen your faith, transforming stress into serenity.

Prayer
Lord, help me find moments of stillness in my busy day. May my time of meditation and reflection bring me closer to You and fill my heart with Your peace.

Affirmation
I find peace in the quiet moments, knowing that God is with me and guiding me through every challenge.

April 22
Overcoming Feelings of Unworthiness

"Since you are precious and honored in my sight, and because I love you, I will give people in exchange for you, nations in exchange for your life." (Isaiah 43:4, NIV)

Devotional Reflection

Have you ever felt like you don't measure up? Perhaps you've doubted your worth, questioning if you are deserving of God's love. These feelings can weigh heavily, especially during tough times or when comparing yourself to others. For many Black women, societal expectations can intensify these doubts.

Imagine a diamond buried under layers of dirt. The dirt doesn't change its value, it just hides it from view. Similarly, our worth doesn't change based on circumstances or feelings. Like the diamond, our value is constant and unchanging.

God sees us as precious and honored. No matter the challenges or feelings of inadequacy, His love for us remains unchanged. Embracing this truth can transform how we see ourselves—valuable, cherished, and worthy of His love.

When feelings of unworthiness arise, remember this verse. Take time to reflect on God's love and how He sees you as precious. Through this lens, you can overcome feelings of doubt and embrace your true worth in God's eyes.

Prayer

Lord, thank You for reminding me of my worth in Your eyes. Help me to see myself as You see me—precious and loved. Strengthen me to overcome any feelings of unworthiness and to trust in Your love and grace. Amen.

Affirmation

I am precious and valued in God's sight, and His love for me never changes.

April 23
The Role of Faith in Navigating Career Transitions

"Trust in the Lord with all your heart and lean not on your own understanding; in all your ways submit to him, and he will make your paths straight." (Proverbs 3:5-6, NIV)

Devotional Reflection

Career changes can feel like standing at a crossroads with no clear path. Whether starting a new job, switching fields, or facing unexpected changes, it's normal to feel uncertain. For many Black women, these transitions come with added challenges and expectations.

Consider a woman who lost her job, feeling lost and unsure. She leaned into her faith, praying for guidance and trusting in God's plan. As she did, new opportunities emerged. Her faith didn't make the path clear, but it gave her the strength to navigate through the uncertainty.

When facing a career transition, remember that God is with you. By trusting in Him and not relying solely on your own understanding, you allow His wisdom to guide your decisions. Trusting God means knowing He has a plan, even if it's not immediately clear. As you navigate these changes, seek His guidance through Prayerand reflection.

Faith doesn't promise an easy path, but it assures us that God will make the way straight. Trust His plan as you move through your career transition, knowing it's greater than your own.

Prayer

Dear God, I trust You with my career transition. Help me to lean not on my own understanding but to rely on Your guidance. Give me clarity and confidence as I navigate this change, and show me the path You have prepared for me. Amen.

Affirmation

I trust in God's plan for my career and believe that He will guide me through every transition with wisdom and grace.

April 24
Embracing Spiritual Growth During Parenthood

"These commandments that I give you today are to be on your hearts. Impress them on your children. Talk about them when you sit at home and when you walk along the road, when you lie down and when you get up." (Deuteronomy 6:6-7, NIV)

Devotional Reflection

Parenting is a full-time job that demands energy and attention, making it challenging to find time for personal spiritual growth. For many Black women, balancing family responsibilities and personal faith can feel overwhelming.

Picture a mother juggling work, household duties, and parenting, all while trying to maintain her spiritual life. It may seem like there's no time for Bible study or prayer. Yet, this verse shows us how to weave faith into daily life.

Imagine discussing Bible stories with your children while cooking or praying together before bedtime. These moments not only teach your children about faith but also reinforce your spiritual journey. Every interaction becomes an opportunity to live out your faith and grow spiritually.

Integrating spiritual practices into parenting doesn't have to be separate from daily tasks. By making faith a natural part of your routine, you nurture both your own and your children's spiritual growth. Embrace these moments as part of your own spiritual journey.

Prayer

Lord, help me to weave my faith into my daily life as I raise my children. Guide me to find moments to teach and grow spiritually together with them. Strengthen me to balance my responsibilities with my spiritual journey. Amen.

Affirmation

I embrace my role as a parent and use every moment as an opportunity for spiritual growth, knowing that my faith journey enriches my life and my family's.

April 25
The Importance of Spiritual Mentorship

"As iron sharpens iron, so one person sharpens another."

(Proverbs 27:17, NIV)

Devotional Reflection

Have you ever tried to sharpen a knife without a sharpening stone? It's hard to make it effective alone. Similarly, spiritual growth can be challenging without guidance and support. Many Black women face unique challenges in their spiritual journeys, and having a mentor can make a big difference.

Imagine a young woman feeling lost in her faith. She seeks out a mentor—a wise woman who has walked a similar path and offers guidance and encouragement. This relationship becomes a source of strength, helping her navigate her spiritual journey with clarity and confidence.

Mentorship goes beyond advice; it's about sharing experiences, offering support, and holding each other accountable. A spiritual mentor provides insights, shares their own journey, and prays with you. They encourage commitment to your faith.

Finding a mentor who understands your experiences can be crucial. Seek someone who can relate to your life and offer guidance that resonates. Their wisdom and support can help you grow stronger and overcome obstacles along your spiritual path.

Prayer

Lord, thank You for the mentors who have guided me and those who will guide me in the future. Help me to seek out and value mentorship in my spiritual growth. Grant me the wisdom to choose the right mentors and the humility to learn from them. Amen.

Affirmation

I am open to seeking and valuing spiritual mentorship, knowing that it will help me grow stronger in my faith and navigate my spiritual journey with greater wisdom and clarity.

April 26
Navigating Faith Challenges in Education

"If any of you lacks wisdom, you should ask God, who gives generously to all without finding fault, and it will be given to you."

(James 1:5, NIV)

Devotional Reflection

Pursuing education can be both exciting and challenging. For many Black women, balancing academic demands with personal faith can feel overwhelming. You might wonder how to align your educational goals with your spiritual values or face challenges that test your faith.

Consider a young woman excelling in her studies but feeling conflicted between academic pressures and spiritual beliefs. She felt stressed, unsure of how to maintain her faith while striving for success. Through Prayerand seeking guidance from mentors, she found ways to integrate her faith into her education, using her academic journey as an opportunity for spiritual growth.

Navigating these challenges means asking God for wisdom and guidance, trusting Him with your academic decisions, and seeking ways to honor your faith. Whether it's handling stress, making ethical choices, or finding balance, know that God is there to support you.

Embrace education as a chance to strengthen your faith, trusting that God's wisdom will guide your choices and reflect your values.

Prayer

Heavenly Father, grant me wisdom as I navigate the challenges of my educational journey. Help me to balance my studies with my faith and to seek Your guidance in every decision I make. Strengthen me to stay true to my values while pursuing my goals. Amen.

Affirmation

I seek God's wisdom in my education and trust that He will guide me through every challenge, helping me to grow spiritually and academically.

April 27
Building Resilience Through Spiritual Practices

"God is our refuge and strength, an ever-present help in trouble."
(Psalm 46:1, NIV)

Devotional Reflection

Building resilience is like strengthening a muscle—it takes practice and dedication. For many Black women, coping with stress involves not just physical effort but also spiritual strength. Spiritual practices, such as prayer, meditation, and reading the Bible, are powerful tools for building inner strength.

Imagine a woman feeling overwhelmed by work, family, and personal challenges. By setting aside time for Prayerand reflection, she taps into a deeper source of strength. Each moment of Prayerand quiet reflection helps her recharge and face her troubles with renewed courage.

Spiritual practices create a space to connect with God and draw on His strength. These practices help you stay grounded and resilient, even when life feels difficult. They remind you that you are not alone—God is with you, offering support and strength.

Incorporating spiritual practices into your daily routine builds resilience. You learn to turn to God in difficult moments, finding comfort and strength in His presence. Embrace these practices to strengthen your resilience and find inner peace.

Prayer

Lord, I turn to You for strength and resilience. Help me to build a strong spiritual foundation through Prayerand reflection. Guide me to rely on Your support during times of trouble and to find comfort in Your presence. Amen.

Affirmation

I am resilient and strong through my faith in God. His support and strength are my refuge in times of trouble, helping me to overcome challenges with courage and peace.

April 28
Finding Joy in Your Spiritual Journey

"Weeping may stay for the night, but rejoicing comes in the morning."

(Psalm 30:5, NIV)

Devotional Reflection

Sometimes, the journey of faith can feel like a long, difficult road filled with doubt and struggle. For many Black women, finding joy amid these challenges can seem tough, but joy is an essential part of our spiritual journey.

Imagine a woman facing obstacles in her life—stress at work, challenges at home, and personal struggles. Yet, she finds moments of joy through spiritual practices—whether it's a heartfelt prayer, a comforting Bible verse, or the support of her faith community. These moments remind her that her journey is also filled with blessings and hope.

Finding joy involves celebrating small, meaningful moments. It's about recognizing the positive growth and changes that come from your faith. Whether through prayer, a supportive conversation, or a sense of purpose from following God's path, joy can be found and cherished.

Celebrate these moments of joy. They remind you of God's love and presence in your life, uplifting you and reinforcing that joy is a natural and important part of your spiritual journey.

Prayer

Lord, help me to find and celebrate the joy in my spiritual journey. Even in times of struggle, let me see the moments of blessing and happiness that come from my faith. Fill my heart with Your joy and peace. Amen.

Affirmation

I embrace the joy in my spiritual journey, knowing that even in challenges, God's blessings and love bring me happiness and peace.

April 29
The Impact of Faith on Mental Health

"Do not be anxious about anything, but in every situation, by Prayerand petition, with thanksgiving, present your requests to God. And the peace of God, which transcends all understanding, will guard your hearts and your minds in Christ Jesus." (Philippians 4:6-7, NIV)

Devotional Reflection

Life can sometimes feel overwhelming, with stress and worries weighing heavily on your mind. As a Black woman navigating daily challenges, it's easy to feel anxious or burdened. But faith offers a way to ease these worries and find inner peace.

When you face moments of anxiety, turning to Prayercan be a powerful relief. By talking to God about your concerns, you invite His peace into your heart. This isn't just about seeking comfort; it's about letting go of the pressure and trusting that God is in control.

Remember that God's peace isn't just a fleeting feeling; it's a deep, lasting calm that helps you face life's stresses with confidence. It guards your mind against the chaos and provides a steady foundation, even when circumstances are tough.

Embracing faith in your daily life means finding strength in Prayerand letting God's peace soothe your worries. It's about creating a space where you can release anxiety and experience a profound sense of calm, knowing that you're not alone.

Prayer

Lord, I bring my worries to You and ask for Your peace to fill my heart and mind. Help me to trust in Your support and find calm amid my stress. Guide me with Your strength and comfort me with Your presence. Amen.

Affirmation

My faith in God brings peace and support to my mental health. I trust in His guidance to ease my anxieties and find calm in His loving presence.

April 30
Reflecting on Your Spiritual Growth Over the Month

"Let us examine our ways and test them, and let us return to the Lord."

(Lamentations 3:40, NIV)

Devotional Reflection

As April comes to a close, take a moment to look back and reflect on your spiritual journey this month. Each day, you have faced challenges, celebrated victories, and grown in faith. Reflecting on this progress is an important part of nurturing your spiritual life.

Think about the times this month when you leaned into your faith for strength and guidance. How did God's word support you? What lessons have you learned about yourself and your spiritual growth? Recognize the small victories and the ways you have drawn closer to God.

Reflecting on these experiences helps you see the ways in which your faith has impacted your life. It also provides an opportunity to celebrate how far you've come and to set intentions for continued growth. Embrace the moments when you felt God's presence guiding you and acknowledge the areas where you can seek further development.

By taking time to review your spiritual progress, you affirm your commitment to your faith journey and open your heart to further growth. This reflection not only honors your journey but also strengthens your path forward.

Prayer

Lord, thank You for guiding me through this month. Help me to reflect on my growth and learn from my experiences. Lead me to continue growing in faith and aligning my life with Your will. Amen.

Affirmation

I reflect with gratitude on my spiritual growth, celebrating how far I've come and looking forward to further development in my faith.

May
Health and Wellness

May 1
Cultivating a Peaceful Mindset

"You will keep in perfect peace those whose minds are steadfast, because they trust in you." (Isaiah 26:3, NIV)

Devotional Reflection

As black women, we often carry the weight of the world on our shoulders. From managing our families to advancing in our careers, the constant juggling act can feel overwhelming. Life's demands can sometimes steal our peace, leaving us feeling anxious and drained. But in the midst of it all, God offers us a peace that passes all understanding.

Cultivating a peaceful mindset doesn't mean we ignore the chaos around us. It means we choose to lean on God and find rest in Him. The world may be loud, pulling us in many directions, but when we place our trust in God, He provides a calm in the storm. Imagine starting your day with this assurance: no matter what comes your way, you have a refuge in Him. This isn't just a Thursday morning peace; it's an everyday peace, available to you wherever you are. Trusting God with your worries allows you to release what you can't control, giving you the freedom to live with a mind at ease.

Today, choose to breathe deeply and let go of the need to handle everything on your own. God's got you, and His peace will keep you steady when life feels shaky. Keep your mind fixed on Him, and let His peace flow into your day.

Prayer

Lord, I ask for Your peace to fill my mind and heart today. Help me trust You in every situation, knowing You are in control. When life feels overwhelming, remind me to lean on You for strength and peace. Amen.

Affirmation

I trust God to keep my mind in perfect peace, no matter what I face today.

May 2
Spiritual Renewal Through Rest

"Come to me, all you who are weary and burdened, and I will give you rest." (Matthew 11:28, NIV)

Devotional Reflection

In a world that constantly pushes us to do more, be more, and achieve more, rest can feel like a luxury we can't afford. As black women, we often feel the pressure to excel in all areas of life—our families, careers, and communities—leaving little time for ourselves. But God calls us to rest, not just physically, but spiritually too.

Rest is a gift from God. It's not a sign of weakness, but an opportunity for renewal. Think about how you feel after a good night's sleep—your body feels refreshed, ready to take on the day. Now imagine what spiritual rest could do for your soul. When we pause and rest in God, we allow Him to restore us from the inside out. It's in those quiet moments that we can hear Him speak to us, feel His presence, and regain our strength.

Today, give yourself permission to rest, knowing that even God rested after creating the world. You don't have to do everything by yourself. Rest in God's promise that He will carry your burdens and refresh your spirit. When we allow ourselves to pause, we find the strength to continue our journey with renewed purpose and energy.

Prayer

Dear Lord, help me to embrace rest as a necessary part of my spiritual journey. Teach me to pause and find peace in You, trusting that You will restore my strength. Amen.

Affirmation

I give myself permission to rest, knowing that God refreshes my soul and gives me strength.

May 3
Guarding Your Mental Health in Relationships

"Above all else, guard your heart, for everything you do flows from it."
(Proverbs 4:23, NIV)

Devotional Reflection

Relationships, whether with family, friends, or partners, can bring us joy, support, and companionship. But sometimes, they can also be sources of stress or emotional strain. As black women, we may feel the pressure to be the backbone in our relationships, often prioritizing others' needs while ignoring our own well-being. However, God calls us to protect our hearts, which includes our mental health.

Guarding your mental health doesn't mean distancing yourself from those you care about, but rather recognizing when boundaries are necessary. Some relationships may require you to draw clear lines to protect your peace. Whether it's stepping back from someone who drains you emotionally or addressing issues that have been weighing you down, your mental health matters to God. You are worthy of relationships that nourish, not deplete, you.

It's important to remember that you are not called to carry the weight of others at the expense of your own well-being. Healthy boundaries are not selfish; they're essential for maintaining a sound mind and heart. Seek wisdom from God as you navigate your relationships, and trust that He will guide you toward what brings peace and protects your mental health.

Prayer

Father, I ask for Your guidance in protecting my mental health while maintaining healthy relationships. Help me set boundaries that bring peace and honor You. Amen.

Affirmation

I guard my mental health by creating healthy boundaries, trusting God to guide my relationships.

May 4
Nourishing Your Body with Faith

"So whether you eat or drink or whatever you do, do it all for the glory of God." (1 Corinthians 10:31, NIV)

Devotional Reflection

Food is more than just fuel for our bodies; it's a blessing from God, a gift meant to nourish and sustain us. However, in the rush of daily life, we can often forget the spiritual significance of what we put into our bodies. As black women, many of us carry cultural traditions around food—whether it's a family recipe or a shared meal that brings loved ones together. But how often do we take the time to pause and see food as a blessing from God, provided for our well-being?

Nourishing your body isn't just about eating healthy; it's about cultivating a mindset of gratitude for what you have. Every meal is an opportunity to honor your body and give thanks for the way God provides. Consider the power of praying before each meal—not as a ritual, but as a moment to reflect on the nourishment you're about to receive. When you view food with faith and gratitude, you shift your focus from just "eating to survive" to "eating to thrive."

Today, invite God into your meals. Whether it's a simple snack or a full meal, remember to nourish not only your body but your soul with gratitude and prayer. Let your approach to food be an extension of your faith.

Prayer

Lord, thank You for providing me with food to nourish my body. Help me to approach each meal with gratitude and honor You through what I eat. Amen.

Affirmation

I nourish my body with gratitude and faith, recognizing each meal as a blessing from God.

May 5
Managing Loneliness with Faith

"The Lord is close to the brokenhearted and saves those who are crushed in spirit." (Psalm 34:18, NIV)

Devotional Reflection

Loneliness can be one of the most difficult emotions to navigate, especially when we feel disconnected from others. As black women, we often carry many responsibilities, which can sometimes make us feel isolated even when we're surrounded by people. Whether it's physical distance from loved ones or emotional distance from those who may not understand your struggles, loneliness can creep in quietly. But in those moments, faith reminds us that we are never truly alone.

God sees you, and He is near to those who feel lonely and brokenhearted. Faith provides a comfort that no human companionship can fully offer. When the world feels distant, God's presence remains close. He is always ready to listen, comfort, and embrace you in His love. Moments of loneliness can actually deepen our connection with Him as we turn to Him for strength and companionship. He reminds us that we are valued and cherished, even when we feel unseen by the world.

Today, if you are feeling lonely or isolated, take time to rest in God's presence. Speak to Him openly about your feelings, and let His love fill the spaces where loneliness resides. Trust that He is with you, and He will carry you through the moments of solitude.

Prayer

Lord, in my moments of loneliness, remind me that I am never truly alone because You are always with me. Help me to find comfort and peace in Your presence. Amen.

Affirmation

Even in my loneliness, I am never alone, for God is always near, offering me love and peace.

May 6
Finding Strength in Physical Weakness

"But he said to me, 'My grace is sufficient for you, for my power is made perfect in weakness.' Therefore I will boast all the more gladly about my weaknesses, so that Christ's power may rest on me."

(2 Corinthians 12:9, NIV)

Devotional Reflection

Physical weakness, whether from illness, aging, or fatigue, can be frustrating and disheartening. As black women, we are often expected to carry a heavy load, appearing strong even when our bodies feel anything but. When physical limitations arise, it can feel like we are being held back from our responsibilities, leaving us discouraged. Yet, in these moments of weakness, God's strength shines the brightest.

God doesn't require us to be physically strong to accomplish His will. In fact, He often works through our weakness to demonstrate His power and grace. When your body feels weak, remember that you don't have to carry everything on your own. God's strength is enough to sustain you when your own energy runs out. It's in these times that we learn to rely fully on Him, allowing His power to be our source of strength. There is beauty in surrendering our physical struggles to God and trusting that His grace will carry us through.

Today, instead of being frustrated by your physical limitations, lean into God's strength. Let Him show you that in your weakness, His power is perfect. Trust that even when your body is tired, your spirit can remain strong in Him.

Prayer

Father, when I feel physically weak or ill, remind me that Your strength is all I need. Help me to embrace Your grace in my times of weakness, knowing You will carry me through. Amen.

Affirmation

In my physical weakness, I find strength in God's grace, knowing His power is made perfect in my limitations.

May 7
Practicing Gratitude for Your Health Journey

"Give thanks in all circumstances; for this is God's will for you in Christ Jesus." (1 Thessalonians 5:18, NIV)

Devotional Reflection

Navigating health challenges, whether big or small, can be overwhelming and sometimes discouraging. It's easy to focus on what's not going well, whether it's physical pain, setbacks in treatment, or feeling like you're not as strong as you once were. But in the midst of these struggles, practicing gratitude can uplift your spirit and shift your mindset.

Gratitude isn't about ignoring the reality of your challenges, but rather choosing to focus on the blessings that are still present. Even in the hardest moments, there's always something to be thankful for—whether it's the support of loved ones, the ability to take small steps forward, or the fact that God is with you through every part of your journey. Gratitude has the power to renew your mind and bring peace to your heart, allowing you to see beyond the current difficulties and appreciate the strength you've been given to keep going.

Today, take a moment to reflect on your health journey, no matter where you are in it. What can you be thankful for? It may not always be easy, but practicing gratitude can help you stay grounded in faith, trusting that God is guiding you toward healing and renewal.

Prayer

Lord, thank You for the blessings that I sometimes overlook, especially during challenging times. Help me to see Your goodness in every part of my health journey, and fill my heart with gratitude. Amen.

Affirmation

I choose gratitude in my health journey, knowing that God's blessings are present in every step, and He is guiding me toward strength and healing.

May 8
Emotional Healing Through Worship

"The Lord is my strength and my shield; my heart trusts in him, and he helps me. My heart leaps for joy, and with my song I praise him."

(Psalm 28:7, NIV)

Devotional Reflection

There's something powerful about worship that goes beyond just singing songs or raising your hands. Worship is a direct connection to God, where we pour out our hearts and invite His presence to work in us. As black women, we often carry a lot of emotional burdens—past hurts, stress, and worries about the future. But in moments of worship, we have the opportunity to lay those burdens down and experience healing that can only come from God.

When we worship, we release our pain, sadness, and struggles into God's hands, and in return, He pours peace and emotional healing into us. Worship is a space where we can be vulnerable, honest, and open before God. It's not about having all the answers or being perfect; it's about letting go and trusting that God is already working in our hearts. The act of worship can soften even the heaviest of burdens and renew our spirits in ways we may not fully understand.

Today, make time for worship. It doesn't have to be in a church or a formal setting—it can be as simple as singing a song in your kitchen or whispering words of praise in your quiet time. Let worship be the pathway for God to bring emotional healing and restoration to your heart.

Prayer

Lord, I thank You for the gift of worship. As I lift my heart to You today, I ask that You heal my emotions and renew my spirit through Your love and grace. Amen.

Affirmation

In worship, I find emotional healing and spiritual renewal, trusting God to restore my heart and bring peace into my life.

May 9
Breaking Free from Unhealthy Habits

"So if the Son sets you free, you will be free indeed." (John 8:36, NIV)

Devotional Reflection

Unhealthy habits, whether physical, emotional, or spiritual, can sometimes feel like chains holding us back from living fully in God's purpose. Whether it's negative self-talk, relying on unhealthy coping mechanisms, or patterns of behavior that no longer serve us, these habits can keep us from the abundant life God desires for us. As black women, we may face unique pressures, but through faith, we can find the strength to break free from what no longer serves us.

The journey of letting go of unhealthy behaviors isn't always easy, but with God's help, it is possible. When we surrender our struggles to Him, He gives us the strength to overcome and guides us toward healthier paths. Freedom starts with acknowledging that change is needed and trusting that God is ready to walk with us as we make those changes. Breaking free is not about perfection; it's about progress. Each step you take to release an unhealthy habit is a step toward the freedom God has already promised you.

Today, reflect on any habits or patterns that are holding you back. Ask God for the strength to let them go and the wisdom to replace them with healthy, life-giving practices. Trust that with faith, you can break free and move toward a better version of yourself.

Prayer

Lord, I ask for Your strength and guidance as I seek to break free from the habits that hold me back. Help me let go and embrace the freedom You have promised me. Amen.

Affirmation

With God's help, I am breaking free from unhealthy habits and stepping into the freedom and purpose He has for me.

May 10
Listening to Your Body's Needs

"Do you not know that your bodies are temples of the Holy Spirit, who is in you, whom you have received from God? You are not your own."

(1 Corinthians 6:19, NIV)

Devotional Reflection

In the hustle of everyday life, it's easy to overlook the signals our bodies send us. Whether it's feeling tired, overwhelmed, or even experiencing physical pain, we often push through, ignoring the very temple God has given us. As black women, many of us have been conditioned to always "keep going," no matter the cost. But God calls us to care for our bodies, honoring them as vessels that carry His Spirit.

Listening to your body isn't just about recognizing when you're hungry, tired, or stressed—it's about acknowledging those signals as divine messages urging you to slow down, rest, or nourish yourself. Trusting your body's signals is an act of faith, a way of saying, "Lord, I honor the temple You've entrusted to me." It's okay to rest when you're weary, to fuel your body when it needs energy, and to give yourself the care you deserve. By listening to your body's needs, you're aligning yourself with the care God desires for you.

Today, take a moment to tune in to what your body is telling you. Are you in need of rest, nourishment, or quiet time? Trust that God is guiding you to respond to those needs, and honor the temple He's blessed you with.

Prayer

Father, thank You for this body You've given me. Help me to listen to my body's signals and honor it as a temple of Your Spirit. Give me wisdom to care for myself through faith. Amen.

Affirmation

I listen to my body's needs and honor it as a sacred temple, trusting that God guides me in caring for myself with love and wisdom.

May 11
Spiritual Detox for a Healthier Mind

"Finally, brothers and sisters, whatever is true, whatever is noble, whatever is right, whatever is pure, whatever is lovely, whatever is admirable—if anything is excellent or praiseworthy—think about such things." (Philippians 4:8, NIV)

Devotional Reflection

Just as our bodies need a detox to remove harmful substances, our minds require a spiritual cleanse to rid ourselves of negative influences and toxic thoughts. We can become bogged down by worry, doubt, fear, or the words of others, leaving our minds cluttered and weighed down. As black women, we may face additional stressors and challenges, but through faith, we can clear away what doesn't serve us and make room for God's truth.

A spiritual detox involves more than just letting go of harmful thoughts; it's about replacing them with things that are good, pure, and worthy of praise. Faith-based spiritual detoxing means seeking God's truth over the lies the world tells us. It means being intentional about what we allow into our minds—whether it's what we watch, read, or engage in daily. By focusing on the goodness of God and filling our minds with His promises, we begin to transform how we think, react, and approach challenges.

Today, take a moment to reflect on what thoughts or influences might be holding you back from a healthier mindset. Ask God to help you remove these and replace them with His truth, allowing you to experience peace, clarity, and renewal.

Prayer

Lord, I ask for Your help in removing negative thoughts and influences from my mind. Fill me with Your truth and guide me toward a healthier, faith-filled mindset. Amen.

Affirmation

I detox my mind from negativity, focusing on God's truth and filling my thoughts with what is good, pure, and worthy of praise.

May 12
Faith-Based Approach to Managing Anxiety

"Cast all your anxiety on him because he cares for you."

(1 Peter 5:7, NIV)

Devotional Reflection

Anxiety can creep into our lives in subtle ways, making everyday situations feel overwhelming. As black women, the pressures of life—work, family—can make it hard to find peace. But God invites us to release our anxiety and trust in Him. While the world may tell us to handle everything on our own, scripture reminds us that we are not meant to carry the weight of our worries alone.

Leaning on scripture and Prayerprovides a way to manage anxiety with faith at the center. God's Word is filled with promises that offer comfort and strength in times of fear. When anxious thoughts arise, turning to Prayerallows us to lay those burdens at God's feet, trusting Him to provide peace that goes beyond our understanding. Instead of spiraling in worry, we can remind ourselves of God's love and care, knowing that He holds every situation in His hands.

Today, when anxiety knocks on your door, answer it with scripture and prayer. Let God's promises calm your mind and heart, and trust that He is with you in every moment of uncertainty.

Prayer

Lord, I surrender my anxieties to You. Help me to trust in Your care and lean on Your Word when worry takes over. Give me peace and remind me that You are in control. Amen.

Affirmation

I release my anxiety to God, trusting Him to bring peace and strength to my heart through scripture and prayer.

May 13
Releasing Control to God for Emotional Freedom

"Trust in the Lord with all your heart and lean not on your own understanding; in all your ways submit to him, and he will make your paths straight." (Proverbs 3:5-6, NIV)

Devotional Reflection

Many of us find comfort in control. We want to plan every detail, manage every outcome, and steer our lives in the direction we think is best. But the truth is, holding on to control can create more stress, anxiety, and emotional burden than freedom. As black women, the weight of managing everything—whether it's our homes, careers, or relationships—can feel overwhelming. But God calls us to let go and trust Him with the details.

Releasing control to God isn't about giving up; it's about finding emotional freedom in knowing that we don't have to carry everything alone. When we cling too tightly to control, we block God's ability to work fully in our lives. By surrendering our plans, our worries, and even our pain, we open ourselves to the healing and freedom only He can provide. Trusting God means believing that His way is better, even when we don't see the full picture.

Today, take a step back and ask yourself: What are you holding on to that you need to release? Trust that as you surrender control, God will not only guide your path but also free your heart from the weight of trying to manage everything on your own.

Prayer

Lord, I surrender my need for control to You. Help me to trust in Your plan and find emotional freedom in releasing my worries and burdens to You. Amen.

Affirmation

I release control to God, trusting that He will guide my path and provide emotional freedom and peace.

May 14
Reclaiming Joy in Your Daily Life

"The joy of the Lord is your strength." (Nehemiah 8:10, NIV)

Devotional Reflection

Life's busy pace and challenges can sometimes rob us of the simple joys that once brightened our days. As black women, we often carry the weight of responsibility—caring for others, managing tasks, and striving to meet expectations. In the middle of it all, joy can feel distant, buried beneath stress and fatigue. But joy is a gift from God, and it can be reclaimed when we reconnect with Him in our daily lives.

Finding joy doesn't always come from grand moments. It's often found in the small, quiet blessings we experience each day. When we slow down and reconnect with God, we open ourselves to see the beauty in simple things—a moment of laughter, the warmth of the sun, or a kind word from a loved one. True joy comes from a deep connection with God, who fills our hearts with strength and peace no matter what we are facing. It's about allowing His presence to refresh your spirit and bring light into the everyday moments.

Today, make space to reconnect with God and rediscover the joy He has placed around you. Whether it's through prayer, a walk in nature, or simply pausing to breathe, let God's joy flow through your life and lift your spirit.

Prayer

Lord, help me to reclaim the joy that comes from You. Open my eyes to the simple blessings around me, and let Your joy strengthen my heart today. Amen.

Affirmation

I embrace the joy of the Lord in my daily life, finding strength and peace in His presence every day.

May 15
Prioritizing Sleep as a Form of Worship

"In peace I will lie down and sleep, for you alone, Lord, make me dwell in safety." (Psalm 4:8, NIV)

Devotional Reflection

In a world that glorifies constant hustle and busyness, it can be easy to forget that rest is part of God's design. As black women, we are often expected to keep pushing, even when we're exhausted—giving our all to everyone around us while neglecting our own well-being. But sleep is not a luxury; it's a necessity that God has built into our lives as a way to restore and renew us. In fact, prioritizing sleep can be seen as an act of worship.

When we allow ourselves to rest, we are trusting God with our time, our worries, and our responsibilities. It's an acknowledgment that He is in control, not us, and that it's okay to step away and rest in His care. By valuing sleep, we are obeying God's design for our well-being. Just as He rested on the seventh day, He calls us to honor our bodies and minds by embracing the gift of rest. Proper sleep allows us to recharge, remain strong, and serve Him better in our daily lives.

Tonight, as you prepare for bed, see sleep as more than just rest—it is an opportunity to trust in God's provision, to let go of your burdens, and to restore your body and mind as He intended.

Prayer

Lord, thank You for the gift of sleep and rest. Help me to prioritize sleep as a way to honor and obey Your design for my well-being. I trust You with my worries as I rest in Your care. Amen.

Affirmation

I honor God's design for my well-being by prioritizing rest, trusting Him with my time and responsibilities.

May 16
Faith and Emotional Boundaries

"Above all, love each other deeply, because love covers over a multitude of sins." (1 Peter 4:8, NIV)

Devotional Reflection

Setting emotional boundaries can sometimes feel like a balancing act between protecting your heart and extending grace to others. As black women, we often feel the pull to give more than we receive, pouring ourselves into relationships that may leave us emotionally drained. But faith teaches us that while love and grace are essential, so is the ability to protect our emotional well-being.

Emotional boundaries are not about building walls; they are about creating healthy spaces where love, respect, and understanding can thrive. God doesn't call us to be everything to everyone. He wants us to show love, but He also wants us to guard our hearts with wisdom. Boundaries allow us to remain emotionally whole, enabling us to give from a place of fullness rather than depletion. They help us manage our emotional energy and ensure that we are not overextending ourselves in ways that harm our mental and spiritual health.

Today, consider where you may need to establish or reinforce emotional boundaries in your life. Doing so with grace doesn't mean shutting people out—it means protecting the emotional space God has given you to flourish. Trust that God will guide you in maintaining boundaries while still loving others deeply.

Prayer

Lord, help me to set healthy emotional boundaries that protect my heart while extending grace to others. Give me wisdom and strength to love well without overextending myself. Amen.

Affirmation

I honor my emotional well-being by setting healthy boundaries with grace and faith, trusting God to guide me in love and protection.

May 17
Dealing with Physical Pain Through Prayer

"The Lord sustains them on their sickbed and restores them from their bed of illness." (Psalm 41:3, NIV)

Devotional Reflection

Physical pain, whether from illness or chronic conditions, can wear down not only the body but the spirit as well. As black women, we often push through pain, believing we must stay strong no matter what. But when discomfort lingers, and we feel weighed down by it, we may start to question our strength and wonder if relief will ever come. In these moments, Prayerbecomes our lifeline, connecting us to the One who understands our suffering.

God invites us to bring our pain to Him, not just in hope for healing but for comfort and peace through the process. When we pray through our physical discomfort, we acknowledge that God is our strength even when our bodies feel weak. Prayerdoesn't always take away the pain instantly, but it brings us closer to the One who can provide relief, both physically and emotionally. It allows us to rest in His care, knowing that He is with us, sustaining us through each difficult moment.

Today, as you face any physical pain or discomfort, remember to lean into prayer. Speak to God openly about your struggles, and trust that He is working in ways you may not yet see. Let His presence bring peace to your mind and body as you navigate the challenges of pain.

Prayer

Lord, I come to You with my physical pain, trusting that You will sustain me through this time. Please bring comfort to my body and peace to my spirit as I lean on You for strength and healing. Amen.

Affirmation

I trust God to sustain me through physical pain, finding comfort and strength through Prayerand His healing presence.

May 18
The Power of Affirmations in Self-Healing

"The tongue has the power of life and death, and those who love it will eat its fruit." (Proverbs 18:21, NIV)

Devotional Reflection

The words we speak over ourselves have incredible power. As black women, we often face challenges that can leave us feeling worn down mentally, emotionally, and spiritually. In these moments, the thoughts we choose to dwell on can either uplift or break us further. But through faith-filled affirmations, we can begin to speak healing into our lives, one word at a time.

Affirmations are more than just positive statements—they are declarations rooted in faith. When we speak God's promises over ourselves, we are aligning our thoughts and words with His truth. Affirmations such as "I am loved by God," "I am strong in Christ," or "God is my healer" can transform how we see ourselves and approach challenges. Repeating these faith-filled affirmations helps retrain our minds, breaking free from negative self-talk and replacing it with God's truth. Each Affirmationbecomes a step toward healing—mentally, emotionally, and spiritually.

Today, practice speaking life over yourself through affirmations grounded in faith. Remind yourself of God's promises and let those words take root in your heart. Healing often begins with the words you choose to speak over your life.

Prayer

Lord, help me to speak words of healing and truth over myself. Guide me in using affirmations rooted in faith to strengthen my mind, heart, and spirit. Amen.

Affirmation

I speak words of life and healing over myself, trusting in God's promises to bring restoration to my mind, body, and spirit.

May 19
Trusting God During Health Scares

"When I am afraid, I put my trust in you." (Psalm 56:3, NIV)

Devotional Reflection

Health scares can bring a wave of uncertainty and fear, shaking the foundation of even the strongest faith. As black women, we may often feel the pressure to be resilient in the face of such trials, but the truth is, these moments can be overwhelming. Whether it's waiting for test results or navigating an unexpected diagnosis, the unknown can lead to anxiety. However, it's in these moments of fear and uncertainty that God calls us to lean on Him fully.

Trusting God during health scares doesn't mean pretending we aren't afraid or worried. It means acknowledging the fear but choosing to place it in God's hands. He is the ultimate healer, the one who knows our bodies inside and out, and who sees the path ahead even when we don't. Leaning on Him brings comfort in uncertainty and strengthens our faith as we navigate the unknown. God promises to walk with us through every trial, offering peace that surpasses all understanding.

Today, if you are facing a health scare or uncertainty about your well-being, take a deep breath and hand it over to God. Trust that He is in control, and let His presence calm your heart as you place your health in His capable hands.

Prayer

Lord, I trust You with my health, especially in moments of fear and uncertainty. Calm my anxious heart and remind me that You are with me, guiding me through every step. Amen.

Affirmation

I trust God with my health, knowing that He is in control and will guide me through every moment of uncertainty.

May 20
Finding Balance in a Busy Life

"Come to me, all you who are weary and burdened, and I will give you rest." (Matthew 11:28, NIV)

Devotional Reflection
Life can often feel like a never-ending juggling act, especially when we're balancing work, family, personal goals, and relationships. As black women, the weight of responsibility can sometimes feel heavier, with expectations to constantly show up strong and capable in all areas. But living in a constant state of busyness can leave us drained and disconnected from the peace God desires for us. Finding balance isn't just about time management—it's about leaning on God to help prioritize what truly matters.

God calls us to rest in Him, to release the burdens we carry and trust Him with the details of our lives. When we allow faith to guide us, we gain the wisdom to make decisions that promote balance and well-being. It's okay to say no when necessary, to pause when we need rest, and to seek moments of quiet in the midst of the chaos. By trusting God with our time, we allow Him to direct our steps and restore the energy we need to fulfill our responsibilities without losing ourselves.

Today, ask God for wisdom in finding balance. Let Him show you how to manage your time, energy, and focus in a way that honors your well-being while fulfilling the callings He has placed on your life.

Prayer
Lord, help me find balance in my busy life. Guide my steps and give me wisdom to prioritize what truly matters, trusting You to lead me toward rest and peace. Amen.

Affirmation
I seek balance in my life through faith, trusting God to guide my priorities and give me strength for each day.

May 21
Maintaining Spiritual Wellness Amid Health Struggles

"The Lord is my strength and my defense; he has become my salvation."
(Exodus 15:2, NIV)

Devotional Reflection

Facing health struggles can often take a toll not only on your body but also on your spirit. It's easy to feel discouraged, questioning why you're going through such trials. As black women, we're often expected to be strong, even in moments of personal struggle, but health challenges can push us beyond our limits. Maintaining spiritual wellness in the midst of these difficulties becomes essential for finding peace and hope.

Spiritual wellness means staying connected to God even when your physical body feels weak. It's about leaning into your faith and trusting that God is still with you, working through the challenges. Though health struggles can make you feel isolated or weary, turning to prayer, scripture, and the comfort of God's presence provides the spiritual nourishment you need to keep going. Your faith becomes a source of strength that lifts your spirit, even when the body feels frail.

Today, if you are experiencing health challenges, remind yourself that your spiritual wellness is a source of strength. Continue to nourish your spirit by spending time with God, knowing that He is your defender and your source of healing.

Prayer

Lord, help me to keep my faith strong, even in the midst of health challenges. Remind me that You are my strength and that You are with me through every struggle. Amen.

Affirmation

I maintain my spiritual wellness by trusting in God's strength and believing that He is with me, even during health struggles.

May 22
Faith and Healthy Friendships

"As iron sharpens iron, so one person sharpens another."
                                        (Proverbs 27:17, NIV)

Devotional Reflection

Friendships play a vital role in our lives, offering support, encouragement, and companionship. However, not all friendships are created equal. Some can nurture and uplift, while others may drain us emotionally or cause stress. As black women, the value of healthy friendships that bring joy, peace, and understanding cannot be overstated. Building friendships rooted in faith can significantly contribute to our mental well-being, helping us grow spiritually and emotionally.

Healthy friendships are those that reflect God's love and support, where both parties encourage one another in faith and personal growth. When our friendships are based on trust, respect, and mutual care, we experience the positive effects on our emotional health. These connections give us safe spaces to share our burdens, celebrate victories, and walk through life's challenges. God desires us to cultivate friendships that sharpen us, making us stronger and more grounded in Him.

Today, reflect on the friendships in your life. Are they nurturing your mental and spiritual health? Seek God's guidance in building and maintaining friendships that align with His purpose for your life, and allow your relationships to be sources of joy and peace.

Prayer

Lord, help me to build and maintain healthy friendships that nurture my mental and spiritual well-being. Guide me in choosing relationships that reflect Your love and grace. Amen.

Affirmation

I build healthy friendships rooted in faith, knowing they nurture my mental well-being and strengthen my spirit.

May 23

Creating a Routine that Honors God and Your Body

"Do you not know that your bodies are temples of the Holy Spirit, who is in you, whom you have received from God? You are not your own." (1 Corinthians 6:19, NIV)

Devotional Reflection
Creating a daily routine that honors both God and your body is a powerful way to live in alignment with your faith and your well-being. As black women, we often prioritize others, leaving little time for ourselves or our spiritual growth. However, God calls us to care for the body and mind He has given us, ensuring that our daily habits reflect His love and care.

A routine that honors God and your body doesn't have to be complicated. It starts with small, intentional choices—whether it's starting the day with prayer, moving your body to stay healthy, or making time for rest. It's about recognizing that self-care is not selfish, but a reflection of honoring the temple God has entrusted to you. When we develop routines rooted in faith, we create space for God's presence in our daily lives while nurturing our physical and emotional health.

Today, reflect on your daily routine. Are there ways you can incorporate more faith and self-care into your day? Trust that when you prioritize both God and your well-being, you'll find balance and peace in your daily life.

Prayer
Lord, help me to create a daily routine that honors both You and my body. Guide me in making choices that reflect Your love and care, and give me the strength to prioritize my well-being. Amen.

Affirmation
I create a routine that honors God and my body, recognizing that self-care and faith are both important in my daily life.

May 24
Overcoming Guilt in Your Health Journey

"Therefore, there is now no condemnation for those who are in Christ Jesus." (Romans 8:1, NIV)

Devotional Reflection

Guilt can be a heavy burden, especially when it comes to our health. Whether it's skipping a workout, eating something we feel we shouldn't, or not taking care of our bodies the way we hoped, guilt has a way of creeping in. As black women, we often face added pressures to meet certain standards, and when we fall short, the guilt can feel overwhelming. But God does not call us to live under the weight of guilt—He offers grace.

Your health journey is not about perfection; it's about progress and finding balance. God sees your efforts, your struggles, and your heart. He wants you to embrace grace and let go of the guilt that holds you back. Just as God extends grace to us when we fall short in other areas of life, He also offers it in our health journey. You are allowed to have setbacks, to make mistakes, and to start fresh each day without condemning yourself.

Today, release any guilt you may be carrying about your health and wellness path. Remember that God's grace covers all things, and each day is a new opportunity to care for your body and spirit with love and kindness.

Prayer

Lord, help me to let go of the guilt I feel in my health journey. Remind me that Your grace is always present, and guide me to embrace it fully as I take care of the body You've given me. Amen.

Affirmation

I release guilt and embrace grace in my health journey, trusting that God's love and compassion guide me each day.

May 25
Handling Stress with Spiritual Maturity

"Cast your cares on the Lord and he will sustain you; he will never let the righteous be shaken." (Psalm 55:22, NIV)

Devotional Reflection

Stress is an inevitable part of life, and as black women, we often face unique challenges that can add to the pressure. Whether it's balancing work, family, or personal expectations, stress can feel like a constant companion. However, spiritual maturity gives us the tools to handle life's stresses in a way that honors God and protects our well-being.

Spiritual maturity is about trusting God even when things feel overwhelming. It's about recognizing that we don't have to bear the weight of life's difficulties on our own. By leaning on God through prayer, scripture, and faith, we rise above stress, knowing that He is in control. Spiritual maturity helps us pause, reflect, and respond rather than react. It allows us to approach challenges with a calm heart, confident that God's strength is enough to carry us through.

Today, when stress arises, choose to handle it with spiritual maturity. Bring your concerns to God, trust Him to sustain you, and let His peace fill your heart as you face life's challenges with faith.

Prayer

Lord, help me to handle stress with spiritual maturity. Teach me to trust You with my cares and to find peace in Your presence, knowing that You are always in control. Amen.

Affirmation

I handle stress with spiritual maturity, trusting God to sustain me and guide me through life's challenges with peace and strength.

May 26
The Connection Between Faith and Fitness

"For physical training is of some value, but godliness has value for all things, holding promise for both the present life and the life to come."

(1 Timothy 4:8, NIV)

Devotional Reflection

Faith and fitness may seem like two separate parts of life, but they are more connected than you might think. As black women, we often take on multiple roles and responsibilities, sometimes forgetting to prioritize both our physical and spiritual well-being. However, the discipline required for physical fitness can also strengthen our faith and deepen our spiritual connection to God.

When we care for our bodies through exercise, we are honoring the temple that God has given us. Physical activity helps clear our minds, reduce stress, and improve our mood, all of which can enhance our spiritual well-being. Fitness requires commitment, patience, and perseverance—traits that are also necessary for a strong faith. By staying physically active, we create a space where both our bodies and spirits can thrive, enabling us to serve God with energy and joy.

Today, view your fitness routine as an opportunity to connect with God. Whether it's a walk, a workout, or stretching, take time to thank Him for your body and the strength He provides to keep moving forward.

Prayer

Lord, thank You for the gift of my body. Help me to honor it through fitness and care, and remind me that physical activity can draw me closer to You. Strengthen me both physically and spiritually. Amen.

Affirmation

I honor my body and strengthen my faith through fitness, knowing that both my physical and spiritual well-being are important to God.

May 27
Honoring God Through Your Diet

"So whether you eat or drink or whatever you do, do it all for the glory of God." (1 Corinthians 10:31, NIV)

Devotional Reflection

Our relationship with food is deeply personal, and as black women, we often carry rich cultural traditions that involve food. While it's important to enjoy those traditions, it's also essential to reflect on how our eating habits impact both our physical and spiritual well-being. Mindful eating allows us to pause and make intentional choices about what we consume, understanding that our bodies are temples of the Holy Spirit.

Honoring God through your diet is not about strict rules or deprivation; it's about caring for the body He has given you. When you approach food with gratitude and mindfulness, you make decisions that nourish your body and soul. Eating in a way that honors God involves balance—choosing foods that fuel your body and support your health while still enjoying the blessings of delicious meals. It's about recognizing that food is a gift from God and treating it as such.

Today, as you make choices about what to eat, consider how those choices reflect your commitment to honoring God with your body. Let your meals be a time of thankfulness and nourishment, both physically and spiritually.

Prayer

Lord, help me to honor You through my food choices. Guide me in making decisions that nourish my body and bring glory to You. Thank You for the gift of food and the strength it provides. Amen.

Affirmation

I honor God by making mindful choices about what I eat, caring for my body as a temple of the Holy Spirit.

May 28
Fostering Mental Clarity Through Scripture

"Your word is a lamp for my feet, a light on my path."

(Psalm 119:105, NIV)

Devotional Reflection

In the midst of a busy and chaotic world, mental clarity can feel out of reach. The constant demands of life, paired with internal worries and distractions, can create a sense of mental fog. As black women, we often juggle multiple responsibilities, and the pressure to always be "on" can cloud our thoughts. But God offers us a way to find clarity and focus through His Word.

Scripture has the power to cut through the noise and bring peace to our minds. When we turn to God's Word, we are reminded of His promises, His direction, and His guidance. It helps us refocus on what truly matters and align our thoughts with His will. Whether it's through a verse that brings peace or a passage that offers wisdom, the Bible provides the clarity we need to navigate life's distractions and hear God's voice clearly.

Today, when you feel mentally overwhelmed, pause and open the Word of God. Let scripture guide your thoughts and bring you the clarity that only He can provide. His Word will light your path and help you focus on His voice, no matter how loud the world may seem.

Prayer

Lord, when my mind feels cluttered, help me turn to Your Word for clarity and focus. Guide my thoughts and help me hear Your voice through the scriptures You have provided. Amen.

Affirmation

I find mental clarity and peace through God's Word, trusting it to guide my thoughts and help me focus on His voice.

May 29
Embracing Emotional Freedom in Christ

"So if the Son sets you free, you will be free indeed." (John 8:36, NIV)

Devotional Reflection

Emotional burdens, whether from past hurts, ongoing stress, or lingering fears, can weigh heavily on our hearts. As black women, we often feel the pressure to keep it all together, hiding our emotional struggles behind a strong exterior. But Christ offers us true freedom, not just from sin, but from the emotional chains that may keep us bound.

In Christ, there is freedom to release the pain, the fear, and the worry that may have taken root in your heart. He doesn't just call us to manage our emotions—He calls us to be free from those burdens, replacing them with His peace. When you embrace the emotional freedom that Christ offers, you allow Him to heal your heart, release you from bitterness, and fill you with joy. The weight of emotional struggles no longer defines you because your identity is rooted in Christ's love and freedom.

Today, take a moment to reflect on any emotional burdens you've been carrying. Bring them to Christ and let Him free you from those chains. Embrace the emotional freedom that comes with being loved, seen, and fully known by the Savior.

Prayer

Lord, I bring my emotional struggles to You, trusting that You will set me free. Heal my heart and help me embrace the freedom and peace that only You can provide. Amen.

Affirmation

In Christ, I find emotional freedom and release from the burdens that have weighed me down. I am free indeed.

May 30
Celebrating Your Health Wins with God

"I will give thanks to you, Lord, with all my heart; I will tell of all your wonderful deeds." (Psalm 9:1, NIV)

Devotional Reflection

Often in our health journeys, we focus on what we haven't yet achieved or the obstacles that still lie ahead. But it's important to pause and celebrate the progress we've made, no matter how small it may seem. As black women, we face unique challenges in maintaining our health, but each step forward is a victory worth acknowledging. These wins, whether big or small, are evidence of God's grace and strength working in us.

God desires us to rejoice in our progress and to thank Him for the ability to move forward. Whether it's improving your fitness, managing stress better, or making healthier food choices, these are moments where God has provided strength and guidance. Celebrating these wins with gratitude reminds us that we are not alone on this journey—God is with us every step of the way, cheering us on. Acknowledging progress, no matter how incremental, is a reflection of His faithfulness in our lives.

Today, take time to recognize your health wins. Reflect on how far you've come, thank God for His support, and celebrate your progress with joy and gratitude.

Prayer

Lord, I thank You for the progress I've made in my health journey. Help me to see each win, big or small, as a reflection of Your grace. Guide me to continue moving forward with strength and gratitude. Amen.

Affirmation

I celebrate every health win with gratitude, knowing that God has been with me every step of the way, providing strength and guidance.

May 31
Preparing for a New Season of Health

"Forget the former things; do not dwell on the past. See, I am doing a new thing! Now it springs up; do you not perceive it?"

(Isaiah 43:18-19, NIV)

Devotional Reflection

As we approach a new season, it's natural to reflect on where we've been and where we're headed. For many of us, our health journeys have been filled with ups and downs, progress and setbacks. But today, God invites you to look ahead with hope and faith, trusting that He is doing something new in your health and wellness. The past, with all its struggles and victories, has led you to this moment—but it doesn't define the future God has planned for you.

Preparing for a new season of health means releasing any guilt, frustration, or disappointment from the past. It's about embracing the opportunity for renewal, knowing that God is still working in you, guiding you toward wholeness. With each new day, God gives us the strength to keep moving forward, trusting Him to guide us toward greater health—physically, mentally, and spiritually. Whatever lies ahead, you can face it with confidence, knowing that God's hand is on your journey.

Today, step into this new season with faith, trusting God to continue leading you. Whether you're setting new goals or simply recommitting to taking care of yourself, know that God is with you, bringing fresh strength and grace for the days ahead.

Prayer

Lord, as I prepare for a new season of health, I trust You to guide me every step of the way. Help me let go of the past and embrace the new things You are doing in my life. Thank You for Your constant presence and strength. Amen.

Affirmation

I step into this new season of health with faith, trusting God to guide my wellness journey and provide the strength I need for each day.

June
Relationships and Community

June 1
Understanding the Power of Sisterhood

"Two are better than one, because they have a good return for their labor: If either of them falls down, one can help the other up."
(Ecclesiastes 4:9-10, NIV)

Devotional Reflection

Sisterhood is a powerful and necessary bond, especially for black women who navigate unique challenges in their personal and professional lives. True sisterhood is more than just friendship—it's a deep connection rooted in mutual love, trust, and understanding. When you have sisters by your side, you gain a source of strength, comfort, and encouragement that lifts you up when you feel weighed down by the world.

There is something special about friendships with other black women. These relationships allow you to be your authentic self, free from judgment. In a world where black women are often expected to be strong, sisterhood creates a safe space where you can be vulnerable and supported. Your sisters can help bear the weight of your struggles, celebrate your victories, and remind you of your worth when you forget. Through these bonds, you experience the power of collective strength and love.

Today, take a moment to reflect on the women in your life who embody sisterhood. Thank God for their presence, and if you are feeling isolated, ask Him to bring meaningful friendships into your life. Embrace the beauty of having sisters who uplift and encourage you through every season of life.

Prayer

Lord, thank You for the gift of sisterhood. Help me to nurture and cherish the friendships that uplift and strengthen me. Guide me to be a supportive and loving sister to others. Amen.

Affirmation

I embrace the power of sisterhood, knowing that together, we uplift and support one another with love and strength.

June 2
Navigating Conflict with Grace

"A gentle answer turns away wrath, but a harsh word stirs up anger."
(Proverbs 15:1, NIV)

Devotional Reflection

Conflict is an inevitable part of any relationship, whether with friends, family, or coworkers. Disagreements can arise from misunderstandings, unmet expectations, or even different perspectives. As black women, we are often expected to be strong and handle conflicts head-on, but sometimes, that strength can lead us to react with frustration or anger. However, God calls us to a higher standard—He asks us to approach conflict with grace and wisdom, leaning on our faith to guide us through challenging moments.

Navigating conflict with grace means choosing to respond with calm and understanding rather than reacting with harshness. It's about pausing to seek God's wisdom before you speak and asking for patience when emotions run high. Grace allows you to listen, empathize, and communicate without letting anger take control. When you approach disagreements with a heart centered on God's peace, you create space for healing, understanding, and reconciliation.

Today, if you find yourself in the midst of conflict, take a step back and seek God's guidance. Ask Him to help you handle the situation with grace, allowing His love to guide your words and actions. Trust that through His wisdom, you can navigate conflict with faith and emerge with stronger, healthier relationships.

Prayer

Lord, help me to navigate conflict with grace. Give me the wisdom to respond with love and understanding, and guide me through disagreements with a calm spirit. Amen.

Affirmation

I handle conflict with grace and wisdom, trusting God to guide my words and actions as I seek peace and understanding.

June 3
Setting Boundaries in Relationships

"Above all else, guard your heart, for everything you do flows from it."
                                            (Proverbs 4:23, NIV)

Devotional Reflection

Setting boundaries can be one of the most loving actions you take for yourself and others. As black women, we often find ourselves giving and sacrificing in our relationships, sometimes to the point of emotional and mental exhaustion. We feel the pressure to be everything for everyone, but God has not called us to neglect our own well-being. Establishing healthy boundaries is essential for protecting your emotional and mental health, while still allowing love and grace to flow in your relationships.

Boundaries aren't about shutting people out; they are about creating spaces where you can thrive without being drained. When you set clear boundaries, you teach others how to respect your time, energy, and emotional capacity. It's not selfish—it's an act of self-care and self-preservation that allows you to show up fully in your relationships without losing yourself in the process. Boundaries help you protect your peace and ensure that your needs are met as well.

Today, reflect on where you may need to establish or reinforce boundaries in your life. Ask God for wisdom and strength to protect your emotional and mental well-being while nurturing healthy, balanced relationships. Trust that setting boundaries will allow you to experience more peace, joy, and fulfillment in your relationships.

Prayer

Lord, help me to set healthy boundaries that protect my emotional and mental well-being. Give me the wisdom to know when and how to establish these boundaries with love and grace. Amen.---

Affirmations

I honor my emotional and mental health by setting healthy boundaries, trusting God to guide me in nurturing balanced and fulfilling relationships.

June 4
Supporting Your Sisters in Christ

"Carry each other's burdens, and in this way you will fulfill the law of Christ." (Galatians 6:2, NIV)

Devotional Reflection

As black women, we know the power of community and sisterhood. There is a unique bond that forms when women come together, sharing their joys, challenges, and dreams. In Christ, this bond is even stronger. God calls us to be pillars of strength for one another, lifting up our sisters in times of need, celebrating their victories, and walking alongside them in both good times and bad.

Supporting your sisters in Christ means offering love, encouragement, and a listening ear when needed. It's about being present, not just when it's convenient, but when they need you the most. We are called to reflect Christ's love by standing in the gap for one another—through prayer, words of affirmation, and acts of kindness. Sometimes, being a pillar of strength isn't about having all the answers, but simply offering your presence and reminding them that they are not alone.

Today, take a moment to consider the women in your life. How can you be a pillar of strength for them? Whether through a phone call, prayer, or offering your time, allow God to use you to uplift and encourage your sisters in Christ.

Prayer

Lord, help me to be a source of strength and encouragement for the women in my life. Show me how I can support them in ways that reflect Your love and grace. Amen.

Affirmation

I am a pillar of strength for my sisters in Christ, offering love, encouragement, and support as we walk together in faith.

June 5
Healing from Broken Friendships

"The Lord is close to the brokenhearted and saves those who are crushed in spirit." (Psalm 34:18, NIV)

Devotional Reflection

The pain of losing a close friendship can be just as deep as any other form of heartbreak. When a friendship breaks apart, whether through conflict, distance, or growing apart, it leaves a void in our hearts. As black women, friendships often serve as lifelines—safe spaces where we share our deepest thoughts, dreams, and fears. So when a friendship ends, it can feel like losing a piece of ourselves. But in these moments of pain, God is present, ready to heal our hearts and restore our spirits.

Healing from the loss of a friendship takes time, and it requires trust in God's ability to mend what feels broken. Just as He is close to the brokenhearted, He promises to heal those wounds, bringing peace and comfort as you grieve what was lost. Trusting God through this process allows Him to guide you toward emotional healing, showing you that your value is not defined by one relationship, but by His love for you. As you heal, God may bring new connections into your life or restore relationships in unexpected ways.

Today, if you're dealing with the pain of a broken friendship, give your heart to God. Trust Him to carry you through the healing process, knowing that He is with you every step of the way.

Prayer

Lord, I bring the pain of my broken friendship to You. Heal my heart and help me trust in Your love as I navigate this season of loss. Guide me toward peace and healing. Amen.

Affirmation

I trust God to heal my heart from the pain of broken friendships, knowing He will restore my spirit and bring peace into my life.

June 6
Celebrating Each Other's Success

"Rejoice with those who rejoice; mourn with those who mourn."

(Romans 12:15, NIV)

Devotional Reflection

In a world that often promotes competition and comparison, it can sometimes feel difficult to celebrate the successes of others without reflecting on our own journeys. As black women, we carry many aspirations and dreams, and seeing others achieve what we also long for can stir feelings of envy or inadequacy. However, God calls us to a higher standard—one that embraces true joy for others without comparing their victories to our own paths.

Celebrating another woman's success doesn't take away from your own progress. In fact, rejoicing with your sisters strengthens the bonds of sisterhood and allows love and grace to flourish. When we cheer each other on, we're reminding ourselves that God has a plan for each of us, and that there is no limit to His blessings. What God has for you is meant for you, and celebrating someone else's moment of victory is an act of faith that your time will come too.

Today, choose to celebrate the success of others wholeheartedly, knowing that their wins do not diminish your journey. Trust that God's timing is perfect and that your victories will come in their season.

Prayer

Lord, help me to celebrate the successes of others with a pure heart, free of envy or comparison. Remind me that You have a perfect plan for my life, and I trust in Your timing. Amen.

Affirmation

I rejoice in the success of others, knowing that God has a unique and perfect plan for my life as well.

June 7
Managing Expectations in Relationships

"Be completely humble and gentle; be patient, bearing with one another in love." (Ephesians 4:2, NIV)

Devotional Reflection

We all enter relationships—whether with family, friends, or romantic partners—with certain expectations. Sometimes, these expectations are rooted in our desires for how we want others to behave or what we believe relationships should look like. However, unrealistic expectations can set us up for disappointment, frustration, and even resentment. As black women, carrying the weight of these expectations, both for ourselves and others, can leave us feeling let down when people don't meet the standards we've created.

God calls us to approach relationships with grace, patience, and love, rather than a rigid set of expectations. When we let go of the need for others to fit into our ideals, we open ourselves to seeing them as God sees them—flawed, yet deeply loved. Learning to love others as they are means accepting their imperfections and trusting God to work in their lives, just as He is working in ours. It frees us from the pressure of expecting others to meet our every need and allows us to focus on building healthy, balanced relationships grounded in love.

Today, reflect on the expectations you may be placing on the people in your life. Ask God for the wisdom and grace to let go of unrealistic demands and to love others as they are, trusting Him to guide and strengthen your relationships.

Prayer

Lord, help me to release unrealistic expectations in my relationships. Teach me to love others with grace and patience, accepting them as they are. Guide me in building relationships that honor You. Amen.

Affirmation

I release unrealistic expectations and embrace grace and love in my relationships, trusting God to guide me in accepting others as they are.

June 8
Being a Godly Influence in Your Community

"In the same way, let your light shine before others, that they may see your good deeds and glorify your Father in heaven."

(Matthew 5:16, NIV)

Devotional Reflection

As black women, many of us are seen as pillars in our communities, whether through our roles in the family, church, or workplace. But being a positive influence goes beyond just holding a title or position—it's about living out your faith in a way that inspires and uplifts those around you. Your actions, words, and presence can reflect God's love and grace, serving as a beacon of hope and encouragement in your community.

Being a godly influence means letting your light shine, not for recognition, but so that others can see the goodness of God through your life. It's about using your gifts, talents, and resources to build up others, offering support where needed and standing firm in your faith, even when it's challenging. Your influence isn't limited to big moments—it's often in the small, everyday interactions where your faith makes the biggest impact.

Today, consider how you can be a godly influence in your community. Whether through a kind word, an act of service, or simply leading by example, allow your faith to shine brightly, knowing that God can use your light to draw others closer to Him.

Prayer

Lord, help me to be a godly influence in my community. Let my actions, words, and presence reflect Your love and inspire those around me to draw closer to You. Amen.

Affirmation

I live out my faith boldly, allowing my life to be a godly influence that inspires and uplifts those around me.

June 9
Overcoming Loneliness in Community

"God sets the lonely in families, he leads out the prisoners with singing." (Psalm 68:6, NIV)

Devotional Reflection
It's possible to be surrounded by people—family, friends, coworkers—and still feel a deep sense of loneliness. As black women, we often carry many responsibilities, and sometimes, the weight of those responsibilities can make us feel isolated, even in the midst of community. Feeling disconnected or out of place can make it hard to find your true sense of belonging, even among those who love you. But God sees you in your loneliness and promises to place you in spaces where you can thrive and be valued.

Overcoming loneliness starts with understanding that you are never truly alone. God is always with you, guiding you toward the people and places that align with His purpose for your life. Finding your place and purpose in a community doesn't always happen overnight—it's a process of trusting God to connect you with those who will support and uplift you. Sometimes, it's about being open to new relationships or stepping out of your comfort zone to engage with others. Trust that God will lead you to the right spaces and that you have a purpose within the community, even if it's not immediately clear. Today, if you're feeling lonely, turn to God and ask Him to guide you to your place in the community. Trust that He has a purpose for you and that He will place people in your life who will support and encourage you.

Prayer
Lord, in moments of loneliness, remind me that You are always with me. Guide me to the people and places where I can find connection, support, and purpose in my community. Amen.

Affirmation
I trust God to lead me to my place and purpose in my community, knowing that I am never truly alone with Him by my side.

June 10
Forgiveness as a Path to Healing

"Bear with each other and forgive one another if any of you has a grievance against someone. Forgive as the Lord forgave you."

(Colossians 3:13, NIV)

Devotional Reflection

Forgiveness is one of the hardest acts of love we're called to practice, especially when the hurt runs deep. As black women, we may have experienced wounds from family, friends, or even societal pressures that leave us holding on to resentment. These grudges, though justified at times, can weigh down our hearts and prevent us from experiencing the freedom and peace God desires for us. Forgiveness is not about excusing someone's behavior, but about releasing yourself from the burden of holding on to pain.

When we choose to forgive, we open the door for healing—both emotionally and spiritually. God calls us to forgive because it reflects His own grace toward us. By letting go of grudges, we make space for His peace to fill our hearts. Forgiveness is a process that may take time, but as we surrender our hurt to God, we allow Him to work in us, bringing freedom from the chains of bitterness and anger.

Today, consider who or what you need to forgive. Ask God to give you the strength to release any grudges you've been holding on to and to help you experience the healing and peace that comes with forgiveness.

Prayer

Lord, help me to forgive those who have hurt me. Give me the strength to let go of any grudges I've been holding, and fill my heart with Your peace and healing. Amen.

Affirmation

I choose forgiveness as a path to healing, releasing grudges and allowing God's peace to fill my heart and relationships.

June 11
The Strength of a Praying Friend

"Therefore confess your sins to each other and pray for each other so that you may be healed. The Prayerof a righteous person is powerful and effective." (James 5:16, NIV)

Devotional Reflection

There's something truly powerful about a friend who prays for you. As black women, we often serve as pillars of strength for those around us, but it's in moments of shared Prayerthat we are reminded we don't have to carry the weight alone. A friend who prays with and for you creates a spiritual bond that transcends the ordinary, deepening trust and connection in your relationship. Prayerstrengthens relationships because it invites God into the midst of your friendship, allowing Him to work in ways you both may not even realize.

Praying for a friend shows that you care about their well-being, both spiritually and emotionally. It's an act of love that demonstrates you are willing to stand in the gap for them, lifting them up in moments of need, and celebrating with them in moments of joy. Through prayer, your bond becomes rooted in faith, and you find strength in knowing that God is at the center of your relationship.

Today, take time to pray for a friend. Reach out and let them know that you are praying for them, and if possible, pray together. Watch how God strengthens and deepens your relationship as you bring your friendship before Him.

Prayer

Lord, thank You for the gift of friendships rooted in prayer. Help me to be a praying friend, lifting up my sisters in Christ and strengthening our bonds through faith and love. Amen.

Affirmation

I am a praying friend, strengthening my relationships through faith and the power of prayer, knowing that God is at the center of every bond.

June 12
Embracing Diversity in Friendships

"There is neither Jew nor Gentile, neither slave nor free, nor is there male and female, for you are all one in Christ Jesus."

(Galatians 3:28, NIV)

Devotional Reflection

Friendship is a gift, and one of its beauties is the chance to connect with people from diverse backgrounds. As Black women, shared experiences often bring us closer to those who understand our unique journeys, but it's equally important to embrace diversity in friendships. Valuing differences enriches our lives, opens our hearts, and offers new perspectives that strengthen our faith and understanding of God's love.

God created each of us uniquely, and embracing diversity in friendships reflects His creativity and inclusivity. Building relationships with people from various cultures and backgrounds allows us to experience the richness of life and grow in empathy. These friendships challenge us to think beyond our experiences and remind us that, in Christ, we are all part of one body, united by His love.

Consider how you can embrace diversity in your friendships today. Be open to connecting with others who are different, and ask God to help you see the beauty in those differences. Valuing diversity strengthens your ability to love as Christ loves us.

Prayer

Lord, help me to embrace diversity in my friendships. Open my heart to connect with people from different backgrounds and experiences, and teach me to value the richness that comes from those relationships. Amen.

Affirmation

I embrace diversity in my friendships, valuing the differences that make each person unique and growing in love and understanding through Christ.

June 13
Restoring Trust After Betrayal

"The Lord is close to the brokenhearted and saves those who are crushed in spirit." (Psalm 34:18, NIV)

Devotional Reflection

Betrayal by someone you trust can cut deeply, leaving wounds that are hard to heal. As black women, we often invest deeply in our relationships, so when betrayal occurs, it can feel especially personal and devastating. Whether it's a friend, family member, or loved one who has hurt you, the pain can cause you to guard your heart, making it difficult to trust again. But God specializes in restoration—both of the heart and of relationships.

Restoring trust after betrayal requires time, healing, and divine intervention. It's important to remember that forgiveness doesn't happen overnight, and trust doesn't automatically return. However, God is able to work in the hearts of both the one who was hurt and the one who caused the hurt, bringing reconciliation and healing in ways we may not think possible. Trusting God to rebuild broken relationships doesn't mean ignoring the pain or rushing the process, but allowing Him to guide you through it with grace and wisdom.

Today, if you're struggling with the aftermath of betrayal, bring your pain to God. Ask Him to heal your heart and show you the steps needed to restore trust, whether that means reconciling the relationship or simply finding peace within yourself.

Prayer

Lord, I bring my hurt and betrayal to You. Heal my heart and help me trust You to guide the process of restoring broken relationships. Give me wisdom, grace, and peace as You rebuild what has been lost. Amen.

Affirmation

I trust God to heal my heart and restore relationships, knowing that He can rebuild trust and bring peace after betrayal.

June 14
How to Uplift a Sister in Crisis

"Carry each other's burdens, and in this way you will fulfill the law of Christ." (Galatians 6:2, NIV)

Devotional Reflection

When someone you care about is going through a difficult time, it's natural to want to help. As black women, we understand the importance of sisterhood and community, especially during moments of crisis. Whether it's a personal loss, financial hardship, or emotional pain, being a source of support can make all the difference. However, it's not always easy to know what to do or say when a sister is struggling. Sometimes, the most powerful thing you can offer is simply your presence and encouragement.

Uplifting a sister in crisis means being there without judgment or pressure, providing a safe space for her to express her emotions. Listening without offering immediate solutions can be a source of comfort, reminding her that she is not alone. Encouragement doesn't always require grand gestures; a heartfelt prayer, a kind word, or a shoulder to cry on can mean the world to someone in distress. Most importantly, lifting her up in Prayerand standing in faith with her invites God's healing and peace into the situation.

Today, think about how you can uplift a sister in crisis. Whether through prayer, a phone call, or simply being there for her, let her know that she is not alone. Your support, rooted in love and faith, can help her find strength in the midst of her struggles.

Prayer

Lord, help me to be a source of encouragement and support for my sisters who are in crisis. Guide my words and actions so that I can uplift them in their time of need and remind them of Your love and presence. Amen.

Affirmation

I am a source of strength and encouragement, uplifting my sisters in times of crisis through love, prayer, and support.

June 15
Communicating with Love and Honesty

"Instead, speaking the truth in love, we will grow to become in every respect the mature body of him who is the head, that is, Christ."

(Ephesians 4:15, NIV)

Devotional Reflection

Effective communication is essential to building strong, lasting relationships. As black women, we often find ourselves balancing multiple roles, and within those roles, communication can be challenging. Whether it's with family, friends, or coworkers, speaking truth with love requires both courage and grace. While honesty is necessary for genuine relationships, how we deliver that truth can either strengthen or strain our connections.

God calls us to speak truth in love, not to avoid difficult conversations but to approach them with kindness and respect. Love and honesty go hand in hand—honesty without love can come across as harsh, while love without honesty can lead to misunderstandings and unresolved issues. When you communicate from a place of love, even difficult truths are easier to hear and more likely to bring about positive change. Your words have the power to build others up, so choose them wisely and let your heart be led by compassion.

Today, reflect on how you communicate with those around you. Are there areas where you need to speak the truth with more love or honesty? Ask God to guide your words so that they reflect His grace and strengthen your relationships.

Prayer

Lord, help me to communicate with both love and honesty. Give me the wisdom to speak truth in a way that strengthens my relationships and brings peace, understanding, and growth. Amen.

Affirmation

I speak truth with love and honesty, allowing my words to build stronger, healthier connections with those around me.

June 16
Finding Balance Between Family, Friends, and Self

"Let all that you do be done in love." (1 Corinthians 16:14, NIV)

Devotional Reflection

Balancing the demands of family, friends, and personal well-being can often feel overwhelming. As black women, we are often expected to be everything to everyone—caring for our families, supporting our friends, and giving of ourselves in countless ways. While it's important to show up for others, it's equally essential to take care of yourself. Neglecting your own needs for the sake of others can lead to burnout and resentment, making it harder to be the supportive presence you want to be.

God desires for us to live balanced lives, where we can nurture our relationships while also honoring the care we need for ourselves. Finding balance requires setting boundaries, prioritizing time for self-care, and recognizing that it's okay to say no when necessary. When you take time to rest and recharge, you are better equipped to love and serve those around you with a full heart. It's not selfish to prioritize your well-being—it's an act of love that allows you to show up fully in all areas of your life.

Today, take a moment to assess how you're balancing your relationships with family, friends, and your own needs. Ask God for guidance in setting boundaries and maintaining the balance that brings peace and health to every part of your life.

Prayer

Lord, help me find balance in my relationships. Give me the wisdom to care for my family and friends while also prioritizing my own well-being. Teach me how to set healthy boundaries and to trust You with my time and energy. Amen.

Affirmation

I create balance in my life by caring for my family, friends, and myself, trusting that God will guide me to maintain peace and well-being.

June 17
Recognizing When It's Time to Walk Away

"Do not be misled: 'Bad company corrupts good character.'"
(1 Corinthians 15:33, NIV)

Devotional Reflection

Letting go of a toxic relationship can be one of the most challenging decisions you face. As black women, we are often taught to persevere, to hold on, and to give our all to relationships, whether they are friendships, family ties, or romantic connections. But there are times when continuing to invest in a relationship causes more harm than good, and walking away becomes a necessary step toward protecting your peace and well-being.

Recognizing when it's time to walk away requires deep reflection and seeking God's wisdom. Toxic relationships drain you emotionally, mentally, and spiritually, often leaving you feeling unworthy or conflicted. God calls us to nurture relationships that bring love, support, and mutual respect. When a relationship consistently brings pain, manipulation, or harm, it may be time to step back and let go. Trusting God with your heart means knowing that He will guide you toward healthier connections and will provide peace as you navigate the difficult process of letting go.

Today, if you're struggling with whether to walk away from a toxic relationship, ask God for clarity and strength. Trust that He will lead you in making the right decision, bringing healing and peace as you move forward.

Prayer

Lord, I seek Your wisdom in recognizing when it's time to let go of relationships that no longer serve my well-being. Help me to trust You with my heart and guide me toward peace and healing in all my relationships. Amen.

Affirmation

I trust God to guide me in knowing when to walk away from toxic relationships, believing that He will bring peace, healing, and healthier connections into my life.

June 18
Giving Grace to Yourself and Others

"Be kind and compassionate to one another, forgiving each other, just as in Christ God forgave you." (Ephesians 4:32, NIV)

Devotional Reflection

Giving grace is often easier when extended to others, but what about showing that same grace to yourself? As black women, many of us strive for excellence in our work, relationships, and personal goals. In the process, we may be quick to forgive others but harsh in judging ourselves when we fall short. However, God's grace is not just for those around us—it's also for us. Just as we are called to show compassion and kindness to others, we are invited to extend that same gentleness to ourselves.

Offering grace means recognizing that everyone, including yourself, makes mistakes and needs room to grow. It means forgiving others when they hurt or disappoint you and releasing yourself from the burden of perfection. When we give ourselves permission to receive grace, we allow God's love to fill the spaces where shame, guilt, or frustration once lived. This grace empowers us to move forward with a renewed sense of peace, embracing our humanity while trusting God's guidance in our growth.

Today, reflect on how you can show grace to both yourself and those around you. Ask God to help you release self-criticism and embrace the same kindness you so freely offer to others.

Prayer

Lord, help me to give grace to those around me and to myself. Teach me to show kindness and compassion, forgiving myself and others as You have forgiven me. Amen.

Affirmation

I offer grace to myself and others, knowing that kindness and compassion are gifts from God that bring healing and peace to my life and relationships.

June 19
Rebuilding Relationships After Hurt

"Make every effort to live in peace with everyone and to be holy; without holiness no one will see the Lord." (Hebrews 12:14, NIV)

Devotional Reflection

When relationships are fractured by misunderstandings or hurt, restoring them can seem impossible. Many Black women have experienced the pain of broken friendships or family ties, and the rebuilding process can be emotionally draining and spiritually challenging. Yet, God calls us to pursue peace and reconciliation. With His guidance, even the most damaged relationships can be healed.

Rebuilding doesn't mean ignoring the pain; it's about addressing hurt with honesty, seeking forgiveness, and trusting God to mend what's broken. It requires patience, grace, and a willingness to listen. Though the journey to healing may take time, God can soften hearts and bring renewal where there was once strife.

If you're facing a broken relationship today, ask God to guide you toward reconciliation. Trust that He will provide the wisdom, courage, and grace to rebuild the bond. Rely on His timing, and know that healing can happen through His power.

Prayer

Lord, I ask for Your guidance in rebuilding relationships that have been broken by hurt. Help me to approach these situations with grace and a spirit of reconciliation. Give me the strength to forgive, seek peace, and trust You to restore what has been lost. Amen.

Affirmation

I trust God to guide me in rebuilding broken relationships, knowing that He can restore peace and bring healing to my heart and connections.

June 20
Using Your Voice for Good

"The mouth of the righteous is a fountain of life, but the mouth of the wicked conceals violence." (Proverbs 10:11, NIV)

Devotional Reflection

Your voice holds power—power to inspire, uplift, and influence the lives of those around you. As black women, we often carry the weight of history, culture, and our communities on our shoulders. Our voices matter, and God has given us the ability to use them for good, to speak life into others and to stand for truth. Whether you're engaging in everyday conversations, leading in your community, or advocating for justice, your words have the potential to create lasting change.

Using your voice for good means speaking with wisdom, kindness, and intention. It's about knowing when to offer encouragement, when to challenge harmful ideas, and when to stand up for those who cannot speak for themselves. God calls us to be voices of love and truth, and when we align our words with His guidance, we become instruments of His will, bringing light into difficult situations and hope into dark spaces.

Today, reflect on how you can use your voice for good. Whether it's through conversations with loved ones, sharing your story, or advocating for positive change in your community, trust that God will guide your words and use them to bless others.

Prayer

Lord, help me to use my voice for good. Guide my words so that they reflect Your love, wisdom, and truth. Empower me to speak boldly and lovingly, uplifting others and making a positive impact in my community. Amen.

Affirmation

I use my voice for good, speaking truth, love, and wisdom into my community, knowing that God guides my words and uses them to bless others.

June 21
Embracing Your Role in the Community

"For just as each of us has one body with many members, and these members do not all have the same function, so in Christ we, though many, form one body, and each member belongs to all the others."

(Romans 12:4-5, NIV)

Devotional Reflection

You have a unique role in your community, and your presence is valuable. As Black women, we often wear many hats—nurturers, leaders, caregivers, and advocates—each with a profound impact. It's easy to overlook our contributions or feel like they're not enough, but God has placed each of us in our communities for a purpose. The gifts He's given you are designed to strengthen those around you.

Embracing your role means recognizing the importance of what you bring, whether leading, serving, or offering a listening ear. It's not about comparing yourself to others but understanding that every contribution is essential to the body of Christ. When you use the gifts God has given you, your community is enriched, and your faith grows. Your willingness to step into your role with faith and love helps create a strong, supportive environment for everyone.

Take time today to reflect on the role God has given you in your community. Embrace your unique contributions, and trust that God is using you to make a difference.

Prayer

Lord, thank You for the role You've given me in my community. Help me to embrace it fully and use my gifts to build a strong, faith-filled environment. Teach me to see the value in what I offer and to trust that You are using me for Your purpose. Amen.

Affirmation

I embrace my unique role in my community, knowing that God has placed me here with purpose to build and strengthen those around me.

June 22
Encouraging a Sister's Faith Journey

"And let us consider how we may spur one another on toward love and good deeds." (Hebrews 10:24, NIV)

Devotional Reflection

Encouraging a sister in her faith journey is one of the most powerful and loving things you can do. As black women, we understand the importance of community and the need for support as we walk through life's challenges. When it comes to faith, that support becomes even more significant. By walking alongside another woman in her spiritual growth, you create a space where she can feel empowered, strengthened, and loved as she deepens her relationship with God.

Supporting a sister's faith journey doesn't require grand gestures; sometimes, the most impactful encouragement comes from simply listening, praying together, or offering a word of wisdom in a moment of doubt. We are called to lift one another up, to spur each other on toward love, and to help each other grow in faith. When you offer support, you not only help your sister draw closer to God, but you also strengthen your own faith as well.

Today, think about the women in your life who are on their own faith journeys. How can you be a source of encouragement to them? Whether it's through prayer, sharing scripture, or simply being present, your support can make a difference in their walk with God.

Prayer

Lord, help me to encourage and support my sisters in their faith journeys. Give me the wisdom to know how to walk alongside them and the love to lift them up in their times of need. Thank You for the opportunity to grow together in faith. Amen.

Affirmation

I encourage and support my sisters in their faith journeys, walking alongside them with love and faith as we grow closer to God together.

June 23
The Importance of Mentorship and Guidance

"For lack of guidance a nation falls, but victory is won through many advisers." (Proverbs 11:14, NIV)

Devotional Reflection

Mentorship is essential for spiritual growth and personal development. As Black women, we often draw strength from those who have walked the path before us—wise elders, trusted friends, or community leaders. Learning from others who've faced similar challenges provides valuable insight and encouragement. Mentorship reminds us that we don't have to walk this journey alone.

As we grow, we're also called to mentor others. God uses our experiences to guide those just starting their journey. By being a mentor, you offer wisdom, support, and Christ's love to those seeking direction. Your story, challenges, and victories become a roadmap for someone else, helping them move forward. Mentorship is a cycle—receiving guidance and passing it on to others.

Today, reflect on the mentors who have poured into your life and thank God for them. Also, ask God how you can be a mentor to someone else, using your experiences to offer guidance and encouragement.

Prayer

Lord, thank You for the mentors You've placed in my life. Help me to be a source of wisdom and guidance to others, sharing what I've learned to support their growth. Teach me how to walk in love and faith as I guide those who look to me for direction. Amen.

Affirmation

I honor the guidance I've received from mentors and commit to being a mentor, sharing my wisdom and experiences to help others grow in their faith and life journey.

June 24
Being a Peacemaker in Your Circle

"Blessed are the peacemakers, for they will be called children of God."
(Matthew 5:9, NIV)

Devotional Reflection

In a world often filled with conflict and division, being a peacemaker is a powerful calling. As black women, we are sometimes placed in situations where we are called to bridge gaps, mediate disputes, and promote harmony. Whether in family, friendships, or our broader communities, the role of peacemaker allows us to reflect God's love and bring healing where there is discord.

Being a peacemaker isn't about avoiding conflict, but rather about addressing it with grace, wisdom, and compassion. It means stepping into difficult situations with a heart for reconciliation, seeking to understand others, and helping them come together in mutual respect. True peace isn't just the absence of conflict—it's the presence of God's love in relationships. When you work to promote peace, you are building a foundation of trust, understanding, and forgiveness in your relationships and community.

Today, ask God to give you the strength and wisdom to be a peacemaker in your circle. Whether it's in your home, workplace, or community, trust Him to guide you in fostering reconciliation and unity.

Prayer

Lord, help me to be a peacemaker in my relationships and community. Give me the wisdom to approach conflict with grace and the courage to promote reconciliation. Let Your love guide me as I work to build peace wherever I go. Amen.

Affirmation

I am a peacemaker in my circle, promoting reconciliation and unity through God's love and wisdom in every relationship and community I encounter.

June 25
The Gift of Vulnerability in Friendship

"Therefore encourage one another and build each other up, just as in fact you are doing." (1 Thessalonians 5:11, NIV)

Devotional Reflection

True friendship requires more than shared experiences; it requires vulnerability. As Black women, we often carry the weight of being strong, guarding our hearts to protect ourselves from hurt. However, the deepest friendships are formed when we allow ourselves to be open and authentic, even when it feels risky. Vulnerability strengthens relationships and allows for deeper healing and understanding.

When you share your fears, struggles, and joys with friends, you invite them into your heart, giving them the chance to uplift and support you. Authentic friendships flourish when both people feel safe to be their true selves, without fear of judgment. Though vulnerability may seem like weakness, it is a strong act of trust in a relationship.

Today, consider how you can be more vulnerable in your friendships. Be open about your needs, emotions, and struggles, trusting that God will surround you with friends who uplift and build you up in love.

Prayer

Lord, give me the courage to be vulnerable in my friendships. Help me to open my heart, knowing that true friendship requires trust and authenticity. Surround me with friends who will support and encourage me as we grow together in faith and love. Amen.

Affirmation

I embrace vulnerability in my friendships, knowing that openness and authenticity deepen my connections and allow God's love to work through me and my friends.

June 26
Learning to Receive Support

"Carry each other's burdens, and in this way you will fulfill the law of Christ." (Galatians 6:2, NIV)

Devotional Reflection

Many black women are raised to be strong, resilient, and self-sufficient. While strength is a gift, constantly being the one who supports others can become overwhelming if you never allow yourself to be supported in return. The "strong woman" narrative often makes it difficult to admit when you need help or to open yourself up to receiving care. However, true strength also lies in vulnerability, in knowing when to accept help and allowing others to share in your burdens.

Learning to receive support is not a sign of weakness but an acknowledgment that you, too, deserve care, rest, and encouragement. God created us for community and calls us to both give and receive. By letting others support you, you are allowing them to fulfill their role in loving you as God intended. Letting go of the need to always be strong enables you to find comfort in the love and support of those who genuinely care for your well-being.

Today, reflect on areas of your life where you may need to let go of the "strong woman" narrative and be open to receiving support. Trust that God has placed people in your life who are willing and able to help lift you up when you need it most.

Prayer

Lord, help me let go of the need to always be strong and self-reliant. Teach me to receive support from those You've placed in my life, and remind me that I am worthy of care and love. Amen.

Affirmation

I let go of the "strong woman" narrative and allow myself to receive support, trusting that God has placed people in my life to share in my burdens and uplift me.

June 27
Building Lasting Friendships with Faith

"A friend loves at all times, and a brother is born for a time of adversity." (Proverbs 17:17, NIV)

Devotional Reflection

Lasting friendships are often grounded in something deeper than shared interests. As Black women, we value meaningful connections built on respect, trust, and love. The strongest friendships are rooted in faith, with God at the center. These relationships provide a foundation that can endure the trials and challenges life brings.

Friendships built on faith offer more than just support—they encourage spiritual growth, prayer, and guidance rooted in God's word. They become sources of strength during adversity and joy in times of celebration. A faith-based friendship reminds you that you're never alone—God is present, guiding and nurturing your bond.

Today, reflect on your friendships and how you can strengthen them through faith. Consider praying with your friends, sharing scripture, or being intentional about placing God at the center of your relationships. Trust that He will sustain and bless these friendships for years to come.

Prayer

Lord, thank You for the gift of friendships rooted in faith. Help me to build lasting connections that honor You and strengthen me spiritually. Guide me in nurturing these relationships so that they reflect Your love and grace. Amen.

Affirmation

I build lasting friendships grounded in faith, trusting that God will sustain and strengthen these connections through love, prayer, and spiritual growth.

June 28
Balancing Family Relationships with Faith

"If any of you lacks wisdom, you should ask God, who gives generously to all without finding fault, and it will be given to you."

(James 1:5, NIV)

Devotional Reflection

Family relationships are some of the most important yet complex dynamics we navigate in life. As black women, family often plays a central role, and balancing these relationships with our faith can sometimes feel challenging. Whether it's dealing with misunderstandings, differing beliefs, or unresolved conflicts, managing family dynamics requires patience, prayer, and godly wisdom.

Faith is the anchor that can guide us through these complexities. When we approach our family relationships with prayer, we invite God into our interactions, allowing Him to give us the patience and understanding we need to handle difficult situations with grace. Asking for wisdom in navigating these relationships helps us to respond with love, even when circumstances are tough. By keeping God at the center of our family interactions, we strengthen these bonds and allow His peace to flow through our homes.

Today, bring your family relationships before God. Ask for wisdom and guidance in balancing the dynamics that may feel challenging, trusting that He will provide the grace you need to foster peace and unity.

Prayer

Lord, I ask for Your wisdom and guidance as I navigate the complexities of my family relationships. Help me to approach every situation with faith and love, trusting You to lead me with grace and understanding. Amen.

Affirmation

I balance my family relationships with faith, trusting God's wisdom to guide me in navigating complex dynamics with love and grace.

June 29
Recognizing and Releasing Envy in Relationships

"Let us not become conceited, provoking and envying each other."
                                            (Galatians 5:26, NIV)

Devotional Reflection

Envy can quietly creep into even the most loving relationships, often without us realizing it. As black women, we may feel the weight of expectations—whether it's personal accomplishments, career success, or family dynamics—and when we see others achieving what we desire, comparison can take root. Left unchecked, envy can strain relationships and prevent us from celebrating the successes of those we care about. However, God calls us to let go of envy and embrace a heart of love, support, and genuine joy for others.

Releasing envy begins with recognizing it and bringing it to God in prayer. By shifting our focus from comparison to gratitude, we allow God to transform our hearts and free us from the destructive cycle of envy. True peace and fulfillment come from trusting God's unique plan for our lives, rather than measuring our worth against someone else's journey. When we release envy, we open the door to deeper, more supportive relationships built on mutual respect and love.

Today, ask God to help you recognize any feelings of envy you may be harboring in your relationships. Release those emotions to Him, and trust that He will provide you with peace, contentment, and joy as you foster healthier, more supportive connections with others.

Prayer

Lord, help me to recognize and release any envy in my heart. Teach me to celebrate the successes of others with love and support, trusting in Your plan for my life. Fill my heart with peace and contentment, knowing that my worth is found in You alone. Amen.

Affirmation

I release envy and embrace a heart of love and support in my relationships, trusting God's unique plan for my life and celebrating the successes of others with joy.

June 30
The Power of Women Coming Together in Christ

"For where two or three gather in my name, there am I with them."

(Matthew 18:20, NIV)

Devotional Reflection

There is a special strength when Black women come together in faith, supporting one another and praying together. Sisterhood, centered in Christ, goes beyond friendship—it becomes a spiritual bond, a community of women uplifting one another in love, faith, and grace. When we gather in Christ's name, His presence strengthens our unity and empowers us to be a source of encouragement and wisdom.

Coming together in faith creates a safe space for vulnerability, where we can share struggles, celebrate victories, and lean on each other. The power of sisterhood in Christ influences not just our relationships but also families and communities. Our faith-filled sisterhood reflects God's love and strength, showing the world the beauty of unity, compassion, and purpose.

Today, celebrate the power of women coming together in Christ. Reflect on the beauty of the sisterhood around you and how, through faith, you can continue to uplift and strengthen one another.

Prayer

Lord, thank You for the gift of sisterhood and community in Christ. Help me to cherish the women in my life and to continue building relationships grounded in faith, love, and support. May we come together in Your name, lifting each other up and reflecting Your love. Amen.

Affirmation

I celebrate the power of women coming together in Christ, knowing that our sisterhood strengthens us, uplifts us, and reflects God's love and purpose.

July
Joy and Gratitude

July 1
Choosing Joy in Difficult Seasons

"Consider it pure joy, my brothers and sisters, whenever you face trials of many kinds, because you know that the testing of your faith produces perseverance." (James 1:2-3, NIV)

Devotional Reflection

Finding joy during difficult seasons may feel impossible, especially when life's challenges seem overwhelming. As black women, we face unique struggles and pressures that can weigh heavily on our hearts. Whether it's personal loss, financial hardship, or the stresses of daily life, joy can feel like it's out of reach. Yet, God calls us to choose joy, even in the face of trials, because it's through these moments that our faith is strengthened.

Choosing joy doesn't mean ignoring pain or pretending everything is perfect. It means trusting that God is with you through the hardship, working all things for your good. Joy is rooted in the deep belief that God's love and presence are constant, even when circumstances are difficult. When you focus on His goodness and promises, joy becomes a steady source of strength, lifting your spirit even when the world feels heavy.

Today, ask God to help you choose joy in the midst of whatever challenges you are facing. Trust Him to guide you through difficult seasons, knowing that He is using them to build your faith and perseverance.

Prayer

Lord, help me to choose joy even in the hardest seasons of my life. Remind me of Your constant presence and the strength You provide through every trial. Give me the faith to see beyond my circumstances and to trust in Your goodness. Amen.

Affirmation

I choose joy in difficult seasons, trusting that God is with me, strengthening my faith and guiding me through every challenge.

July 2
Finding Gratitude in Small Blessings

"Give thanks in all circumstances; for this is God's will for you in Christ Jesus." (1 Thessalonians 5:18, NIV)

Devotional Reflection

In a fast-paced world, it's easy to overlook the small blessings that surround us every day. As black women, many of us carry the weight of responsibilities, striving for goals and caring for others. In the midst of all this, the simple moments of beauty—like a kind word, a warm sunrise, or a quiet cup of coffee—can go unnoticed. Yet, it is in these small blessings that God's presence often shines the brightest, reminding us of His love and provision in the ordinary moments of life.

Gratitude for small blessings transforms how we see the world. When we intentionally pause to recognize the little things, we begin to see God's hand in every part of our lives. Gratitude shifts our focus from what's missing or challenging to what's already there, offering us peace and joy in the present. Whether it's the smile of a loved one, the sound of laughter, or the comfort of a quiet moment, these small blessings are gifts from God, placed in our lives to lift our spirits and remind us of His goodness.

Today, take a moment to reflect on the small blessings in your life. Ask God to open your eyes to the beauty around you, and offer thanks for the ways He shows His love in the everyday moments.

Prayer

Lord, thank You for the small blessings You place in my life each day. Help me to notice and appreciate the beauty in the ordinary moments, and remind me that Your love is present in every detail of my life. Amen.

Affirmation

I am grateful for the small blessings in my life, recognizing God's presence and love in every moment, big and small.

July 3
Joy in the Morning: Starting the Day with Praise

"Let the morning bring me word of your unfailing love, for I have put my trust in you. Show me the way I should go, for to you I entrust my life." (Psalm 143:8, NIV)

Devotional Reflection

Starting the day with joy and praise can be transformative. As Black women, we often wake up with responsibilities and concerns that weigh us down before the day begins. However, by choosing to start the morning with praise, we shift our focus from stress to gratitude, from worry to trust in God. Morning praise sets the tone for the day, reminding us that, no matter the challenges ahead, God's love and presence are already with us.

When we begin the day thanking God for His faithfulness, we invite His peace and joy into our hearts. Praise realigns our thoughts with His promises, allowing us to walk in confidence and joy, even in the face of difficulty. Whether through prayer, worship, or meditating on God's goodness, starting the day with praise fills us with hope and purpose.

Today, take a moment to start your day with praise. Reflect on God's goodness, His unfailing love, and His presence in your life, allowing joy to guide your steps.

Prayer

Lord, I thank You for this new day and for Your unfailing love. Help me to start each morning with praise, knowing that Your joy and peace will carry me through whatever challenges I may face. Guide my steps and fill my heart with joy today. Amen.

Affirmation

I choose to start each day with praise, trusting in God's love and allowing His joy to fill my heart and guide my steps throughout the day.

July 4
Practicing Gratitude Despite Disappointment

"Give thanks to the Lord, for he is good; his love endures forever."

(Psalm 136:1, NIV)

Devotional Reflection

Life doesn't always go as we expect. Disappointments—whether big or small—can leave us feeling discouraged and frustrated. As black women, we often face setbacks that test our strength and resilience, whether in our personal lives, careers, or relationships. It's in these moments of disappointment that practicing gratitude becomes both a challenge and a necessity. Gratitude shifts our perspective, reminding us that even when things don't go according to plan, God is still good and His love for us never changes.

Choosing gratitude in the face of disappointment doesn't mean ignoring the pain or pretending everything is fine. It's about recognizing that even when life throws us unexpected challenges, there are still reasons to give thanks. God's faithfulness is present, even in our hardest moments. When we focus on the blessings we still have—the love of family, the beauty of nature, the gift of another day—our hearts begin to heal, and we find strength to move forward with hope.

Today, reflect on an area of disappointment in your life. Ask God to help you practice gratitude, even in the midst of your frustration, and thank Him for His unwavering love and grace that sustains you.

Prayer

Lord, help me to maintain a grateful heart even when life doesn't go as I hoped. Teach me to see Your goodness in all circumstances and to trust in Your plan, knowing that Your love endures forever. Amen.

Affirmation

I practice gratitude despite disappointment, trusting in God's goodness and His unfailing love to guide me through every challenge.

July 5

Embracing Joy in the Journey

"You make known to me the path of life; you will fill me with joy in your presence, with eternal pleasures at your right hand."

(Psalm 16:11, NIV)

Devotional Reflection

As black women, we often set high goals and expectations for ourselves, striving for success in our personal and professional lives. While it's important to pursue our dreams, we sometimes get so focused on reaching the destination that we forget to find joy in the journey. Embracing joy in the process allows us to appreciate each step of growth, learning, and experience along the way.

God's purpose for your life isn't just about the final outcome; it's about the moments in between—the lessons, the relationships, the small victories. The journey is where transformation happens. When we focus only on the end goal, we miss the joy God provides in the everyday moments. Embracing joy in the journey means trusting that God is with you through each twist and turn, and He is working all things for your good. Every challenge you face is shaping you into the woman He has called you to be.

Today, choose to find happiness in the process, not just in the destination. Reflect on how far you've come and trust that God is guiding you every step of the way. Let joy fill your heart, knowing that your journey is a beautiful part of His plan.

Prayer

Lord, help me to embrace joy in the journey, trusting that You are with me every step of the way. Teach me to find happiness in the process and to appreciate the lessons and blessings that come with each season of life. Amen.

Affirmation

I embrace joy in the journey, trusting that God is guiding my steps and finding happiness in the process, not just the destination.

July 6

Reclaiming Joy After Loss

"Those who sow with tears will reap with songs of joy."

(Psalm 126:5, NIV)

Devotional Reflection

Loss, whether it's the loss of a loved one, a job, a dream, or a relationship, can leave an empty space in our hearts that feels impossible to fill. As black women, we often carry the weight of grief quietly, trying to remain strong for those around us. But grief doesn't just go away, and reclaiming joy after loss can feel like an overwhelming task. Yet, God promises that joy can return—even after the darkest seasons of our lives.

Grief is a journey, and joy doesn't always come immediately. But trusting God through the process allows healing to begin. God knows your pain, and He is with you in your sorrow. Over time, as you lean into His presence, you will find that joy slowly returns—not necessarily in the way it existed before, but in a new, deeper form. Reclaiming joy after loss doesn't mean forgetting what or whom you've lost; it means allowing God to fill your heart with hope and peace, even as you continue to heal.

Today, if you are grieving, trust that God is walking with you. Ask Him to restore joy to your life, in His time and in His way. Believe that even in your sorrow, songs of joy will rise again.

Prayer

Lord, I trust You to restore my joy after loss. Help me to heal and to find peace in Your presence. Even in my grief, I believe that You will fill my heart with hope and joy once again. Amen.

Affirmation

I trust God to restore my joy after loss, knowing that He is with me in my grief and will bring hope and healing in His perfect time.

July 7

The Power of Gratitude to Heal

"Give thanks to the Lord, for he is good; his love endures forever."
(Psalm 107:1, NIV)

Devotional Reflection

Gratitude has a unique power to heal our hearts and souls. As black women, we face many challenges—both visible and invisible—and it's easy to become overwhelmed by the weight of life's demands. However, when we choose to focus on the blessings in our lives, gratitude shifts our perspective and opens the door to emotional and spiritual healing. Being thankful in the midst of challenges doesn't deny the reality of pain; instead, it reminds us that God is with us through it all.

Gratitude helps us release negative emotions like bitterness, anger, and sadness by shifting our focus from what we lack to what we have. It's a reminder of God's constant provision, His love, and His grace. As you thank God for even the smallest blessings—a kind word, a new opportunity, the beauty of a new day—your heart begins to heal, and your spirit is uplifted. Gratitude is not just an emotional practice; it's a spiritual tool that aligns us with God's goodness and brings peace and healing to our souls.

Today, take time to reflect on the things you are thankful for, even in the midst of life's challenges. Let gratitude become a healing balm for your heart as you thank God for His faithfulness and love.

Prayer

Lord, thank You for Your goodness and for the many blessings You have placed in my life. Help me to embrace gratitude daily, knowing that it brings healing and peace to my heart. Teach me to see Your love and provision, even in the small things. Amen.

Affirmation

I embrace the healing power of gratitude, knowing that thankfulness opens my heart to God's love and brings emotional and spiritual peace.

July 8

Joy in Community

"How good and pleasant it is when God's people live together in unity!" (Psalm 133:1, NIV)

Devotional Reflection

Community is one of the greatest gifts God has given us. As Black women, we often carry the weight of various responsibilities and expectations. In these moments, community becomes a source of strength, joy, and comfort. True joy is found not just in our individual accomplishments but in the connections we share with others—our sisters, friends, family, and church.

Joy in community means finding happiness in the support and love we give and receive. Whether through a kind word, shared laughter, or someone praying for you, the connections we make lift our spirits in ways solitude cannot. God designed us to live in unity, to build each other up, and to experience joy in relationships. The beauty of community is that we don't have to carry life's burdens alone; love and support bring joy.

Today, embrace the joy that comes from connection. Reach out to a friend or loved one, and reflect on how your community has supported you. Let the joy of these relationships fill your heart with gratitude and peace.

Prayer

Lord, thank You for the gift of community and the joy that comes from connection. Help me to embrace and nurture the relationships in my life, and remind me that I don't have to walk this journey alone. Fill my heart with joy as I experience the love and support of those around me. Amen.

Affirmation

I find joy in community, celebrating the love and support I receive and share, knowing that God created us to thrive in connection with one another.

July 9
Overcoming Negative Thoughts with Gratitude

"Finally, brothers and sisters, whatever is true, whatever is noble, whatever is right, whatever is pure, whatever is lovely, whatever is admirable—if anything is excellent or praiseworthy—think about such things." (Philippians 4:8, NIV)

Devotional Reflection

Negative thoughts can take root in our minds, affecting how we see ourselves and the world. As Black women, the challenges we face—whether personal, professional, or societal—can sometimes leave us feeling overwhelmed or inadequate. These negative thoughts can grow if left unchecked, making it hard to see the blessings in our lives. However, gratitude is a powerful tool to shift our mindset and break the cycle of negativity.

When we focus on thankfulness, we replace negative thoughts with reminders of God's goodness. Gratitude realigns our minds with what is true and praiseworthy. It doesn't ignore struggles but helps us see beyond them, reminding us of the countless ways God blesses us. Practicing gratitude cultivates a positive mindset rooted in faith and joy.

Today, if negative thoughts take over, pause and reflect on what you are thankful for. List your blessings, big and small, and allow gratitude to transform your mindset and fill your heart with peace.

Prayer

Lord, help me overcome negative thoughts by focusing on Your goodness. Teach me to replace negativity with gratitude, and remind me of the many blessings You have given me. Fill my mind and heart with peace as I cultivate a spirit of thankfulness. Amen.

Affirmation

I replace negative thoughts with gratitude, focusing on the blessings in my life and allowing thankfulness to shape a positive, faith-filled mindset.

July 10
Gratitude for Growth

"Consider it pure joy, my brothers and sisters, whenever you face trials of many kinds, because you know that the testing of your faith produces perseverance." (James 1:2-3, NIV)

Devotional Reflection

Growth often comes through the trials we face. As Black women, life's obstacles can feel heavy, but these experiences also shape and strengthen us. It's easy to get caught up in frustration, but when we step back, we can see how difficulties have contributed to our growth. Gratitude for growth means recognizing that every challenge is an opportunity to become wiser, stronger, and more resilient.

God uses trials to stretch us, deepen our faith, and equip us for the future. While it's hard to feel thankful during hardship, gratitude helps us see the bigger picture. Growth isn't just about enduring tough times; it's about becoming more aligned with God's purpose. When we shift our perspective to thankfulness, we realize that struggles have shaped us into women equipped with wisdom and perseverance.

Today, reflect on the growth that has come from your challenges. Ask God to help you be grateful for the lessons learned and the strength gained. Embrace the growth, knowing He is guiding you every step of the way.

Prayer

Lord, thank You for the growth that comes through life's challenges. Help me to embrace every lesson and trust that You are shaping me into the woman You've called me to be. Give me a heart of gratitude for the strength and wisdom I've gained along the way. Amen.

Affirmation

I am grateful for the growth that comes from life's challenges, knowing that God is using every trial to strengthen me and shape me for His purpose.

July 11

Joyful in the Waiting

"But those who hope in the Lord will renew their strength. They will soar on wings like eagles; they will run and not grow weary, they will walk and not be faint." (Isaiah 40:31, NIV)

Devotional Reflection

Waiting is not always easy, especially when we long for answers or breakthroughs. As black women, we may often feel like we are waiting—waiting for opportunities, for healing, for change. Seasons of waiting can test our patience and faith, but they are also times when God is doing His greatest work in us. Learning to maintain joy during these periods is an act of faith, trusting that God's timing is perfect, even when it doesn't align with our own.

Joyful waiting doesn't mean ignoring the frustrations of delay; rather, it means trusting God's process and finding contentment in the present. When we focus on the goodness of God and the strength He provides, we begin to see that waiting is not wasted time. It is a season of preparation, growth, and renewal. Choosing joy in the waiting means believing that God is working all things together for our good, even when we cannot see it yet.

Today, if you find yourself in a season of waiting, ask God to help you remain joyful and patient. Trust that He is working behind the scenes, and that this season will lead to something greater than you can imagine.

Prayer

Lord, help me to find joy in the waiting. Strengthen my faith and teach me to trust Your timing. Even when I cannot see the outcome, help me to find peace and contentment in knowing that You are at work in my life. Amen.

Affirmation

I choose joy in the waiting, trusting God's perfect timing and believing that He is preparing me for something greater.

July 12
Gratitude for God's Provision

"And my God will meet all your needs according to the riches of his glory in Christ Jesus." (Philippians 4:19, NIV)

Devotional Reflection

In the busyness of life, it can be easy to overlook the countless ways God provides for us each day. As black women, many of us carry the weight of responsibilities, whether in our homes, workplaces, or communities. Sometimes, we may focus on what we lack or what we are striving for, forgetting to pause and acknowledge God's faithful provision. Yet, every breath we take, every meal we eat, and every opportunity we encounter is a reminder of His blessings and care.

God's provision isn't just about material things. It's about the peace He gives in the middle of chaos, the strength to endure difficult days, and the love that surrounds us even when we feel alone. Gratitude for God's provision helps us to see the bigger picture and to trust that He is always meeting our needs. When we take time to reflect on how He has provided in the past, we can rest assured that He will continue to do so in the future.

Today, reflect on the many ways God has provided for you. Thank Him for both the tangible and intangible blessings in your life, and trust that He will continue to supply all your needs.

Prayer

Lord, thank You for Your constant provision in my life. Help me to recognize and be grateful for all the ways You meet my needs, both big and small. Teach me to trust in Your faithful care, knowing that You are always with me. Amen.

Affirmation

I am grateful for God's provision, recognizing the many ways He blesses my life and trusting that He will continue to meet all my needs.

July 13

Joy in Serving Others

"Each of you should use whatever gift you have received to serve others, as faithful stewards of God's grace in its various forms."

(1 Peter 4:10, NIV)

Devotional Reflection

There is a special kind of joy that comes from serving others. As black women, we often find ourselves in positions where we are naturally nurturing and giving. But beyond the roles we play, acts of service bring fulfillment and purpose. When we serve others with love, we not only make a difference in their lives, but we also reflect God's grace and goodness. Service shifts our focus from our own challenges to the needs of those around us, allowing us to see the beauty in helping others.

Serving others doesn't always require grand gestures. It can be as simple as offering a listening ear, giving encouragement, or helping someone with a small task. These acts of kindness have the power to bring light to someone's day and remind them of God's love. The joy in serving comes from knowing that we are being used by God to bless others and that through service, we are living out our purpose. Serving isn't just about what we give; it's also about the joy and growth we receive in return.

Today, reflect on how you can serve those around you. Whether in small or big ways, find opportunities to bless others and discover the joy that comes from giving selflessly.

Prayer

Lord, thank You for the opportunity to serve others. Help me to find joy in the acts of kindness I offer and to recognize the purpose You've placed in my life through service. Teach me to serve with love and grace, reflecting Your goodness in everything I do. Amen.

Affirmation

I find joy and purpose in serving others, knowing that my acts of kindness reflect God's love and bring happiness to both myself and those I serve.

July 14
Thankful for the Strength of Your Ancestors

"Therefore, since we are surrounded by such a great cloud of witnesses, let us throw off everything that hinders and the sin that so easily entangles. And let us run with perseverance the race marked out for us." (Hebrews 12:1, NIV)

Devotional Reflection

The strength of our ancestors is a legacy that continues to inspire us today. As Black women, we stand on the shoulders of those who came before us—women who endured unimaginable hardships with resilience, grace, and dignity. Their strength and unwavering faith paved the way for us to live, dream, and thrive. Reflecting on their courage reminds us that the strength we possess today is part of a long legacy of powerful Black women.

Our ancestors faced adversity but overcame it, often leaning on God for strength. As we encounter our own challenges, it's important to remember the prayers and sacrifices that built the foundation we stand on. Their resilience fuels our courage, and their faith strengthens our own. Honoring the strength of our ancestors reminds us of the power within us and the spiritual connection we share with them.

Today, celebrate the strength of your ancestors. Thank God for the women who came before you, whose resilience and faith continue to inspire you. Reflect on how their strength shapes your own journey.

Prayer

Lord, I thank You for the strength and resilience of my ancestors. Help me to honor their legacy by walking in faith, perseverance, and courage. May their strength continue to inspire me as I navigate my own challenges, trusting that You are guiding me just as You guided them. Amen.

Affirmation

I celebrate the strength of my ancestors, embracing the resilience they passed down and using it to fuel my faith, courage, and perseverance in my own journey.

July 15
Cultivating Joy Through Worship

"Come, let us sing for joy to the Lord; let us shout aloud to the Rock of our salvation." (Psalm 95:1, NIV)

Devotional Reflection

Worship is a powerful way to connect with God and experience joy, no matter what life brings. As black women, we carry many burdens—emotional, physical, and spiritual. Yet, when we enter into worship, we are invited to release those burdens and focus our hearts on God's goodness. Worship shifts our perspective from our circumstances to the greatness of God, allowing joy to rise within us even in the most difficult times.

Through worship, we find renewal for our spirits. It doesn't have to be confined to Sunday mornings at church; daily worship and praise can transform your home, your commute, or even a quiet moment in nature. Singing praises, speaking prayers, or simply reflecting on God's love can fill your heart with a joy that transcends circumstances. Worship is more than just a ritual—it's an act of drawing closer to God, inviting His presence into every part of your day. In those moments, His peace and joy overflow into your heart, refreshing and renewing your soul.

Today, take time to cultivate joy through worship. Whether through song, prayer, or quiet reflection, lift your heart to God in praise and allow His joy to fill your spirit.

Prayer

Lord, thank You for the gift of worship. Help me to find joy in praising You, even in my busiest and hardest moments. Renew my spirit as I worship You, and fill my heart with the joy that comes from being in Your presence. Amen.

Affirmation

I cultivate joy through daily worship and praise, knowing that God's presence renews my spirit and fills my heart with joy, no matter my circumstances.

July 16
Grateful for Every Season

"There is a time for everything, and a season for every activity under the heavens." (Ecclesiastes 3:1, NIV)

Devotional Reflection

Life is full of seasons—some filled with joy and success, others with challenges and growth. As black women, we experience life's ups and downs in unique and powerful ways. It's easy to give thanks when things are going well, but God calls us to find gratitude in every season of life, even during the difficult times. Each stage, whether high or low, holds valuable lessons and opportunities for growth.

Gratitude in every season means recognizing that God is present in both the blessings and the challenges. In times of abundance, we celebrate His provision and goodness. In times of struggle, we trust that He is refining us and deepening our faith. Every season serves a purpose, and when we embrace joy in each stage, we open ourselves to God's wisdom and guidance. By being thankful for every season, we acknowledge that God is always working in our lives, shaping us for His divine plan.

Today, reflect on the season you are in—whether it's one of abundance or difficulty. Ask God to help you embrace joy and gratitude, trusting that He is with you in every stage of life.

Prayer

Lord, thank You for being with me in every season of life. Help me to embrace each stage with joy and gratitude, knowing that You are using it to shape me and guide me according to Your plan. Teach me to find peace in Your presence, no matter where I am in life's journey. Amen.

Affirmation

I am grateful for every season of life, embracing the joy and lessons that each stage brings, and trusting that God is with me through it all.

July 17
Joyful Motherhood: Celebrating the Gift of Raising Children

"Children are a heritage from the Lord, offspring a reward from him."
(Psalm 127:3, NIV)

Devotional Reflection

Motherhood is one of life's greatest blessings, yet it can also be one of its most challenging roles. As black women, the journey of raising children often comes with unique experiences, from managing societal pressures to balancing multiple responsibilities. Despite the demands, there is deep joy and fulfillment in nurturing the next generation. Each moment with your children is an opportunity to shape their lives, to guide them, and to witness the beauty of their growth.

Finding joy in motherhood means embracing both the small, everyday moments and the milestones. Whether it's the laughter during playtime, the quiet moments of prayer, or the tough but necessary lessons, each part of the journey reflects God's grace in the lives of both you and your children. As you pour into their lives, know that God is also strengthening and guiding you. Even on the difficult days, there is joy to be found in the privilege of being a mother—a calling filled with love, faith, and purpose.

Today, celebrate the gift of motherhood. Thank God for the children He has entrusted to you, and find joy in the journey, knowing that you are fulfilling a divine role in shaping their lives.

Prayer

Lord, thank You for the gift of motherhood. Help me to find joy and fulfillment in the everyday moments of raising my children. Give me the strength, patience, and wisdom to guide them according to Your will, and let me celebrate the blessing of this beautiful journey. Amen.

Affirmation

I find joy and fulfillment in the journey of motherhood, knowing that God has blessed me with the gift of raising and nurturing the next generation.

July 18
Gratitude for Health

"Do you not know that your bodies are temples of the Holy Spirit, who is in you, whom you have received from God? You are not your own." *(1 Corinthians 6:19, NIV)*

Devotional Reflection

Our health is one of the greatest gifts from God, yet it's often something we take for granted until it's challenged. As black women, we sometimes bear the burden of caring for others, often neglecting our own well-being in the process. But God calls us to honor and care for our bodies, recognizing them as temples of the Holy Spirit. Showing gratitude for our health, no matter its current state, is an act of appreciation for the gift of life and the body that carries us through each day.

Being thankful for your health doesn't mean ignoring any challenges or limitations you may face. Instead, it means appreciating what your body is capable of, acknowledging the small and big ways it supports you daily. From being able to walk, breathe, and move, to the strength it provides in times of illness or recovery, your body is a reflection of God's work in you. Cultivating gratitude for your health encourages you to care for your body with love, recognizing it as a vessel that God has entrusted to you.

Today, take a moment to thank God for your body, health, and well-being. No matter where you are on your health journey, be grateful for the strength you have today, and commit to caring for yourself with love and reverence.

Prayer

Lord, thank You for the gift of health and my body. Help me to care for it as a temple of Your Spirit and guide me in making choices that honor the life You've blessed me with. Amen.

Affirmation

I am grateful for my health and body, recognizing it as a precious gift from God, and I commit to caring for myself with love and respect.

July 19
Rediscovering Joy Through Laughter

"A cheerful heart is good medicine, but a crushed spirit dries up the bones." (Proverbs 17:22, NIV)

Devotional Reflection

Laughter is a powerful and healing gift that God has given us. As black women, the weight of our responsibilities and the challenges we face can sometimes cause us to forget the importance of joy and laughter in our lives. Yet, laughter has the ability to lighten our spirits, heal emotional wounds, and remind us of the beauty in life. It is not just a fleeting emotion but a reflection of God's joy within us.

Laughter can be found in the small moments—a shared joke, a funny memory, or the simple pleasure of being in the company of loved ones. When we allow ourselves to laugh, we release the tension and stress that so often builds up, giving ourselves permission to feel light and joyful. Laughter doesn't mean we ignore life's difficulties, but it allows us to approach them with a sense of peace and perspective. It's a reminder that even in the midst of challenges, joy can still be found.

Today, seek opportunities to rediscover joy through laughter. Surround yourself with people and experiences that bring a smile to your face, and thank God for the gift of laughter that heals and uplifts.

Prayer

Lord, thank You for the gift of laughter and the healing power it brings. Help me to embrace joy in my daily life and to find moments of lightness even in the midst of challenges. Fill my heart with a cheerful spirit and remind me to cherish the joy You have placed in my life. Amen.

Affirmation

I embrace the healing power of laughter, allowing joy to fill my heart and uplift my spirit, knowing that God's joy is present in every moment.

July 20
Grateful for Your Unique Journey

"The Lord will vindicate me; your love, Lord, endures forever—do not abandon the works of your hands." (Psalm 138:8, NIV)

Devotional Reflection

Your life's journey is unlike anyone else's, filled with its own highs, lows, twists, and unexpected turns. As black women, we often navigate a world that presents us with unique challenges, yet God has crafted each of our paths with purpose and intention. Every experience, trial, and victory shapes us into the women He has called us to be. Gratitude for your unique journey means embracing all aspects of it, recognizing that God is using every moment to fulfill His purpose in your life.

No matter where you are on your journey—whether you're walking through a season of joy or challenge—God's hand is guiding you. The struggles you face teach you strength and perseverance, while the victories remind you of His faithfulness. Being grateful for your unique path allows you to release comparison and trust that God's timing for your life is perfect. Every twist and turn is part of a beautiful story that He is writing, one that leads to His ultimate plan for you.

Today, take a moment to reflect on your journey. Thank God for the way He is shaping your life, and celebrate the uniqueness of your path, knowing that it is designed specifically for you.

Prayer

Lord, thank You for the unique journey You have me on. Help me to embrace every season, knowing that You are working all things for my good. Teach me to be grateful for the experiences that shape me and to trust that Your plan for my life is unfolding perfectly. Amen.

Affirmation

I am grateful for my unique journey, trusting that God is guiding every step and using every experience to fulfill His purpose for my life.

July 21

Joy Amidst the Noise

"The Lord gives strength to his people; the Lord blesses his people with peace." (Psalm 29:11, NIV)

Devotional Reflection

In today's fast-paced world, finding peace and joy can feel like a challenge. As black women, we often juggle multiple responsibilities, whether it's work, family, or community obligations. The noise of life—both literal and figurative—can be overwhelming, making it hard to connect with moments of calm and joy. Yet, even in the midst of this chaos, God calls us to find joy by anchoring ourselves in His peace.

Joy doesn't require perfect circumstances or a quiet life; it can be found in the middle of the busyness. When we intentionally seek God's presence and peace, we create space for joy to flourish. Whether it's through a quiet moment of prayer, deep breaths of gratitude, or simply pausing to acknowledge God's goodness, peace is available to us even in the most hectic moments. The world may be chaotic, but God's peace is constant, and it brings joy to our hearts when we focus on Him.

Today, make an effort to find joy amidst the noise. Take moments throughout your day to pause, breathe, and invite God's peace into your heart. In doing so, you'll discover that joy is not far from you, even in the busiest of times.

Prayer

Lord, thank You for the peace You offer me, even in the midst of a chaotic world. Help me to find moments of joy by seeking Your presence and resting in Your peace. Teach me to pause and trust that You are with me, no matter how busy life gets. Amen.

Affirmation

I find joy amidst the noise, seeking God's peace in the busyness of life and allowing His presence to bring calm and joy to my heart.

July 22
Gratitude for Lessons Learned

"Consider it pure joy, my brothers and sisters, whenever you face trials of many kinds, because you know that the testing of your faith produces perseverance." (James 1:2-3, NIV)

Devotional Reflection

Life's hardest lessons are often the ones that shape us the most. As black women, we encounter challenges that test our resilience and faith, and though these trials may feel heavy, they are filled with opportunities for growth. The lessons we learn from adversity build strength, deepen our wisdom, and increase our reliance on God. With time and reflection, we can look back and recognize that the very things we thought would break us have actually made us stronger.

Gratitude for life's lessons allows us to see trials as moments of transformation. While the experience itself may not feel joyful, the growth it produces is a cause for thanksgiving. God uses every challenge to shape our character, mold our faith, and prepare us for greater things. Embracing these lessons with gratitude reminds us that nothing we go through is in vain—God is always working, even in the hardest moments, for our good and His glory.

Today, reflect on the lessons you've learned through life's challenges. Thank God for the strength and wisdom those experiences have given you, and trust that He is continually shaping you for the better.

Prayer

Lord, thank You for the lessons You've taught me through life's challenges. Help me to embrace these lessons with gratitude, knowing that You are shaping me into the person You've called me to be. Give me the strength to continue learning and growing in faith. Amen.

Affirmation

I am grateful for the lessons life has taught me, knowing that each challenge shapes me for the better and brings me closer to fulfilling God's purpose for my life.

July 23
Joy in Overcoming Obstacles

"But thanks be to God! He gives us the victory through our Lord Jesus Christ." (1 Corinthians 15:57, NIV)

Devotional Reflection

There's a special kind of joy that comes from overcoming obstacles. As black women, we often face unique challenges that test our faith, resilience, and determination. Whether the struggle is personal, professional, or emotional, the joy that follows victory is sweeter because it comes from perseverance and trust in God's strength. Every obstacle you overcome is a testimony to God's power at work in your life, turning what seemed impossible into a reason for celebration.

The victories we experience after struggles remind us of God's faithfulness. Obstacles can feel overwhelming, but when we press forward in faith, relying on God's guidance, we find strength we didn't know we had. The joy of overcoming is not just about the success—it's about the growth, lessons, and faith that develop along the way. Celebrating these victories honors the journey, recognizing that through every challenge, God was present, leading you to triumph.

Today, take time to reflect on the obstacles you've overcome and the victories you've achieved. Celebrate those moments with gratitude, and let them remind you that no matter the challenge, God is always with you, bringing you through to victory.

Prayer

Lord, thank You for the strength to overcome obstacles and the victories You've given me. Help me to celebrate these moments with joy and gratitude, knowing that every triumph is a reflection of Your faithfulness and grace. Amen.

Affirmation

I celebrate the victories that come after struggles, knowing that God gives me the strength to overcome every obstacle and fills my life with joy through each triumph.

July 24
Practicing Gratitude in Relationships

"Encourage one another and build each other up, just as in fact you are doing." (1 Thessalonians 5:11, NIV)

Devotional Reflection

Gratitude is a powerful force that can transform relationships. As Black women, our connections with family, friends, and loved ones are central to our lives. However, in the busyness of life, we can sometimes take these relationships for granted. Expressing thankfulness for the people in our lives strengthens our bonds and reminds us of the blessings these connections bring. Gratitude opens the door to deeper understanding, love, and support.

When we take time to appreciate those around us, we create an environment of mutual respect and care. A simple "thank you" can make a world of difference, shifting focus from frustrations to the positive contributions others bring. By expressing our thankfulness, we build stronger relationships and reflect God's love for His creation.

Today, reflect on the relationships in your life. Thank God for the people who support and uplift you, and take a moment to express gratitude to them. Your words will not only strengthen your bonds but also bring joy to others.

Prayer

Lord, thank You for the relationships in my life. Help me to express gratitude for the people You have placed around me, and teach me to strengthen those bonds through thankfulness and love. Guide me in building relationships that honor You. Amen.

Affirmation

I practice gratitude in my relationships, expressing thankfulness for the people in my life and strengthening my connections through love and appreciation.

July 25

The Joy of New Beginnings

"Forget the former things; do not dwell on the past. See, I am doing a new thing! Now it springs up; do you not perceive it?"

(Isaiah 43:18-19, NIV)

Devotional Reflection

New beginnings are a gift from God, filled with fresh opportunities and endless possibilities. As black women, starting something new — whether it's a job, a new chapter in life, or a fresh pursuit — can be both exciting and nerve-wracking. But when we embrace new beginnings with joy and faith, we step into the fullness of God's plan for us. Each new start is a chance to grow, learn, and experience God's grace in ways we may never have imagined.

The joy of new beginnings comes from trusting that God is in control. It's an opportunity to leave behind what no longer serves us and embrace the future with hope and expectation. New ventures, while uncertain, allow us to witness God's faithfulness as we walk into the unknown. He promises to guide us through each new start, offering strength, wisdom, and joy along the way.

Today, if you find yourself on the cusp of a new beginning, embrace it with joy. Thank God for the fresh start, and trust that He will lead you through this new season with grace and purpose.

Prayer

Lord, thank You for the gift of new beginnings. Help me to embrace the joy and excitement of starting fresh, trusting that You are with me every step of the way. Guide me in this new season, and give me the courage to walk into the future with faith and hope. Amen.

Affirmation

I embrace the joy of new beginnings, trusting God to guide me through each fresh start with purpose, faith, and excitement for the future.

July 26

Gratitude in Solitude

"Be still, and know that I am God." (Psalm 46:10, NIV)

Devotional Reflection

In a world filled with constant activity and noise, solitude can feel uncomfortable or unfamiliar. As black women, we often carry multiple roles and responsibilities, making it hard to find time for quiet reflection. Yet, solitude with God is a place where we can recharge, find peace, and express gratitude for His presence. It's in these quiet moments that we can truly feel God's closeness, hear His voice, and reflect on His goodness.

Solitude offers the chance to pause and appreciate the small, still moments where God speaks to our hearts. It is in this quiet space that we can reflect on the blessings of our lives, thank God for His grace, and allow our souls to rest in His peace. Gratitude in solitude is about recognizing that even when we are alone, God is with us, filling the silence with His love and reassurance.

Today, make time for solitude with God. Let the quiet bring you peace, and take a moment to thank Him for His constant presence and love in your life. Through this stillness, you'll find that your heart is filled with gratitude and renewed strength.

Prayer

Lord, thank You for the gift of solitude, where I can draw closer to You. Help me to embrace these quiet moments, finding peace and thankfulness in Your presence. Teach me to cherish the time I spend alone with You, knowing that it brings rest to my soul. Amen.

Affirmation

I find peace and gratitude in solitude, cherishing the quiet moments spent with God and trusting in His presence to renew and guide me.

July 27
Joy in Creative Expression

"For we are God's handiwork, created in Christ Jesus to do good works, which God prepared in advance for us to do." (Ephesians 2:10, NIV)

Devotional Reflection

Creative expression is one of the ways we reflect the image of God. As black women, we often navigate life's challenges with resilience, grace, and creativity. Whether through writing, painting, music, fashion, or any other form of art, creative outlets give us a way to express emotions, ideas, and experiences in ways that bring joy and renewal to our spirits. Creativity connects us to God, the ultimate Creator, and allows us to release stress, celebrate beauty, and find joy in the process.

When we engage in creative activities, we open ourselves to joy in its purest form—creating something new and meaningful from our hearts. Creative expression isn't just about the final product; it's about the journey, the freedom to express ourselves, and the joy that comes from tapping into the gifts and talents God has placed within us. Whether you feel accomplished or simply enjoy the process, creativity is a gift that brings refreshment to the soul and joy to the heart.

Today, explore your creative side, whether through art, music, writing, or any other outlet that brings you joy. Allow yourself to express freely and joyfully, knowing that in these moments, you reflect God's creative nature.

Prayer

Lord, thank You for the gift of creativity. Help me find joy in using the talents You've given me. Guide me as I explore creative outlets that refresh my spirit and draw me closer to You. Amen.

Affirmation

I find joy in creative expression, using the gifts God has given me to refresh my spirit and reflect His creative power and love.

July 28
Thankful for Spiritual Growth

"But grow in the grace and knowledge of our Lord and Savior Jesus Christ. To him be glory both now and forever!" (2 Peter 3:18, NIV)

Devotional Reflection

Spiritual growth is a journey that often comes through moments of stretching, testing, and transformation. As Black women, the experiences we face—challenges, triumphs, and quiet reflections—shape our spiritual lives in unique ways. Recognizing how far God has brought us and how much He has stretched us fills our hearts with gratitude. Every trial, prayer, and step of faith serves a purpose in our spiritual development, drawing us closer to God.

Thankfulness for spiritual growth means appreciating both the difficult moments and the victories. Growth often comes through perseverance, reflection, and learning to trust God more. Looking back, you'll see how God has guided you, deepened your faith, and shaped you. Every season of growth is a testimony to God's grace and His desire for you to flourish.

Today, reflect on how you've grown spiritually. Thank God for the lessons learned, the challenges overcome, and the deepening of your faith, trusting that He will continue to lead you closer to Him.

Prayer

Lord, thank You for the spiritual growth in my life. I'm grateful for Your guidance, even through difficult times. Continue to lead me, helping me grow in faith and closer to You. Amen.

Affirmation

I am thankful for my spiritual growth, recognizing the ways God has stretched and strengthened me, and I trust Him to continue leading me on this journey of faith.

July 29

Joy in Surrender

"Trust in the Lord with all your heart and lean not on your own understanding; in all your ways submit to him, and he will make your paths straight." (Proverbs 3:5-6, NIV)

Devotional Reflection

Surrender is not always easy, but it is one of the most freeing acts of faith. As black women, we often carry the weight of multiple roles, expectations, and responsibilities, and the desire to be in control can sometimes leave us feeling overwhelmed. Yet, when we choose to let go and fully trust God's plan, we find a deep sense of peace and joy. True joy is not found in having everything figured out, but in trusting that God is guiding every step, even when the path is uncertain.

Surrendering to God means releasing the need to control outcomes and allowing Him to work in His perfect timing. It's an act of faith that acknowledges God's wisdom and sovereignty over our lives. When we trust in His plan, we let go of fear, anxiety, and doubt, and joy fills the spaces once occupied by worry. Surrender brings us closer to God, allowing His peace and presence to flow freely in our hearts, knowing that He holds our future securely in His hands.

Today, reflect on areas of your life where you need to surrender. Trust that God's plan is far greater than anything you could imagine, and find joy in letting go and allowing Him to lead.

Prayer

Lord, help me to find joy in surrendering to Your will. Teach me to trust in Your plan for my life, even when I cannot see the full picture. Give me the strength to let go of control and to rest in the peace that comes from fully trusting You. Amen.

Affirmation

I find joy in surrender, trusting God's perfect plan for my life and letting go of control, knowing that His wisdom and guidance will lead me forward in peace and joy.

July 30
Gratitude for the Gift of Sisterhood

"Two are better than one, because they have a good return for their labor: If either of them falls down, one can help the other up."

(Ecclesiastes 4:9-10, NIV)

Devotional Reflection
Sisterhood is a precious gift that brings support, love, and shared faith into our lives. As black women, the bonds we form with other women who walk with us in faith are powerful sources of strength and joy. Whether through shared experiences, encouragement during tough times, or celebrating victories, the sisterhood we experience in Christ is a beautiful reflection of God's love and His design for community.

True sisterhood offers a safe space for vulnerability, a source of comfort, and a network of support that helps us grow spiritually and emotionally. It reminds us that we don't have to navigate life's challenges alone. The friendships we cultivate with fellow women in Christ uplift us and help us see God's faithfulness in new and profound ways. Through prayer, laughter, and shared faith, sisterhood enriches our lives, reminding us that God places others in our lives to walk this journey together.

Today, take a moment to reflect on the gift of sisterhood in your life. Thank God for the women who have stood by you, encouraged you, and walked alongside you in faith. Celebrate the joy and strength that these friendships bring to your life.

Prayer
Lord, thank You for the gift of sisterhood. I am grateful for the friendships and support of the women You have placed in my life. Help me to cherish and nurture these relationships, and may we continue to uplift and encourage one another in faith. Amen.

Affirmation
I am grateful for the gift of sisterhood, celebrating the joy, support, and strength that comes from my friendships with fellow women in Christ.

July 31
Joy in God's Unfailing Love

"The Lord your God is with you, the Mighty Warrior who saves. He will take great delight in you; in his love he will no longer rebuke you, but will rejoice over you with singing." (Zephaniah 3:17, NIV)

Devotional Reflection

God's unfailing love is a source of everlasting joy. As black women, we face many struggles, but knowing that God's love never wavers gives us hope and strength. His love is constant, unconditional, and eternal, offering peace and security in a world that often feels uncertain. No matter what we face, we can find lasting joy in the truth that we are deeply loved by our Creator.

God's love is not dependent on our circumstances, behavior, or achievements. It is a gift, freely given, and it sustains us through life's highs and lows. When we rest in the knowledge of His unfailing love, we experience a joy that transcends the temporary trials and challenges we face. His love fills the empty spaces in our hearts, brings healing to our wounds, and reminds us that we are never alone. Joy in God's love is not fleeting—it is a deep, abiding assurance that we are held by the One who delights in us.

Today, reflect on the never-ending love of God. Let His love bring joy and peace to your heart, knowing that it is a love that will never fail, never fade, and never leave.

Prayer

Lord, thank You for Your unfailing love. Help me to find joy in the constant reminder that Your love for me never changes. Fill my heart with peace and gratitude as I rest in the assurance of Your love, knowing that I am cherished by You. Amen.

Affirmation

I find lasting joy in God's unfailing love, knowing that I am deeply loved and cherished by my Creator, and His love will never leave or forsake me.

August
Courage and Confidence

August 1
Trusting God's Strength Over Your Own

"But he said to me, 'My grace is sufficient for you, for my power is made perfect in weakness.' Therefore I will boast all the more gladly about my weaknesses, so that Christ's power may rest on me."

(2 Corinthians 12:9, NIV)

Devotional Reflection

Life often presents intimidating situations that make us feel weak or inadequate. Whether it's a demanding project, a tough conversation, or stepping into a new opportunity, it's easy to feel overwhelmed. As Black women, we carry multiple responsibilities, and the pressure to always appear strong can be heavy. However, God reminds us that our strength comes from Him, not from ourselves. His power shines when we acknowledge our limitations and rely on His strength.

Trusting God's strength means letting go of control and resting in the assurance that He is with us. In moments of vulnerability, His power gives us the courage to face what we thought we couldn't. When we lean on God, we are never truly weak; we are empowered by His strength.

Today, let go of the pressure to carry it all on your own. Reflect on situations where you feel unsure, and ask God to fill you with His strength and grace, knowing His power is working through you.

Prayer

Lord, thank You for reminding me that Your strength is enough. Help me to let go of the need to rely on my own power and to trust in Your strength when I feel weak or overwhelmed. Fill me with confidence, knowing that You are with me in every situation I face. Amen.

Affirmation

I trust in God's strength over my own, knowing that His power is made perfect in my weaknesses. He gives me the courage and confidence to face intimidating situations with faith.

August 2
Speaking Boldly in the Workplace

"The Spirit God gave us does not make us timid, but gives us power, love and self-discipline." (2 Timothy 1:7, NIV)

Devotional Reflection

As black women, navigating the workplace can come with its own set of challenges, especially when it comes to finding your voice and speaking boldly. Whether it's addressing issues, sharing ideas, or advocating for yourself, it can sometimes feel intimidating to speak up. Yet, God has not called us to be timid. He has given us a spirit of power, love, and self-discipline—qualities that equip us to step into professional spaces with confidence and assertiveness.

Speaking boldly in the workplace isn't about dominating conversations or always having the last word. It's about trusting that your perspective, experience, and voice are valuable and worth sharing. When you speak with confidence, you not only advocate for yourself, but you also create space for others to recognize your worth. God has given you gifts, talents, and wisdom, and He calls you to use them boldly, even in professional settings. Trust that He will guide your words and give you the courage to speak up when it matters.

Today, reflect on areas in your workplace where you feel hesitant to speak up. Ask God for the confidence to use your voice, knowing that He is with you and will empower you to speak boldly and with grace.

Prayer

Lord, thank You for the spirit of power and confidence You have given me. Help me to speak boldly in the workplace, trusting that my voice matters and that You are with me in every conversation. Guide my words and give me the courage to use my voice for good. Amen.

Affirmation

I speak boldly in the workplace, trusting in the power, love, and confidence that God has given me. My voice is valuable, and I use it to advocate for myself and others with grace and wisdom.

August 3
Overcoming Fear of Failure

"For I know the plans I have for you," declares the Lord, "plans to prosper you and not to harm you, plans to give you hope and a future."
(Jeremiah 29:11, NIV)

Devotional Reflection

Fear of failure can be paralyzing, making it difficult to take steps forward, especially when the outcome is uncertain. As black women, societal pressures and expectations can sometimes intensify this fear, leading to self-doubt and hesitation. However, God calls us to trust His plan, even when the path ahead is unclear. His plans for us are good, filled with hope and a future designed with purpose.

Overcoming fear of failure begins with recognizing that our success does not rest solely in our hands but in God's. We may not always see the full picture, but God does. When we trust in His guidance, we can move forward confidently, knowing that even if we stumble, He is there to pick us up and redirect our path. Every setback is an opportunity for growth, and every challenge a chance to deepen our faith. Trusting God's plan allows us to release the fear of failure and walk in the assurance that He is guiding our steps.

Today, reflect on areas of your life where fear of failure is holding you back. Surrender that fear to God and trust that His plan for you is greater than any mistake or setback you might face.

Prayer

Lord, help me to overcome the fear of failure and trust in Your perfect plan for my life. Even when the path ahead feels uncertain, give me the confidence to move forward, knowing that You are guiding my steps. Remind me that my worth is found in You, not in my successes or failures. Amen.

Affirmation

I release the fear of failure and trust in God's plan for my life. I move forward with confidence, knowing that He is guiding my steps, and even in uncertainty, I am secure in His love and purpose.

August 4
Embracing Your Unique Gifts

"We have different gifts, according to the grace given to each of us."

(Romans 12:6, NIV)

Devotional Reflection

Each of us has been blessed with unique gifts and talents that reflect God's creativity and purpose for our lives. As black women, it's easy to feel pressure to conform to certain expectations or compare ourselves to others. However, God created you with specific gifts that only you can offer the world. Embracing your unique talents means recognizing their value and using them confidently for the glory of God.

Your gifts—whether they are creative, intellectual, or relational—are meant to be used to uplift others and fulfill the purpose God has for you. There is power in fully embracing what makes you special and leaning into the abilities God has entrusted to you. By doing so, you honor the One who gave you these gifts and build a life filled with purpose and confidence. You don't need to be like anyone else; your uniqueness is a reflection of God's plan for your life.

Today, take time to reflect on the talents and abilities God has given you. Celebrate your uniqueness and seek opportunities to use your gifts to bless others, knowing that you are fully equipped to make a meaningful impact.

Prayer

Lord, thank You for the unique gifts You have given me. Help me to embrace and use these talents with confidence, knowing that they are valuable and have been entrusted to me for a purpose. Guide me in using my gifts to serve others and glorify You. Amen.

Affirmation

I embrace my unique gifts with confidence, knowing that God has given me these talents for a purpose. I use them to bless others and fulfill the calling God has placed on my life.

August 5
Stepping Out of Your Comfort Zone

"Have I not commanded you? Be strong and courageous. Do not be afraid; do not be discouraged, for the Lord your God will be with you wherever you go." (Joshua 1:9, NIV)

Devotional Reflection

Stepping out of your comfort zone can be intimidating, especially when faced with uncertainty or the fear of failure. As black women, we may feel the weight of expectations or doubts that hold us back from taking bold steps forward. Yet, God calls us to be strong and courageous, knowing that He is with us in every situation. Faith means trusting that even when we venture into the unknown, God is guiding us every step of the way.

Growth and transformation happen when we take risks and step into new opportunities, despite our fears. Whether it's pursuing a new career path, moving to a new city, or simply trying something unfamiliar, God encourages us to trust Him in the process. When we lean on faith, we can push past the limits of our comfort zone, knowing that God will equip us for whatever lies ahead.

Today, reflect on areas of your life where God might be calling you to step out of your comfort zone. Ask Him for the courage and strength to move forward in faith, trusting that He is walking with you into the unfamiliar.

Prayer

Lord, give me the courage to step out of my comfort zone and trust You as I take bold steps forward. Help me to overcome fear and uncertainty, knowing that You are with me wherever I go. Strengthen my faith as I walk into new and unfamiliar territory, relying on Your guidance and grace. Amen.

Affirmation

I step out of my comfort zone with faith and confidence, trusting that God is guiding me through every new opportunity and challenge. He is with me, giving me the strength to move forward boldly.

August 6
Building Confidence in Your Appearance

"I praise you because I am fearfully and wonderfully made; your works are wonderful, I know that full well." (Psalm 139:14, NIV)

Devotional Reflection

In a world that constantly pushes unrealistic beauty standards, it can be difficult to feel confident in your appearance. As black women, we are often subjected to pressures about how we should look, from our hair to our skin tone. However, God reminds us that we are fearfully and wonderfully made. You were created with intention, and every part of you is a reflection of His craftsmanship.

Building confidence in your appearance means embracing the beauty that God has placed in you. It's about recognizing that your worth is not defined by society's standards but by the way God sees you—unique, beautiful, and strong. When you accept and celebrate your appearance as a creation of God, you reflect His glory and gain the confidence to walk in the fullness of who you are. Confidence is not just about how you look, but about recognizing the inner strength and beauty that comes from being made in God's image.

Today, take a moment to reflect on the parts of yourself you struggle to appreciate. Ask God to help you see yourself through His eyes and to build confidence in the beauty and strength He has placed in you.

Prayer

Lord, thank You for creating me fearfully and wonderfully. Help me to embrace the beauty and strength that You have placed within me. Teach me to see myself through Your eyes and to walk confidently, knowing that I am a reflection of Your love and creativity. Amen.

Affirmation

I am fearfully and wonderfully made. I find confidence in my appearance, knowing that God has created me beautifully and with purpose. My beauty and strength come from Him, and I walk confidently in that truth.

August 7
Conquering Self-Doubt

"For we are God's handiwork, created in Christ Jesus to do good works, which God prepared in advance for us to do." (Ephesians 2:10, NIV)

Devotional Reflection

Self-doubt can creep into our minds and make us question our worth and abilities. As black women, the weight of societal expectations, past failures, or negative experiences may cause us to question our purpose or talents. However, God reminds us that we are His handiwork, created with purpose and equipped for good works. Self-doubt has no place when we remember that we are fearfully and wonderfully made, fully capable of accomplishing the plans God has for us.

Overcoming self-doubt begins with silencing the internal voices that challenge your worth. These doubts are often rooted in fear, comparison, or past mistakes, but God's truth tells a different story. You are chosen, equipped, and empowered by God to fulfill His purpose for your life. When you focus on His promises, you gain the strength to push past self-doubt and step confidently into the roles and responsibilities He has called you to.

Today, take time to reflect on areas where self-doubt is holding you back. Ask God to renew your confidence and replace those doubts with His truth, reminding you that you are fully capable and called to greatness.

Prayer

Lord, help me conquer self-doubt and embrace who I am in You. Remind me of my purpose and give me the confidence to silence thoughts that challenge my worth. Thank You for creating me to fulfill Your plans. Amen.

Affirmation

I conquer self-doubt by trusting in God's truth about who I am. I am His handiwork, created with purpose and fully capable of accomplishing the good works He has prepared for me. My worth and abilities are rooted in Him.

August 8
Speaking Truth in Difficult Conversations

"Instead, speaking the truth in love, we will grow to become in every respect the mature body of him who is the head, that is, Christ."

(Ephesians 4:15, NIV)

Devotional Reflection

Difficult conversations can be uncomfortable, yet they are often necessary for growth and healing. As black women, we may find ourselves in situations where speaking up feels risky—whether it's addressing injustice, conflict, or personal boundaries. However, God calls us to speak the truth in love. It's not about winning an argument or proving a point but about communicating honestly with grace, aiming to build others up, even in tough situations.

When we approach difficult conversations with love and courage, we honor God's desire for peace and reconciliation. It takes boldness to speak up, but when we lean on God for strength, He helps us find the right words. Speaking truth doesn't mean avoiding the hard topics, but rather addressing them with compassion, respect, and faith in God's guidance. By trusting Him, you can confront challenging issues with both honesty and a heart full of love, knowing that the outcome is in His hands.

Today, reflect on any difficult conversations you may need to have. Ask God for the courage to speak with honesty, wisdom, and love, and trust that He will guide you through it.

Prayer

Lord, give me the courage to speak the truth in love, even when it's hard. Help me to address difficult conversations with honesty and compassion, trusting that You will guide my words. Teach me to approach every situation with grace, seeking peace and reconciliation in all I do. Amen.

Affirmation

I speak the truth with courage and love, trusting God to guide my words and actions. I address difficult conversations with honesty and grace, seeking to build others up and create peace in all situations.

August 9
Navigating Imposter Syndrome

"For the Spirit God gave us does not make us timid, but gives us power, love and self-discipline." (2 Timothy 1:7, NIV)

Devotional Reflection

Imposter syndrome is the nagging feeling that you're not good enough, that somehow you don't deserve your accomplishments, or that you're just one step away from being "found out." As black women, we may sometimes experience this even more intensely in environments where we feel like we have to prove ourselves. But God's Word reminds us that we are not meant to live in fear or doubt. He has equipped us with power, love, and self-discipline, and we have been placed exactly where we are by His design.

Rejecting imposter syndrome means embracing the truth that God has chosen and positioned you for a reason. You are not an accident or a fluke. You carry gifts and talents that are necessary for the work you're called to do, whether in your career, family, or community. God doesn't make mistakes, and He has already given you everything you need to succeed in your role. When you let go of feelings of inadequacy and embrace your God-given purpose, you step fully into the power He has given you.

Today, reflect on the areas of your life where you feel like an imposter. Ask God to replace those feelings of inadequacy with confidence in His plan and purpose for you, knowing that He has fully equipped you for every task.

Prayer

Lord, help me reject inadequacy from imposter syndrome. Remind me of my purpose and that You've equipped me to succeed. Strengthen my confidence, and help me walk boldly in my calling. Amen.

Affirmation

I reject imposter syndrome and embrace my God-given position and purpose. I trust that God has equipped me with power, love, and self-discipline, and I walk confidently in the purpose He has set for my life.

August 10
Confidently Setting Boundaries

"Above all else, guard your heart, for everything you do flows from it."
(Proverbs 4:23, NIV)

Devotional Reflection

Setting boundaries is an essential part of protecting your peace and well-being, yet it can feel uncomfortable or difficult, especially if you fear disappointing others. As black women, we often carry multiple roles and responsibilities, which can make it challenging to prioritize our own needs. However, establishing healthy boundaries is not only necessary but also a way to honor the life and well-being God has given you.

God calls us to guard our hearts, which includes protecting our emotional, spiritual, and physical health. Setting boundaries allows you to maintain balance and keep relationships and situations from becoming overwhelming. It's an act of self-love and stewardship, recognizing that your well-being matters to God. Healthy boundaries help you preserve your energy for the things that truly matter, allowing you to give more fully when you choose to do so, without feeling depleted or resentful.

Today, reflect on the areas of your life where boundaries are needed. Ask God for the confidence and wisdom to set healthy limits, knowing that in doing so, you are caring for yourself and honoring Him.

Prayer

Lord, help me to confidently set boundaries that protect my peace and well-being. Give me the strength to say no when needed and the wisdom to recognize when I need to guard my heart. Teach me that establishing boundaries is an act of honoring the life You've given me. Amen.

Affirmation

I confidently set healthy boundaries that protect my peace and well-being. I guard my heart, knowing that I am honoring God and caring for myself in a way that allows me to serve and love others more fully.

August 11
Facing Criticism with Grace

"Let your conversation be always full of grace, seasoned with salt, so that you may know how to answer everyone." (Colossians 4:6, NIV)

Devotional Reflection

Criticism can be difficult to face, especially when it feels personal or undeserved. As black women, we may often face criticism in various areas of life—whether at work, in relationships, or even within our communities. It's easy to allow critical words to chip away at our confidence and self-worth, but God calls us to handle criticism with grace. When we respond with wisdom and humility, we protect our inner peace and continue to walk in the confidence that comes from knowing who we are in Christ.

Facing criticism with grace means not letting it define you. Instead, you can view it as an opportunity for growth, choosing to evaluate the feedback with a discerning heart. Some criticism may hold valuable lessons, while other comments may need to be released and left behind. Either way, your self-worth is never dependent on the opinions of others but on the unchanging truth that you are loved, valued, and equipped by God.

Today, if you find yourself facing criticism, ask God for the grace to respond with humility and wisdom. Let Him remind you that your identity and confidence are rooted in Him, not in the words of others.

Prayer

Lord, help me face criticism with grace, without it shaking my confidence or self-worth. Teach me to respond with humility and wisdom, knowing my value comes from You. Amen.

Affirmation

I face criticism with grace, knowing that my confidence and self-worth are rooted in God. I respond with wisdom and humility, embracing opportunities for growth while standing firm in the truth of who I am in Christ.

August 12
Owning Your Achievements

"Let your light shine before others, that they may see your good deeds and glorify your Father in heaven." (Matthew 5:16, NIV)

Devotional Reflection

As Black women, we may feel pressured to downplay our achievements for fear of being seen as boastful. Yet, God calls us to let our light shine and not hide the gifts He's given us. Owning your achievements is about recognizing that your success reflects God's grace and your hard work. It's a chance to celebrate what God has done through you and inspire others.

By owning your achievements, you honor God for the doors He's opened and the strength He's provided. Acknowledging your successes encourages other women to rise confidently in their own journeys. Shrinking back doesn't serve anyone, least of all God, who has blessed you with victories. You can celebrate your wins while remaining humble, knowing they are a testament to God's faithfulness.

Today, reflect on your recent accomplishments. Celebrate them without shrinking back, and thank God for guiding you. Let your light shine so others may see His work in you and be encouraged.

Prayer

Lord, thank You for the blessings and achievements You've placed in my life. Help me to own my successes without shrinking back or feeling the need to minimize them. Teach me to celebrate with humility, giving You all the glory for the victories You've helped me achieve. Amen.

Affirmation

I own my achievements with confidence, knowing that they reflect God's grace and faithfulness. I celebrate my wins, shining my light for others to see, and give all glory to God for His work in my life.

August 13
Trusting God's Timing in Career Moves

"There is a time for everything, and a season for every activity under the heavens." (Ecclesiastes 3:1, NIV)

Devotional Reflection

Career transitions can be exciting yet filled with uncertainty. Whether you are pursuing a new opportunity, waiting for a promotion, or navigating an unexpected change, trusting God's timing in your career can be challenging. As black women, we often feel the need to take control of our paths, but God calls us to wait on Him with confidence, knowing that His timing is perfect. There is a season for every step in our journey, and God is working behind the scenes, even when it feels like nothing is happening.

When we trust God's timing, we release the pressure to figure everything out on our own and allow Him to guide our steps. His plans are greater than our own, and He knows exactly when and where to position us for the greatest impact. Waiting on God doesn't mean being passive—it means continuing to do the work, praying for guidance, and trusting that when the time is right, the doors will open.

Today, reflect on any career decisions or transitions you may be facing. Ask God for patience and trust in His timing, knowing that He is leading you to where you are meant to be.

Prayer

Lord, help me to trust Your timing in my career moves. Give me patience as I wait on Your direction, and remind me that You have a plan and purpose for every season of my life. Teach me to release control and trust that You are guiding my steps to where I need to be. Amen.

Affirmation

I trust God's perfect timing in my career, knowing that He is guiding me to the right opportunities and leading me through every transition. I wait with confidence, trusting that His plans for me are good.

August 14
Courage to Walk Away from Toxic Relationships

"Do not be misled: 'Bad company corrupts good character.' "

(1 Corinthians 15:33, NIV)

Devotional Reflection

Letting go of toxic relationships can be one of the hardest decisions, especially when emotional attachment or history is involved. As Black women, we often nurture and invest deeply in relationships. However, when a relationship becomes toxic—draining your energy, disturbing your peace, or pulling you away from your purpose—God gives us the courage to release what no longer serves us. Walking away isn't weakness; it's a step toward protecting your well-being and honoring the life God has called you to live.

Toxic relationships can take many forms, whether in friendships, family, or romantic ties. God desires relationships that build us up, encourage growth, and reflect His love. Staying in harmful environments limits the joy and peace God intends for us. Trust that He will lead you into life-giving, nurturing relationships.

Today, reflect on any relationships negatively impacting your life. Ask God for the courage to release what no longer serves you and guide you toward healthier, uplifting connections.

Prayer

Lord, give me the courage to walk away from relationships that no longer serve my well-being. Help me trust Your plan, knowing You will provide nurturing connections. Strengthen me as I release toxic influences and guide me toward peace and healthy relationships. Amen.

Affirmation

I have the courage to walk away from toxic relationships, trusting God to guide me toward connections that uplift and nurture my well-being. I release what no longer serves me, stepping into peace and health in my relationships.

August 15
Public Speaking with Faith and Confidence

"The Sovereign Lord has given me a well-instructed tongue, to know the word that sustains the weary. He wakens me morning by morning, wakens my ear to listen like one being instructed." (Isaiah 50:4, NIV)

Devotional Reflection

Public speaking can be daunting, often bringing feelings of nervousness or self-doubt. As Black women, we may feel added pressure to represent ourselves and our communities in a certain way. However, God equips us to speak boldly and confidently. When we trust Him to guide our words, we can stand before any audience with faith, knowing He will speak through us.

Public speaking is more than just having the right words; it's about leaning on God for strength, clarity, and boldness. He gives us the ability to inspire and uplift others through our words. When we surrender our fears to Him, He fills us with wisdom and confidence. Whether speaking in a boardroom, family gathering, or on stage, trust that God will provide the words and the courage to deliver them.

Today, reflect on any upcoming opportunities for public speaking. Ask God to guide your words and give you the confidence to speak boldly, trusting He is with you every step of the way.

Prayer

Lord, thank You for the gift of speech and the ability to share my voice. Help me to trust You fully when I speak in front of others. Fill me with the boldness and confidence to communicate clearly and effectively, knowing that You are guiding my words. Give me peace in those moments and use my words to uplift and inspire others. Amen.

Affirmation

I trust God to guide my words and give me confidence when I speak in front of others. I speak with boldness, faith, and clarity, knowing that God equips me to inspire and uplift through my words.

August 16
Building Confidence in Parenting

"Start children off on the way they should go, and even when they are old they will not turn from it." (Proverbs 22:6, NIV)

Devotional Reflection

Parenting is both rewarding and challenging. As Black women, there may be additional pressures to raise children in a world that doesn't always value their identity. This can lead to self-doubt and make us question our choices. But God has entrusted you with this role and equipped you with the wisdom and instincts to guide your children.

Confidence in parenting doesn't mean having all the answers. It means trusting your God-given instincts and seeking His guidance. You don't have to be perfect—what matters is your willingness to seek God's direction and trust that He is with you in every decision. As you pour love, care, and discipline into your children, remember that God is your strength, providing what you need to be the parent He's called you to be.

Today, reflect on your role as a parent. Ask God to help you trust your instincts and find confidence in your daily decisions, knowing He is walking with you every step of the way.

Prayer

Lord, thank You for the gift of parenting. Help me to trust the instincts You've given me and to rely on Your guidance as I raise my children. Give me confidence and strength, knowing that You are with me in every step of this journey. Teach me to lead my children with love, faith, and wisdom, and help me to trust that You will provide what I need. Amen.

Affirmation

I trust my God-given instincts as a parent, finding confidence in the strength and wisdom God has given me. I raise my children with love, faith, and trust, knowing that God is guiding me every step of the way.

August 17
Balancing Humility and Confidence

"Humble yourselves before the Lord, and he will lift you up."
(James 4:10, NIV)

Devotional Reflection

Humility and confidence may seem like opposites, but in God's eyes, they work together beautifully. As black women, we sometimes feel the pressure to downplay our accomplishments and gifts in the name of humility, believing that it is the "right" or "modest" thing to do. However, true humility isn't about shrinking or hiding your God-given abilities; it's about recognizing that everything you have—your gifts, talents, and successes—comes from God.

Balancing humility and confidence means understanding that you can be both grounded and bold at the same time. Humility keeps you rooted in the truth that your strength comes from God, while confidence allows you to step forward and fully use your gifts for His glory. When you embrace this balance, you can walk confidently in your calling without feeling the need to boast or seek validation from others. Humility in Christ lifts you up, knowing that as you rely on Him, you are empowered to fulfill your purpose.

Today, reflect on areas where you may feel the tension between humility and confidence. Ask God to help you embrace both, knowing that He is the source of your strength and that you can walk boldly in the gifts He has given you.

Prayer

Lord, thank You for the gifts and talents You have placed in me. Help me to balance humility and confidence as I walk in Your calling. Teach me to remain humble, recognizing that my strength comes from You, while also giving me the confidence to boldly use my gifts to serve and glorify You. Amen.

Affirmation

I walk confidently in my God-given gifts while remaining humble, knowing that all my strength comes from the Lord. I embrace both humility and boldness as I fulfill the purpose God has set for me.

August 18
Pursuing Your Dreams Without Fear

"For the Spirit God gave us does not make us timid, but gives us power, love and self-discipline." (2 Timothy 1:7, NIV)

Devotional Reflection

Pursuing your dreams can be both exciting and intimidating, especially when fear creeps in. As Black women, internal doubts may cause us to hesitate or question our ability to achieve the desires God has placed on our hearts. But God has not given us a spirit of fear, but one of power, love, and self-discipline. Stepping forward in faith, trusting God to guide your path, allows you to pursue your dreams with confidence, knowing He is equipping you for the journey.

God places dreams within you for a reason. They align with His purpose for your life. Fear may keep you stuck, but faith propels you forward, relying on God's power to help you overcome obstacles and persevere. Trust that as you step out in faith, God will make a way for your dreams to come to fruition.

Today, reflect on the dreams God has placed on your heart. Ask Him for the strength to move forward without fear, trusting His guidance.

Prayer

Lord, thank You for the dreams and desires You have placed in my heart. Help me to pursue them without fear, trusting that You are guiding my steps. Give me the courage to move forward in faith, knowing that You have equipped me with the power, love, and self-discipline I need to fulfill the purpose You have set before me. Amen.

Affirmation

I pursue my dreams with faith and confidence, trusting that God has placed them in my heart for a purpose. I move forward without fear, knowing that He is guiding me and equipping me for success.

August 19
Overcoming Comparison and Embracing Your Journey

"Let us not become conceited, provoking and envying each other."
(Galatians 5:26, NIV)

Devotional Reflection

Comparison is a common trap that can steal joy and confidence. As Black women, we may face additional pressures to measure up to others' expectations or achievements. Yet, comparison distracts us from the unique path God has designed for each of us. Your journey is filled with purpose, growth, and opportunities tailored for your gifts. Embracing your path means trusting that what God has for you is more than enough.

Overcoming comparison requires recognizing that no two paths are the same. When you focus on others, you miss the beauty of what God is doing in your life. Instead of looking outward, focus on the gifts and experiences God has given you. Trust that His plan for your life is perfect, and your journey, though different, is leading you where you need to be.

Today, reflect on any areas where comparison has crept in. Ask God to help you release those thoughts and find confidence in your unique path.

Prayer

Lord, help me to overcome the trap of comparison and to embrace the unique path You have set for me. Teach me to trust Your plan for my life and to find confidence in the journey You have called me to walk. Strengthen me to focus on Your purpose for me, knowing that I am exactly where I need to be. Amen.

Affirmation

I release the trap of comparison and embrace my unique journey with confidence. I trust that God's plan for my life is perfect, and I focus on the path He has designed specifically for me, knowing that I am right where I need to be.

August 20
Confidence in God's Promises

"Let us hold unswervingly to the hope we profess, for he who promised is faithful." (Hebrews 10:23, NIV)

Devotional Reflection

Life's uncertainties can shake our confidence and make us doubt our path. As Black women, the challenges we face may feel overwhelming, making it easy to lose sight of God's promises. Yet, God's promises are unchanging, even when our circumstances feel unstable. Confidence in His promises means holding onto hope, knowing that what He has spoken will come to pass, no matter how long the wait or how hard the journey.

God's promises offer strength and comfort during uncertain times. Whether waiting for a breakthrough, navigating a tough season, or unsure of what's next, His Word provides the foundation for standing firm in faith. By reminding yourself of His promises—of provision, protection, peace, and purpose—you can walk in boldness, trusting that He will fulfill them in His perfect time.

Today, reflect on the promises God has made to you. Hold onto them with bold faith, trusting that He is working, even when you can't see it. Let His promises guide you through any uncertainty.

Prayer

Lord, thank You for Your unchanging promises. Help me to hold onto them with bold faith, especially during times of uncertainty. Strengthen my confidence in Your Word and remind me that You are faithful to fulfill every promise You have made. Teach me to trust in Your timing and to walk boldly in the hope that You provide. Amen.

Affirmation

I hold onto God's promises with unwavering faith, trusting that He is faithful to fulfill them in His perfect time. I move through life's uncertainties with confidence, knowing that God's Word is true and His promises are unchanging.

August 21
Breaking Free from Past Mistakes

"Therefore, if anyone is in Christ, the new creation has come: The old has gone, the new is here!" (2 Corinthians 5:17, NIV)

Devotional Reflection

Past mistakes can weigh heavily on us, filling our hearts with guilt, shame, and regret. As black women, we may feel the additional pressure to live up to certain standards or expectations, making it even harder to forgive ourselves for our past failures. But God's grace is greater than any mistake we've made. In Christ, we are made new, and the weight of past failures no longer defines us. Walking confidently in God's grace means accepting His forgiveness and embracing the fresh start He has given us.

Breaking free from past mistakes requires us to release the guilt and shame that often hold us back. God does not call us to dwell in our failures but to learn from them, grow, and move forward in His grace. When we let go of the past, we are able to step into the future with confidence, knowing that we are fully loved and forgiven. God's grace covers every shortcoming, and His mercy allows us to walk in freedom, free from the chains of our mistakes.

Today, reflect on any past mistakes that may still be holding you back. Surrender them to God, accepting His grace and forgiveness, and walk confidently into the new life He has given you.

Prayer

Lord, thank You for Your grace and forgiveness. Help me break free from past mistakes and walk confidently in the new life You've given me. Remind me I'm defined by Your love, not my failures. Teach me to embrace Your grace and move forward with faith. Amen.

Affirmation

I break free from the weight of past mistakes and walk confidently in God's grace. I am no longer defined by my failures, but by the new life and freedom that God has given me. I move forward with boldness, trusting in His mercy and love.

August 22
Courage to Make Tough Decisions

"Trust in the Lord with all your heart and lean not on your own understanding; in all your ways submit to him, and he will make your paths straight." (Proverbs 3:5-6, NIV)

Devotional Reflection
Making tough decisions is one of life's greatest challenges. As Black women, we often face difficult choices in our careers, families, or personal lives. The pressure to make the "right" decision can feel overwhelming, and fear of making a mistake can paralyze us. However, God calls us to trust Him fully in the decision-making process. His wisdom is far greater than ours, and when we lean on Him, He promises to guide our steps.

Trusting God's guidance doesn't mean every decision will be easy, but it assures us that He is walking with us through each choice. God sees the bigger picture and knows the path that is best, even when it's unclear in the moment. Courage comes from trusting that He is leading us. When we submit our decisions to God, He promises to guide us toward what is best for our lives and purpose.

Today, if you face a tough decision, bring it to God in prayer. Ask Him for the courage to make the choice, trusting He will lead you, even when the path seems uncertain.

Prayer
Lord, I ask for Your guidance as I face difficult decisions. Help me to trust in Your wisdom, even when the choice is hard. Give me the courage to make decisions in faith, knowing that You are leading me every step of the way. Teach me to lean not on my own understanding, but to trust in Your perfect plan for my life. Amen.

Affirmation
I trust in God's guidance as I make tough decisions, knowing that He is leading me on the right path. I have the courage to make choices with faith and confidence, trusting that God's wisdom will guide me to what is best for my life and purpose.

August 23
Confidence in Your Leadership

"The Lord will make you the head, not the tail. If you pay attention to the commands of the Lord your God that I give you this day and carefully follow them, you will always be at the top, never at the bottom." (Deuteronomy 28:13, NIV)

Devotional Reflection

Stepping into leadership can feel overwhelming, especially when doubt arises about your ability to guide others. As Black women, we often carry the weight of additional expectations, making leadership seem even more daunting. However, God has positioned you for a reason and equipped you with everything you need to lead with faith, courage, and purpose. Leadership isn't just about a title; it's about serving others with the gifts God has given you.

Confidence in leadership begins by knowing God is your strength. You don't have to rely solely on your abilities—God walks with you every step. He has called you to lead with purpose and direction. Trusting in His guidance allows you to embrace your role confidently, knowing He will provide the wisdom and grace needed to inspire and uplift those you lead.

Today, reflect on your leadership roles—whether at home, work, church, or in the community. Ask God for confidence to lead with faith, trusting He has equipped and will guide you in every decision.

Prayer

Lord, thank You for placing me in leadership. Help me embrace this role with faith, courage, and purpose, trusting You've equipped me with the skills and wisdom I need. Strengthen my confidence and guide me to honor You in all I do. Amen.

Affirmation

I embrace my role as a leader with confidence, knowing that God has equipped me to lead with faith, courage, and purpose. I trust in His guidance and wisdom as I serve and inspire others.

August 24
Courage to Advocate for Yourself

"So we say with confidence, 'The Lord is my helper; I will not be afraid. What can mere mortals do to me?'" (Hebrews 13:6, NIV)

Devotional Reflection

Advocating for yourself can be challenging, especially when you've been taught to prioritize others or stay silent in discomfort. As Black women, we often face unique challenges in ensuring our voices are heard and our needs are met. Yet, God calls us to live boldly and confidently, trusting that He is with us when we speak up. Courage to advocate for yourself means recognizing that your needs matter just as much as anyone else's.

Standing up for yourself requires faith and confidence in God's guidance. When you advocate for your needs—whether in relationships, at work, or in daily life—you honor the person God created you to be. Expressing your desires or setting boundaries is an act of self-respect, trusting in the value God has placed on your life. With His strength, you can speak boldly, knowing your voice matters.

Today, reflect on areas where you need to advocate for yourself. Ask God for the courage and confidence to speak up, trusting He will guide you with grace and strength.

Prayer

Lord, give me the courage to advocate for myself in every area of my life. Help me to stand firm in my needs and desires, trusting that You are my helper and that I am worthy of being heard. Strengthen my confidence as I speak up with boldness, knowing that You are with me in every step. Amen.

Affirmation

I have the courage to advocate for myself, trusting that my needs and desires are valuable. I stand confidently, knowing that God is my helper and that my voice deserves to be heard.

August 25
Walking with Confidence in Unfamiliar Spaces

"Have I not commanded you? Be strong and courageous. Do not be afraid; do not be discouraged, for the Lord your God will be with you wherever you go." (Joshua 1:9, NIV)

Devotional Reflection

Walking into unfamiliar spaces—whether it's a new job, environment, or unexpected situation—can feel intimidating. As Black women, we may often find ourselves in spaces where we feel out of place or underrepresented, making it harder to feel confident. Yet, God's promise is clear: He is with us wherever we go. His presence extends to every corner of our lives, giving us strength and courage to move forward with confidence.

When you trust that God is walking beside you, you can embrace unfamiliar spaces with boldness, knowing you are never alone. His presence is your source of confidence, guiding you through the unknown and equipping you for each new challenge. While discomfort may arise, God's assurance allows you to stand tall and move forward with grace. He has a purpose for placing you in these spaces.

Today, reflect on any unfamiliar or uncomfortable spaces you may face. Ask God for the confidence to move forward, trusting that His presence will guide and strengthen you in every moment.

Prayer

Lord, thank You for Your constant presence. Help me walk confidently in unfamiliar spaces, trusting You are with me every step. Give me courage to embrace new challenges, knowing You are guiding and strengthening me. Amen.

Affirmation

I walk with confidence in unfamiliar spaces, trusting that God's presence is with me wherever I go. I face new challenges with boldness, knowing that He is guiding and strengthening me every step of the way.

August 26
Confidence in Your Financial Decisions

"And my God will meet all your needs according to the riches of his glory in Christ Jesus." (Philippians 4:19, NIV)

Devotional Reflection

Managing finances can feel overwhelming, especially when faced with decisions that impact your future. As Black women, we may carry the weight of providing for ourselves, our families, or even our communities, adding pressure to make the "right" financial choices. However, God reminds us that He is our ultimate provider, and we can trust in His provision as we make decisions with wisdom and faith.

Confidence in financial decisions starts with seeking God's guidance. He cares about every aspect of your life, including your financial well-being. When you invite God into decisions—whether budgeting, investing, or giving—you can rest in the assurance that He will provide. Acting with wisdom, trusting in God's provision, and being good stewards of His resources are all ways to honor Him. God's promises assure us He will meet our needs, even when resources seem limited.

Today, reflect on your financial decisions. Ask God for wisdom and guidance, trusting He will provide and give you confidence to make decisions that honor Him.

Prayer

Lord, thank You for being my provider in every aspect of my life. Help me to make financial decisions with wisdom and faith in Your provision. Guide me in being a good steward of the resources You have given me, and remind me that You will meet all my needs according to Your riches and glory. Amen.

Affirmation

I make financial decisions with wisdom and confidence, trusting in God's provision. He will meet all my needs, and I honor Him by being a good steward of the resources He has given me.

August 27
Courage to Start Again

"The righteous may fall seven times, but they rise again."

(Proverbs 24:16, NIV)

Devotional Reflection

Setbacks and disappointments are inevitable, and they can leave us feeling discouraged. As Black women, we may face unique challenges that make the journey harder. Whether it's a career setback, broken relationship, or missed opportunity, starting again can feel daunting. Yet, God reminds us that even when we fall, we can rise again. He gives us the strength to rebuild and move forward, no matter how many times we've been knocked down.

Having the courage to start again requires faith in God's ability to renew, restore, and guide us. Every setback is an opportunity for growth, and with God's help, disappointment can become a stepping stone toward something greater. His grace will carry you through the rebuilding process. Starting again is not failure; it's a testament to your strength and God's unwavering support.

Today, reflect on any setbacks you've experienced. Ask God for the courage to start again, trusting that He is with you and will guide you toward greater opportunities.

Prayer

Lord, give me the courage to start again after setbacks. Help me trust in Your strength as I rebuild, knowing You are with me. Teach me to see setbacks as growth opportunities and give me faith to move forward with hope. Amen.

Affirmation

I have the courage to start again, trusting in God's strength to guide me through setbacks and disappointments. I rise with faith and resilience, knowing that God is with me in the rebuilding process and will lead me to greater opportunities.

August 28
Facing Health Challenges with Confidence

"Lord my God, I called to you for help, and you healed me."

(Psalm 30:2, NIV)

Devotional Reflection

Facing health challenges can be a difficult and emotional journey. As black women, we may feel the pressure to remain strong even when our bodies are struggling. But God reminds us that we are not alone in our health battles. He is a healer, and we can trust His plan for our bodies, even when we don't understand it. Confidence in the face of health challenges comes from knowing that God is with you every step of the way, and His healing power is always available to you.

Trusting God's healing means releasing the fear and anxiety that often accompany health struggles and placing your faith in His ability to restore you. Whether you're dealing with a minor ailment or a more serious condition, God is able to provide peace, strength, and healing according to His will. He may heal instantly, through medical care, or over time, but His plan is always for your good. As you walk through health challenges, lean on God's promises and trust that He will carry you through with love and care.

Today, take a moment to lift your health concerns to God. Ask for His healing power and trust His plan for your body. Rest in the knowledge that He is working in you, even when the path to healing is uncertain.

Prayer

Lord, I trust You with my health and body. Help me to face health challenges with confidence, knowing that Your healing power is at work in me. Guide me through this journey and give me the strength, peace, and faith to trust in Your plan for my healing. Amen.

Affirmation

I face health challenges with confidence, trusting in God's healing power and plan for my body. I rest in His peace, knowing that He is with me every step of the way, guiding me toward healing and restoration.

August 29
Confidence in Building New Relationships

"A friend loves at all times, and a brother is born for a time of adversity." (Proverbs 17:17, NIV)

Devotional Reflection

Building new relationships can feel intimidating, especially after past hurts or rejections. As Black women, we may carry the weight of past experiences, making it harder to open up to new friendships. However, God designed us for community, placing people in our lives to support and uplift us. Confidence in building new relationships starts with trusting that God will guide you to connections that reflect His love and grace.

Opening your heart to new friendships requires faith in God's plan for your relationships. Just as He provides for your physical and spiritual needs, He also provides for your emotional and relational needs. Whether in your career, church, or social circle, trust that God is aligning you with people who will bring growth and joy. He will give you discernment to recognize genuine connections and the courage to open your heart.

Today, reflect on your openness to new relationships. Ask God to guide you to the right friendships and give you confidence to trust His purpose in every connection.

Prayer

Lord, help me trust You as I open my heart to new friendships. Give me confidence to build connections, knowing You will guide me to the right people. Strengthen my faith in Your plan, and help me foster meaningful relationships that reflect Your love. Amen.

Affirmation

I confidently open my heart to new relationships, trusting that God will guide me to meaningful connections that reflect His love and grace. I embrace new friendships with faith, knowing that God has a purpose in every person He brings into my life.

August 30
Courage to Embrace Change

"For I am the Lord your God who takes hold of your right hand and says to you, Do not fear; I will help you." (Isaiah 41:13, NIV)

Devotional Reflection

Change can be challenging, especially when it disrupts comfort and stability. As Black women, we may face various life transitions—whether a career shift, a move, or personal growth—that can stir up fear or anxiety. Yet, God calls us to lean on Him during these moments, promising to be our helper and providing the strength we need to navigate transitions with courage.

Embracing change requires faith in God's plan, even when the path is unclear. Life transitions are opportunities for growth, and God is always at work, shaping us through every season. While change can feel unsettling, we can trust that God will provide guidance and peace as we move forward. When we rely on His strength, we can face change with courage, knowing He is with us every step of the journey.

Today, reflect on any changes or transitions you're currently facing. Ask God for the courage to embrace these moments, trusting that He will provide the strength and guidance you need.

Prayer

Lord, give me the courage to embrace the changes and transitions in my life. Help me to lean on Your strength and trust that You are guiding me through every step. Remind me that I don't have to face change alone, for You are always with me, providing comfort, peace, and direction. Amen.

Affirmation

I embrace change with courage, trusting that God is guiding me through every transition. I lean on His strength, knowing that He holds my hand and walks with me through every life shift.

August 31
Bold Faith in the Face of Uncertainty

"Now faith is confidence in what we hope for and assurance about what we do not see." (Hebrews 11:1, NIV)

Devotional Reflection

Uncertainty can leave us feeling anxious or overwhelmed, especially when the future is unclear. As Black women, navigating an uncertain future can carry extra layers of complexity. Yet, God calls us to have bold faith, even when we can't see the full picture. Faith isn't about knowing every detail, but about trusting God to guide and provide for us along the way. In uncertain times, bold faith anchors us and keeps us moving forward with confidence.

God promises to be with us in every season, including those filled with unknowns. His plan is good, even when it's not immediately visible. Bold faith in uncertainty means surrendering control and trusting that God's wisdom and provision are greater than our fears. Walking in faith opens us to His greater purpose, knowing He is in control and will never leave us.

Today, reflect on any areas of uncertainty in your life. Ask God for bold faith to trust Him completely, knowing He is guiding you, even when the future feels unclear.

Prayer

Lord, strengthen my faith in moments of uncertainty. Help me to trust You completely, knowing that You are guiding me even when the future is unclear. Give me the boldness to walk in faith, trusting that Your plan is greater than my fears. Thank You for being my constant source of hope and assurance. Amen.

Affirmation

I have bold faith in the face of uncertainty, trusting that God is guiding me even when I can't see the full picture. I walk confidently, knowing that His plan for my life is good and He is always with me, providing strength and assurance.

September
Wisdom and Learning

September 1
The Beginning of Wisdom

"The fear of the Lord is the beginning of wisdom, and knowledge of the Holy One is understanding."(Proverbs 9:10, NIV)

Devotional Reflection

True wisdom begins with recognizing God's sovereignty and greatness. As black women navigating life's complexities, we often seek knowledge from many sources, but the Bible reminds us that the foundation of all wisdom is reverence for God. It's not about being afraid of God, but about holding a deep respect and awe for His power, love, and authority. When we start with this understanding, our perspective on life shifts, and we begin to make decisions rooted in God's will, not just our own understanding.

Reverence for God means acknowledging His role as the source of all knowledge, guidance, and truth. It means seeking Him first before relying on our own instincts or the opinions of others. When we honor God in this way, we open ourselves up to receiving divine wisdom that leads us on the right path. True wisdom isn't about knowing all the answers but about knowing the One who holds them.

Today, reflect on your relationship with God. Are you placing Him at the center of your decision-making and seeking His wisdom first? Ask Him to help you develop a deeper reverence for His guidance in every aspect of your life.

Prayer

Lord, help me to recognize that true wisdom starts with reverence for You. Teach me to seek Your guidance in all areas of my life and to trust in Your wisdom above my own. Strengthen my relationship with You, and lead me down the path of righteousness. Amen.

Affirmation

I begin my pursuit of wisdom by honoring God, seeking His guidance in every decision. I trust that He is the source of true knowledge and understanding, and I will walk in His wisdom.

September 2
Learning from Past Mistakes

"My flesh and my heart may fail, but God is the strength of my heart and my portion forever."(Psalm 73:26, NIV)

Devotional Reflection

Mistakes are an inevitable part of life, and while they can be painful or discouraging, they also provide valuable opportunities for growth and wisdom. As black women, the pressures we face may make us feel like we must avoid failure at all costs. However, God doesn't expect perfection—He invites us to learn and grow from our experiences, both good and bad. Past mistakes don't define who we are, but how we respond to them shapes our future.

Reflecting on your mistakes allows you to gain insight into what didn't work, and it offers a chance to adjust your actions moving forward. Each error can be a stepping stone, moving you closer to God's purpose for your life. Learning from mistakes means surrendering the guilt or shame that often follows and embracing the lessons that God is teaching you through these experiences. Instead of dwelling on what went wrong, focus on the strength and wisdom God gives you to overcome and grow.

Today, reflect on the past mistakes that you have been carrying. Ask God to show you the lessons He wants you to learn and to help you turn these missteps into valuable stepping stones for the future.

Prayer

Lord, thank You for turning my past mistakes into opportunities for growth. Help me to reflect on my errors with grace and to gain wisdom from the lessons You are teaching me. Strengthen me as I move forward, trusting in Your guidance and plan for my life. Amen.

Affirmation

I learn from my past mistakes and use them as stepping stones toward growth and wisdom. I trust in God's ability to guide me, knowing that every misstep brings me closer to fulfilling His purpose for my life.

September 3
Seeking God's Guidance in Tough Choices

"If any of you lacks wisdom, you should ask God, who gives generously to all without finding fault, and it will be given to you."

(James 1:5, NIV)

Devotional Reflection

Life is filled with moments of difficult decisions, and the pressure to make the right choice can feel overwhelming. As Black women, we juggle multiple responsibilities, and these choices can impact our families, careers, and personal lives. In these moments, turning to God for guidance is essential. His Word is full of wisdom, and when we seek Him, He promises to provide clarity.

Seeking God's guidance starts with prayer and reading His Word. God's voice is often heard in quiet reflection, scripture, or through the wisdom of trusted, godly people. When we surrender our will and invite God into our decisions, He generously provides the wisdom we need. No decision is too big or small for Him. Trusting God to guide us ensures our choices align with His will, bringing peace even in challenging situations.

Today, take time to seek guidance from God's Word in any tough decisions you face. Ask Him to direct your steps and give you the wisdom to make choices aligned with His purpose.

Prayer

Lord, I ask for Your wisdom and guidance as I face tough choices. Help me to turn to Your Word for direction and to trust in the answers You provide. Guide my steps, and help me make decisions that honor You and align with Your purpose for my life. Amen.

Affirmation

I seek God's guidance in all of my decisions, trusting Him to provide the wisdom I need. I turn to His Word for direction, knowing that His wisdom will lead me down the right path.

September 4
The Power of Listening

"My dear brothers and sisters, take note of this: Everyone should be quick to listen, slow to speak and slow to become angry."

(James 1:19, NIV)

Devotional Reflection

In a world filled with noise, it's easy to overlook the importance of truly listening—to others and to God. As Black women, we often do lot of things, making it hard to pause and be fully present. Yet, listening is a powerful act of love and respect. It deepens our connections and allows us to hear God's voice more clearly. When we practice intentional listening, we open ourselves to greater understanding and alignment with God's will.

Listening to others strengthens relationships and builds empathy. It requires setting aside our own thoughts and distractions. Similarly, listening for God's voice requires quieting our minds and being still. God speaks through scripture, prayer, and the wisdom of others, but we must pause to hear His guidance.

Today, make a conscious effort to listen more intently—to those around you and in your quiet moments with God. Ask Him to help you develop the skill of listening so you may grow in wisdom, understanding, and grace.

Prayer

Lord, teach me the power of listening. Help me to be quick to listen to others with empathy and patience, and to quiet my heart so I can hear Your voice clearly. Guide me in developing the skill of listening, so I can grow in wisdom and draw closer to You. Amen.

Affirmation

I embrace the power of listening, showing love and respect to others while tuning my heart to hear God's voice. I grow in wisdom and understanding by being still and attentive in every moment.

September 5
Learning Patience in Uncertain Seasons

"But if we hope for what we do not yet have, we wait for it patiently."(Romans 8:25, NIV)

Devotional Reflection

Uncertain seasons can test our patience and faith, especially when we don't know how long the waiting will last or what the outcome will be. As black women, we often face seasons of uncertainty, whether it's waiting on career opportunities, relationships, or personal growth. In these moments, it can be easy to become frustrated or anxious. However, God calls us to trust His timing and develop patience, knowing that His plans are always for our good.

Learning patience during uncertain times is not about passive waiting but about actively trusting God's timing and His process. It's in the waiting that God refines us, strengthens our faith, and teaches us valuable lessons. Though we may not see the full picture, God is always at work behind the scenes, preparing us for what lies ahead. Trusting in His timing means believing that everything will unfold according to His perfect plan, and that patience will lead to greater blessings.

Today, reflect on any areas of your life where you are experiencing uncertainty. Ask God to help you develop patience and trust in His timing, knowing that He is working all things together for your good.

Prayer

Lord, help me to be patient during uncertain seasons. Teach me to trust Your timing and to rest in the knowledge that You are always at work in my life. Strengthen my faith as I wait, and remind me that Your plans are perfect, even when I cannot see them clearly. Amen.

Affirmation

I trust God's timing in every season of my life. I embrace patience, knowing that God is working behind the scenes, and I wait with faith, confident that His plan will unfold at the right time.

September 6
Surrounding Yourself with Wise Counsel

"Where there is no counsel, the people fall; but in the multitude of counselors there is safety."(Proverbs 11:14, NIV)

Devotional Reflection

Having wise, godly counsel in your life is essential for growth, guidance, and making sound decisions. As black women, we may feel the need to handle everything on our own, but God encourages us to seek wisdom from others. Surrounding yourself with trusted individuals who share your values and walk in faith can provide clarity, support, and encouragement, especially during challenging times. These individuals can offer perspective and insight that help you stay aligned with God's will for your life.

Building a support system means seeking out those who will speak truth into your life, even when it's hard to hear. Wise counsel not only helps us avoid pitfalls but also strengthens our walk with God. It's important to be intentional about who you allow to influence you. The right people will guide you with wisdom and love, helping you make decisions that reflect God's plan and bring peace.

Today, take a moment to reflect on the people you have in your life. Are you surrounded by wise counsel? If not, pray for God to bring the right individuals into your life—those who will support you with wisdom, faith, and truth.

Prayer

Lord, thank You for the gift of wise counsel. Surround me with godly individuals who offer guidance, support, and encouragement. Help me seek wisdom from those reflecting Your truth, and give me discernment to listen with an open heart. Amen.

Affirmation

I surround myself with wise, godly counsel, trusting in the guidance of those who reflect God's truth and wisdom. I am open to receiving advice that aligns with God's plan for my life and helps me make sound decisions.

September 7
Embracing Humility in the Learning Process

"When pride comes, then comes disgrace, but with humility comes wisdom."(Proverbs 11:2, NIV)

Devotional Reflection

Humility is key to growth and wisdom, but it can be difficult to embrace, especially when we feel the need to have all the answers or to appear strong and capable. As black women, we often carry a lot of responsibility, and the pressure to "know it all" can sometimes lead us to rely solely on our own understanding. However, God calls us to approach the learning process with humility, recognizing that true wisdom comes when we are open to learning from others, from our experiences, and most importantly, from Him.

Humility allows us to admit that we don't know everything and that we can always grow and improve. It keeps us teachable, creating space for God to pour His wisdom into our lives. When we embrace humility, we let go of the need to appear perfect and instead focus on becoming wiser and stronger through the lessons God is teaching us. Growth comes not from pride or self-reliance, but from a humble heart that is willing to learn.

Today, reflect on how humility plays a role in your learning process. Ask God to help you embrace humility so that you can grow in wisdom and be open to the lessons He is bringing into your life.

Prayer

Lord, help me to embrace humility in my journey of growth and learning. Teach me to let go of pride and the need to have all the answers, and open my heart to receive the wisdom that comes from You. Guide me as I learn from my experiences, from others, and from Your Word. Amen.

Affirmation

I embrace humility in the learning process, recognizing that it opens the door to wisdom and growth. I am teachable, knowing that God is continually guiding me to greater understanding and strength.

September 8
Wisdom in Financial Stewardship

"The plans of the diligent lead to profit as surely as haste leads to poverty."(Proverbs 21:5, NIV)

Devotional Reflection

Managing finances is a key part of living a responsible and balanced life. As Black women, we may face financial challenges that require careful planning and wise decision-making. God calls us to be good stewards of the resources He has blessed us with, aligning our spending, saving, and giving with His principles.

Wisdom in financial stewardship means planning diligently, avoiding impulsive decisions, and seeking God's guidance in how we use our money. This includes budgeting, being mindful of debt, and being generous. When we trust God with our finances, we can rest in the assurance that He will guide us to manage them well. Financial wisdom also allows us to bless others and contribute to God's work.

Today, consider your approach to managing finances. Are you inviting God into your financial decisions? Ask Him for wisdom to be a good steward and commit to managing your resources in a way that honors Him.

Prayer

Lord, thank You for the resources You've provided. Help me to manage my finances with wisdom and to be a good steward of what You've entrusted to me. Guide me in planning diligently, avoiding impulsive decisions, and being generous to others. Teach me to trust You with every financial decision I make. Amen.

Affirmation

I manage my finances with wisdom and diligence, trusting God to guide me in every financial decision. I am a good steward of the resources He has provided, using them to honor Him and to bless others.

September 9
The Importance of Lifelong Learning

"Instruct the wise and they will be wiser still; teach the righteous and they will add to their learning."(Proverbs 9:9, NIV)

Devotional Reflection

Life is a continuous journey of growth, and embracing the mindset of lifelong learning is essential to becoming wiser and more fulfilled. As black women, we may often focus on achieving certain milestones or overcoming challenges, but it's important to remember that learning doesn't stop at a certain age or after reaching a particular goal. God invites us to keep growing, to seek knowledge, and to stay open to new lessons and experiences throughout our lives.

Lifelong learning isn't limited to formal education—it includes learning from everyday experiences, people, scripture, and the world around us. When we adopt a mindset of constant learning, we remain humble, teachable, and adaptable to what God wants to show us. This allows us to continue to grow spiritually, emotionally, and mentally, ensuring that we are always evolving into the person God has called us to be.

Today, reflect on how you approach learning in your life. Are you open to new ideas and lessons, even when they come from unexpected places? Ask God to help you cultivate a spirit of lifelong learning, trusting that He will continue to guide you in wisdom.

Prayer

Lord, help me to embrace the mindset of lifelong learning. Teach me to be open to new lessons and experiences, knowing that You are continually guiding me toward growth and wisdom. Keep my heart humble and teachable, and help me to seek knowledge that will enrich my life and strengthen my walk with You. Amen.

Affirmation

I embrace lifelong learning in all areas of my life. I remain open to new lessons and experiences, trusting that God is always guiding me toward greater wisdom, growth, and fulfillment.

September 10
Making Peace with Mistakes

"My grace is sufficient for you, for my power is made perfect in weakness."(2 Corinthians 12:9, NIV)

Devotional Reflection

Mistakes are an inevitable part of life, and learning to make peace with them is essential for growth. As black women, we may feel pressure to excel and avoid failure, but God's grace reminds us that our worth is not tied to perfection. Mistakes are not the end; they are opportunities for valuable lessons that can shape us into wiser, stronger individuals. When we embrace our imperfections and learn from them, we grow closer to God's purpose for our lives.

Making peace with mistakes means letting go of guilt and shame. God's grace is more than enough to cover our shortcomings, and He uses even our errors to teach us important lessons. Every misstep can guide us toward better choices and a deeper understanding of ourselves and God's plan. It's not about avoiding failure, but about how we rise from it, trusting that God is working through every experience for our good.

Today, reflect on any mistakes that are weighing on you. Ask God to help you make peace with them, learning the lessons He wants to teach, and embracing His grace as you move forward.

Prayer

Lord, thank You for Your grace that covers all my mistakes. Help me to make peace with my imperfections and to learn the valuable lessons You have for me. Teach me to trust that even in my weaknesses, Your strength is at work, and guide me to move forward with faith and wisdom. Amen.

Affirmation

I make peace with my mistakes, trusting in God's grace and wisdom. I learn valuable lessons from every misstep, knowing that God's strength is made perfect in my weaknesses. I move forward with confidence and faith.

September 11
Practicing Discernment in Relationships

"Walk with the wise and become wise, for a companion of fools suffers harm."(Proverbs 13:20, NIV)

Devotional Reflection

Relationships deeply affect our spiritual, emotional, and mental well-being. As Black women, we often carry significant relational responsibilities, making it essential to practice discernment in choosing who we allow into our lives. Healthy relationships reflect God's love, while unhealthy connections can drain our energy and pull us from our purpose.

Practicing discernment means seeking God's guidance in all relationships—family, friendships, or romantic connections. Not every relationship is meant to last, and some may require boundaries or even separation. God desires us to walk with those who uplift and encourage us toward His will. Discernment helps us recognize when a relationship is aligned with God's purpose and when it's time to step away for our well-being.

Today, reflect on the relationships in your life. Ask God for wisdom in maintaining the healthy ones and the courage to release any that may be hindering your growth.

Prayer

Lord, grant me discernment to choose and maintain healthy relationships that reflect Your love. Help me recognize those You've placed in my life for growth and set boundaries when needed. Give me wisdom to walk with those who uplift and guide me closer to You. Amen.

Affirmation

I practice discernment in my relationships, choosing to walk with those who reflect God's love and wisdom. I maintain healthy connections and trust God's guidance in setting boundaries when needed.

September 12
Learning Through Adversity

"Consider it pure joy, my brothers and sisters, whenever you face trials of many kinds, because you know that the testing of your faith produces perseverance."(James 1:2-3, NIV)

Devotional Reflection

Adversity is inevitable, and while it brings discomfort and pain, it also offers opportunities for growth. As Black women, we may face unique struggles, but God uses these trials to strengthen our faith and shape us into more resilient individuals. Each difficulty reveals something about ourselves, God, and the world around us. Through adversity, we learn to trust God more deeply and gain wisdom for future challenges.

Learning through adversity requires us to shift our perspective, recognizing God's purpose in each trial. While it's natural to avoid hardship, it's often during difficult seasons that God's presence is most evident, guiding and refining us. Trials test our faith, but they also build perseverance and equip us with the wisdom to face future obstacles. Trusting that God is using adversity for our good helps us endure and emerge stronger.

Today, reflect on any trials you're facing. Ask God to help you find wisdom in these challenges and trust that He is working out His purpose through them.

Prayer

Lord, help me to find wisdom in the adversity I face. Teach me to trust Your purpose in difficult times and to rely on Your strength to carry me through. Amen.

Affirmation

I find wisdom in adversity, trusting that God is using trials to strengthen and refine me. I embrace His purpose in difficult times, knowing that He is guiding me and helping me grow through every challenge.

September 13
Using Your Knowledge to Uplift Others

"Let the wise listen and add to their learning, and let the discerning get guidance."(Proverbs 1:5, NIV)

Devotional Reflection

Our knowledge and experiences are not just for ourselves; they are meant to uplift and empower others. As Black women, our journeys often involve overcoming challenges and gaining wisdom. When we use the knowledge we've gained to help others, we become vessels of God's grace and encouragement. Sharing your wisdom can uplift someone in need of direction or support, and it helps build a stronger sense of community.

God calls us to use what we've learned to bless others. Whether through mentorship, friendships, or casual conversations, sharing your experiences provides encouragement and practical insight to those walking a similar path. Your story can inspire someone to keep going, and your wisdom can guide others to make wise decisions. By uplifting others, you become part of God's greater plan to build His kingdom through love and service.

Today, consider how you can use your knowledge and experiences to uplift others. Ask God for opportunities to share what you've learned to encourage and empower those around you.

Prayer

Lord, thank You for the knowledge and wisdom You've given me through my experiences. Help me to use what I've learned to uplift and empower others. Show me the opportunities where I can share my story and offer encouragement, and guide my words so that they reflect Your love and grace. Amen.

Affirmation

I use my knowledge and experiences to uplift others, sharing wisdom that encourages and empowers those around me. I trust that God is using my story to inspire others and build a stronger community in His love.

September 14
The Value of Quiet Reflection

"Be still, and know that I am God."(Psalm 46:10, NIV)

Devotional Reflection

In a world full of constant activity and noise, the value of quiet reflection is often overlooked. Yet, it is in moments of stillness that we are best able to hear God's voice and gain clarity in our lives. As black women, the demands of daily life can pull us in many directions, making it challenging to find time to pause and reflect. However, God invites us to be still, to quiet our minds, and to seek His presence through reflection. It is through these quiet moments that we can gain wisdom, clarity, and a deeper connection with God.

Quiet reflection allows us to slow down and create space for God's guidance. When we remove distractions and embrace stillness, we can reflect on our thoughts, decisions, and experiences in the light of God's Word. This practice not only brings us peace but also helps us align our hearts and minds with His will. Reflection enables us to see the lessons God is teaching us and provides the wisdom we need to move forward with purpose and direction.

Today, take time to be still and reflect. Ask God to meet you in that quiet space and provide wisdom and clarity for any challenges or decisions you are facing.

Prayer

Lord, help me to embrace the value of quiet reflection. In the stillness, I seek Your wisdom and guidance. Teach me to pause and listen for Your voice, knowing that You speak to me in the silence. Give me clarity and peace as I reflect on Your Word and my life. Amen.

Affirmation

I embrace quiet reflection, seeking God's wisdom and peace in moments of stillness. I trust that God meets me in the silence, providing clarity and direction for my life.

September 15
Applying Biblical Teachings to Daily Decisions

"Your word is a lamp for my feet, a light on my path.
(Psalm 119:105, NIV)

Devotional Reflection

The Word of God is not just for Sunday sermons or spiritual reflection; it is meant to be applied to every part of our lives, including our daily decisions. As black women navigating various roles and responsibilities, we often face choices that affect our families, careers, and personal lives. God has given us His Word to be our guide, offering wisdom and direction for every decision we make. When we turn to scripture, we find guidance that helps us align our choices with God's will.

Applying biblical teachings to daily decisions means making an intentional effort to incorporate God's Word into our thought process. Whether it's a major life choice or a small, everyday decision, the Bible provides principles that can help us discern what is right. God's Word serves as a lamp that lights our way, giving us clarity and helping us to walk in His truth. When we allow scripture to influence our actions, we make decisions that reflect God's love, grace, and wisdom.

Today, consider the decisions you are facing, big or small. Ask God to help you apply His Word to each choice, trusting that His guidance will lead you on the right path.

Prayer

Lord, thank You for giving me Your Word as a guide for my life. Help me to apply biblical teachings to my daily decisions, allowing Your wisdom to shape my actions and choices. Teach me to rely on scripture for guidance, knowing that Your Word is a lamp to my feet and a light to my path. Amen.

Affirmation

I apply God's Word to my daily decisions, trusting in His wisdom to guide my choices. His Word is my constant source of direction, and I walk confidently, knowing that I am following His truth.

September 16
Guarding Your Mind with Wisdom

"The heart of the discerning acquires knowledge, for the ears of the wise seek it out." (Proverbs 18:15, NIV)

Devotional Reflection

Our minds are constantly bombarded with messages from the world around us, many of which can be negative, discouraging, or even harmful. For Black women, navigating these influences can feel overwhelming, especially when society places additional pressures on how we should look, act, and live. But God calls us to protect our thoughts and seek wisdom to guard our minds.

Imagine a woman scrolling through social media, constantly comparing herself to others and feeling less worthy. These subtle influences can cloud our judgment, leading us away from the peace God intends for us. However, when we choose to seek wisdom—whether through scripture, prayer, or wise counsel—we protect our minds from negative thoughts. Wisdom gives us the strength to recognize unhealthy influences and allows us to focus on what is true and good.

Today, remember that your mind is precious. Guard it with wisdom, and allow God's truth to shape your thoughts and actions.

Prayer

Lord, guide me to seek wisdom daily and protect my mind from negativity, filling me with Your truth. Amen.

Affirmation

I guard my thoughts with wisdom, and I choose to focus on what is good, true, and aligned with God's plan for me.

September 17
Wisdom in Parenting Decisions

"Start children off on the way they should go, and even when they are old, they will not turn from it." (Proverbs 22:6, NIV)

Devotional Reflection

Parenting is one of the most important and challenging responsibilities. As Black women, we often feel the weight of raising our children in a world that may not always value their worth. The decisions we make every day—what values to teach, how to discipline, and how to nurture—shape their futures. It's easy to feel uncertain and overwhelmed by the many choices we face, but God promises to guide us through the journey of motherhood.

Imagine standing at a crossroads, unsure which path will best lead your children to success. It can feel like a heavy burden. Yet, God is there, ready to offer His wisdom. By trusting Him with your parenting decisions, you're relying on divine wisdom rather than your own understanding. God knows your child's heart, and He will give you the insight and patience to raise them according to His purpose.

Prayer

Lord, grant me wisdom and strength in parenting, trusting You to guide my decisions for my children's growth. Amen.

Affirmation

I trust God's wisdom in guiding my parenting decisions and nurture my children with love, faith, and strength.

September 18
Growing in Wisdom Through Faith

"The fear of the Lord is the beginning of wisdom, and knowledge of the Holy One is understanding."(Proverbs 9:10, NIV)

Devotional Reflection

Wisdom and faith are deeply intertwined, and as our faith grows, so does our capacity to live wisely. As black women, we may often face challenges that require both strength and discernment. The foundation for making wise decisions in life begins with a deep, unwavering faith in God. When we trust Him fully, we open ourselves to His guidance and understanding, which leads us to make choices that align with His will.

Growing in wisdom through faith means recognizing that true wisdom doesn't come from the world or from our own understanding, but from God. The more we lean on Him, the more we understand His purpose for our lives. As we deepen our faith, we gain insight into how to navigate difficult circumstances, handle relationships, and make sound decisions that reflect our trust in God. Faith leads us to rely on His Word, and in doing so, we become wiser and more grounded in His truth.

Today, reflect on how your faith is influencing your decisions and actions. Ask God to continue growing your faith, knowing that it is the key to living a life filled with wisdom.

Prayer

Lord, help me to grow in wisdom through my faith in You. Strengthen my trust in Your guidance and give me the discernment to make wise decisions that reflect Your will. Teach me to lean on You in all things, knowing that true wisdom comes from You alone. Amen.

Affirmation

I grow in wisdom as I strengthen my faith in God. I trust Him to guide my decisions and actions, knowing that my wisdom is rooted in my relationship with Him.

September 19
Learning to Say "No" with Grace

"Let your 'Yes' be 'Yes,' and your 'No,' 'No'; anything beyond this comes from the evil one." (Matthew 5:37, NIV)

Devotional Reflection

Saying "no" can be difficult, especially when we want to please others or avoid conflict. As Black women, we may often feel the pressure to be everything to everyone, constantly giving of ourselves until we're depleted. However, there is wisdom in knowing when to say "no" and understanding that setting boundaries is essential for protecting your peace and well-being. God calls us to live with clarity and intentionality, which sometimes means knowing when to say "no" with grace.

Setting boundaries is not selfish; it's an act of self-care and stewardship of the life and energy God has given you. Saying "no" allows you to focus on what matters most, ensuring that your "yes" is given to the right people and the right purposes. When done with love and grace, saying "no" can help you maintain balance and peace, allowing you to serve and give from a place of wholeness, rather than exhaustion..

Prayer

Lord, help me to understand the wisdom in setting boundaries and saying "no" when necessary. Give me the courage to protect my peace and well-being, and teach me to say "no" with grace and love. Guide me in using my time and energy wisely, according to Your will for my life. Amen.

Affirmation

I embrace the wisdom of setting boundaries and saying "no" with grace. I protect my peace and well-being, knowing that I am honoring God by using my time and energy wisely.

September 20
Seeking Knowledge in Career Growth

"Do you see someone skilled in their work? They will serve before kings; they will not serve before officials of low rank."(Proverbs 22:29, NIV)

Devotional Reflection

Career growth is a journey that requires intentional learning and dedication. As black women, we often face unique challenges in the workplace, and the pursuit of knowledge can be a powerful tool in advancing your career and fulfilling your purpose. God has given each of us unique talents and skills, and seeking knowledge that aligns with your calling helps you refine those gifts. Whether it's through formal education, mentorship, or personal development, investing in learning opens doors to new opportunities and allows you to serve at a higher level.

It's important to approach your career with both passion and wisdom. Seeking knowledge doesn't just mean gaining new skills—it means aligning your growth with God's purpose for your life. As you pursue learning opportunities, ask God for direction in choosing paths that reflect your values and your calling. He will guide you to opportunities that not only advance your career but also allow you to make a meaningful impact in the lives of others.

Today, reflect on how you can seek knowledge to grow in your career. Ask God for wisdom in pursuing learning opportunities that align with His purpose for your life and help you thrive in your calling.

Prayer

Lord, thank You for my talents and skills. Guide me in seeking knowledge that aligns with Your purpose for my life. Help me pursue growth and learning opportunities to advance and serve others according to Your will. Amen.

Affirmation

I seek knowledge aligned with God's purpose for my life and career. I pursue growth and learning opportunities that allow me to make an impact and serve others.

September 21
Making Wise Decisions in Friendships

"The righteous choose their friends carefully, but the way of the wicked leads them astray."(Proverbs 12:26, NIV)

Devotional Reflection

Friendships are one of the most meaningful aspects of life, but choosing and maintaining the right friendships requires wisdom. As black women, we often navigate multiple roles and responsibilities, making it essential to build friendships that uplift, encourage, and align with God's values. Wise friendships are those that reflect God's love, where mutual respect, support, and spiritual growth thrive. These relationships not only nurture your spirit but also bring peace and joy into your life.

Making wise decisions in friendships means being intentional about who you allow into your inner circle. It's about recognizing the importance of surrounding yourself with people who inspire you to grow in your faith and walk with God. Sometimes, this means letting go of relationships that may no longer serve your spiritual growth or bring peace. God desires for you to have friendships that honor Him and bring out the best in you, creating a space where love, kindness, and wisdom flourish.

Today, reflect on the friendships in your life. Are they building you up spiritually and emotionally? Ask God for wisdom in choosing and maintaining friendships that reflect His love and lead you closer to Him.

Prayer

Lord, guide me in choosing friends that reflect Your love and lead to spiritual growth. Amen.

Affirmation

I choose wise friendships that reflect God's love and bring spiritual growth, peace, and joy.

September 22
The Blessing of Discernment

"For the Lord gives wisdom; from his mouth come knowledge and understanding."(Proverbs 2:6, NIV)

Devotional Reflection

Discernment is a gift from God that allows us to make wise decisions and navigate life's complexities with clarity and confidence. As black women, we often face situations that require careful thought and wisdom, whether in our relationships, careers, or personal lives. Discernment helps us see beyond the surface and understand what truly aligns with God's will. It is a blessing that guides us in making everyday choices, protecting us from harmful decisions and helping us to live in a way that honors God.

Gaining wisdom through discernment means seeking God's guidance in every aspect of life. It involves pausing to pray before making decisions and allowing the Holy Spirit to lead us toward what is right. Discernment helps us distinguish between what is good and what is best, enabling us to make choices that reflect God's wisdom. As we grow in discernment, we become more attuned to God's voice, gaining deeper insight into how to live according to His purpose.

Today, ask God to bless you with the gift of discernment in your daily life. Reflect on areas where you need clarity and wisdom, and trust that God will provide the understanding you need to make wise decisions.

Prayer

Lord, thank You for discernment. Grant me wisdom to make choices that reflect Your will and purpose. Guide my decisions daily, and help me trust Your understanding. Amen.

Affirmation

I embrace discernment, seeking God's wisdom in all choices. I trust His guidance to lead me toward decisions that honor Him and reflect His purpose.

September 23
Learning from Generational Wisdom

"Remember the days of old; consider the generations long past. Ask your father and he will tell you, your elders, and they will explain to you."(Deuteronomy 32:7, NIV)

Devotional Reflection

Generational wisdom is a treasure passed down from those who came before us, providing valuable lessons that can shape how we live today. As black women, many of us have been blessed with the wisdom of mothers, grandmothers, and other elders who have walked through challenges and triumphs, paving the way for us. Their experiences offer insights into resilience, faith, and the strength needed to navigate life's obstacles. Honoring this wisdom means listening to their stories, respecting their knowledge, and applying the lessons they've shared.

The wisdom passed down through generations is a rich resource for understanding how to live with grace, courage, and faith. By embracing these teachings, we honor the legacy of those who have come before us and continue to carry forward the values and principles they lived by. Applying this wisdom to our own lives allows us to build on their experiences, helping us make better choices, face adversity with strength, and grow in our relationship with God.

Today, reflect on the wisdom you've received from elders in your life. How can you honor their legacy by applying their lessons to your own journey? Ask God for guidance in carrying forward the wisdom that has been passed down to you.

Prayer

Lord, thank You for the wisdom passed down from my elders. Help me honor their legacy by applying their lessons and sharing them with future generations. Amen.

Affirmation: I honor my elders' wisdom, applying their lessons with gratitude. I embrace generational wisdom, trusting it guides me in strength and faith.

September 24
Knowing When to Speak and When to Stay Silent

"There is a time for everything, and a season for every activity under the heavens: a time to be silent and a time to speak."

(Ecclesiastes 3:1,7, NIV)

Devotional Reflection

Navigating conversations with wisdom involves knowing when to speak up and when to stay silent. As black women, we often carry the weight of many responsibilities, and there may be times when we feel the urge to defend, explain, or correct. However, true wisdom comes from understanding that not every moment requires our voice. Sometimes the greatest power lies in our ability to listen, observe, and wait for the right time to speak.

Knowing when to speak and when to remain silent requires discernment and sensitivity to God's guidance. Speaking up can bring healing, truth, and clarity, but speaking out of turn or in the wrong moment can create conflict or misunderstanding. In contrast, silence can foster peace, reflection, and wisdom, but remaining silent when a word of truth is needed can hinder growth. The key is allowing God to direct your conversations, ensuring that your words align with His will and that your silence serves a purpose.

Today, ask God to help you discern when to speak and when to stay silent. Reflect on your conversations and interactions, and invite God to guide your words and actions with wisdom.

Prayer

Lord, grant me the wisdom to know when to speak and when to stay silent. Guide my conversations so that my words reflect Your truth, love, and purpose. Teach me to listen with discernment and to speak with grace, ensuring that my voice is used for healing, clarity, and peace. Amen.

Affirmation

I practice wisdom in my conversations, knowing when to speak and when to listen. I trust God to guide my words and actions, ensuring that my voice brings peace, clarity, and truth at the right time.

September 25
Balancing Wisdom and Emotions

"Fools give full vent to their rage, but the wise bring calm in the end."(Proverbs 29:11, NIV)

Devotional Reflection

Emotions are a natural and powerful part of our human experience. As black women, we often carry the emotional weight of our families, communities, and personal challenges. While emotions are valid and should not be dismissed, it is important to balance them with wisdom, especially when we are feeling overwhelmed or reactive. Wisdom allows us to navigate emotional moments with grace, ensuring that our decisions and actions are grounded in God's truth rather than being driven by temporary feelings.

Balancing wisdom and emotions means taking a step back to evaluate a situation before responding. While emotions may urge us to react quickly, wisdom encourages us to pause, pray, and seek God's guidance. This balance allows us to express our emotions in a way that is healthy and constructive, without allowing them to control us. When we lead with wisdom, we can still honor our feelings while making decisions that align with God's will and bring peace to our lives.

Today, reflect on any emotional situations you are facing. Ask God for the wisdom to navigate these moments with clarity, ensuring that your emotions are acknowledged but not controlling your decisions.

Prayer

Lord, help me balance wisdom and emotions. Guide me to respond with grace and clarity, honoring You in every situation. Amen.

Affirmation

I balance wisdom and emotions, navigating emotional moments with grace and clarity. I trust God to guide my responses, ensuring that my actions reflect His peace, love, and wisdom in all situations.

September 26
Seeking God's Word for Clarity

"Your word is a lamp for my feet, a light on my path."
(*Psalm 119:105, NIV*)

Devotional Reflection

Life can sometimes feel confusing, and the path ahead may be unclear. In these moments, it's easy to feel overwhelmed or unsure of which direction to take. As black women, we often juggle multiple roles and responsibilities, making it even more essential to find clarity amidst the noise. God's Word is the ultimate source of clarity, providing guidance, wisdom, and direction when we need it most. Scripture helps us make sense of the uncertainty by reminding us of God's promises and illuminating the steps we need to take.

Turning to the Bible allows us to pause and reflect on God's eternal truths, which can bring peace in times of confusion. His Word is a steady anchor that offers clarity and perspective, even when the world around us seems chaotic. By seeking His guidance through scripture, we can find the answers we need and the reassurance that God is always leading us, even when the path isn't fully visible.

Today, if you're feeling unsure or confused, turn to God's Word for clarity. Ask Him to reveal His truth to you and provide the direction you need to move forward with confidence.

Prayer

Lord, when my path feels unclear, guide me to Your Word for clarity and direction. Help me to trust in Your promises and to rely on scripture to light the way. Teach me to turn to You in moments of confusion, knowing that Your wisdom will guide me forward. Amen.

Affirmation

I seek God's Word for clarity and trust in His wisdom to guide my steps. Even in times of uncertainty, I know that His Word is a light that illuminates my path and leads me toward His purpose for my life.

September 27
Learning to Trust God's Wisdom Over Your Own

"Trust in the Lord with all your heart and lean not on your own understanding; in all your ways submit to him, and he will make your paths straight."(Proverbs 3:5-6, NIV)

Devotional Reflection

As black women, we are often conditioned to handle everything ourselves—balancing work, family, and personal responsibilities. This desire for control can make it hard to trust anyone, even God, with the direction of our lives. Yet, there is peace and freedom in letting go of the need to control everything and trusting God's infinite wisdom over our own limited understanding. God sees the bigger picture and knows what is best for us, even when we don't.

Trusting God's wisdom over our own means acknowledging that He is sovereign and all-knowing. While we may have plans and ideas for our lives, God's plan is always greater and more aligned with His purpose for us. Surrendering control doesn't mean giving up, but rather, it is an act of faith that allows God to guide us toward paths we may not have envisioned for ourselves. His wisdom leads to peace, fulfillment, and purpose that goes beyond what we could achieve on our own.

Today, reflect on any areas where you might be struggling to release control. Ask God to help you trust His wisdom over your own and to guide you with His divine understanding.

Prayer

Lord, help me to trust Your wisdom above my own. Teach me to surrender control, knowing that You see the bigger picture and Your plans are greater than mine. Guide me in faith, and lead me down the path You have prepared for my life. Amen.

Affirmation

I trust in God's infinite wisdom, letting go of the need to control every aspect of my life. I know that His plans are greater than mine, and I walk in faith, allowing Him to lead me on the path He has prepared.

September 28
Practicing Wisdom in Difficult Conversations

"The tongue has the power of life and death, and those who love it will eat its fruit."(Proverbs 18:21, NIV)

Devotional Reflection

Difficult conversations are an inevitable part of life, but approaching them with wisdom and grace is essential to maintaining peace and fostering healthy relationships. As black women, we often face challenging discussions in both personal and professional settings. Whether it's addressing conflicts, setting boundaries, or expressing unmet needs, the way we communicate can either build bridges or create division. Wisdom helps us navigate these conversations with care, ensuring that our words bring life, not harm.

Practicing wisdom in difficult conversations means taking time to prepare, pray, and seek God's guidance before speaking. It involves listening with empathy and responding with grace, even when the subject is sensitive. The goal is not to avoid hard topics but to approach them in a way that reflects God's love and fosters understanding. Wisdom allows us to speak truth in love, handle conflicts with dignity, and promote healing through our words.

Today, think about any difficult conversations you need to have. Ask God for the wisdom to approach them with grace, ensuring that your words are thoughtful, loving, and aligned with His will.

Prayer

Lord, grant me the wisdom to approach difficult conversations with grace and understanding. Help me to speak truth in love, and to handle sensitive topics in a way that reflects Your character. Guide my words and my heart so that I may promote healing and peace in all my interactions. Amen.

Affirmation

I approach difficult conversations with wisdom and grace, allowing God to guide my words and actions. I speak truth in love, using my voice to bring healing, understanding, and peace.

September 29
Finding Wisdom in Nature

"The heavens declare the glory of God; the skies proclaim the work of his hands."(Psalm 19:1, NIV)

Devotional Reflection

Nature is one of the clearest expressions of God's wisdom, offering powerful lessons in patience, growth, and renewal. As black women, we often lead busy lives, and taking the time to observe God's creation can help us slow down and reflect on His power and presence. From the changing of the seasons to the way a tree grows steadily over time, nature reveals God's wisdom in its patterns and cycles. Each element of creation speaks of God's order, patience, and ability to bring renewal.

Nature teaches us that growth is a process. Just as flowers take time to bloom and trees shed their leaves before growing new ones, our own growth requires patience and trust in God's timing. The world around us is full of reminders that even in seasons of waiting or loss, renewal is always on the horizon. Observing the natural world can help us understand God's grace and wisdom, showing us how to approach our own lives with patience, resilience, and hope for the future.

Today, take time to reflect on God's creation. Whether it's a walk outside or simply sitting in a quiet space, allow nature to teach you lessons of patience, growth, and renewal.

Prayer

Lord, thank You for Your creation. Help me learn from the wisdom in nature, reflecting on patience, growth, and renewal. Guide me to live in harmony with Your creation and trust in Your timing. Amen.

Affirmation

I find wisdom in nature, observing God's creation as a reflection of His patience, growth, and renewal. I trust that just as nature follows its course, God is guiding me through every season with His perfect wisdom.

September 30
The Gift of Wisdom Through Prayer

"If any of you lacks wisdom, you should ask God, who gives generously to all without finding fault, and it will be given to you."

(James 1:5, NIV)

Devotional Reflection

Wisdom is one of the greatest gifts we can receive from God, and it is available to us through prayer. As black women, we face daily challenges that require discernment, clarity, and insight. Often, we may rely on our own understanding or the advice of others, but true wisdom comes from seeking God in prayer. When we come before Him, humbly asking for guidance, He generously gives us the wisdom we need to navigate life's complexities.

Prayeris not just a time to present our requests to God; it's an opportunity to seek His heart and receive His divine insight. As we develop a habit of turning to God in prayer, we grow in our ability to make decisions that align with His will. Wisdom gained through Prayerhelps us respond to situations with grace, handle challenges with confidence, and approach every day with a sense of peace, knowing that God is guiding us.

Today, commit to seeking God's wisdom through prayer. Ask Him to fill you with discernment and understanding, trusting that He will guide you in every decision and provide the clarity you need.

Prayer

Lord, thank You for the gift of wisdom that You offer through prayer. Help me to seek You daily, trusting that You will provide the guidance and understanding I need. Teach me to rely on Your wisdom in all areas of my life, knowing that Your insight is greater than my own. Amen.

Affirmation

I seek God's wisdom through prayer, trusting that He will guide me in every decision. I rely on His divine insight and understanding, knowing that true wisdom comes from daily seeking His presence.

October
Healing and Forgiveness

October 1
Letting Go of Past Hurts

"He heals the brokenhearted and binds up their wounds."
(Psalm 147:3, NIV)

Devotional Reflection

Holding on to past hurts can be a heavy burden that prevents you from living in the peace and freedom God desires for you. As black women, the pressures of life and past experiences can leave emotional scars that weigh on our hearts, impacting our mental, emotional, and spiritual well-being. Letting go of those hurts may seem impossible, but God promises to heal your broken heart and bind up your wounds. He sees every tear and knows every pain, and His healing power is greater than any past trauma.

Releasing emotional wounds begins with surrendering them to God. It doesn't mean ignoring or minimizing your pain, but rather allowing God to carry the burden for you. Holding on to past hurts only keeps you bound, while letting go opens the door for God's healing and restoration. Trusting in His ability to heal allows you to move forward in wholeness, with a heart that is free from bitterness and pain. Healing may be a process, but each step toward letting go brings you closer to the peace God desires for your life.

Today, reflect on any past hurts that may still weigh on your heart. Ask God to help you release them and trust Him to heal your heart and restore your joy.

Prayer

Lord, I give You my past hurts and trust You to heal my heart. Help me release the pain and embrace Your healing. Guide me to wholeness and freedom. Amen.

Affirmation

I let go of past hurts and trust in God's healing power. I release the emotional wounds I've carried, knowing that God is binding up my heart and restoring my peace. I walk in the freedom of His healing love.

October 2
The Power of Forgiveness

"Be kind and compassionate to one another, forgiving each other, just as in Christ God forgave you." (Ephesians 4:32, NIV)

Devotional Reflection

Forgiveness is one of the most powerful acts we can engage in, yet it is often one of the most difficult. As black women, the weight of past offenses or disappointments may feel overwhelming, whether from others or even from ourselves. However, holding on to anger, resentment, or guilt only keeps us bound in emotional chains. Forgiveness, on the other hand, is a liberating gift that frees both the giver and the receiver. God calls us to forgive others as we have been forgiven in Christ, and in doing so, we open our hearts to experience His peace and healing.

Forgiving someone doesn't mean excusing their actions or forgetting the hurt. It means releasing the grip that the pain has on your heart and allowing God's grace to flow into that space. The same applies to forgiving yourself. We are often our own harshest critics, holding on to shame and regret for mistakes we've made. But God's grace covers our flaws, and through forgiveness, we can finally experience the freedom to move forward with peace and purpose.

Today, reflect on those you need to forgive, including yourself. Ask God for the strength to release the weight of unforgiveness and embrace the freedom that comes with it.

Prayer

Lord, thank You for the gift of forgiveness. Help me forgive others and myself, releasing anger and regret. Grant me the freedom and healing that comes with forgiveness. Amen.

Affirmation

I embrace the power of forgiveness, releasing the pain of past hurts and mistakes. I forgive others and myself, knowing that forgiveness brings freedom, healing, and peace through God's grace.

October 3
Healing from Betrayal

"The Lord is close to the brokenhearted and saves those who are crushed in spirit." (Psalm 34:18, NIV)

Devotional Reflection

Betrayal is one of the deepest wounds we can experience, especially when it comes from someone we trusted. As black women, betrayal in relationships, friendships, or even within our communities can leave scars that feel impossible to heal. The pain of being let down, lied to, or deceived can create feelings of isolation, anger, and grief. However, God's promise is that He is close to the brokenhearted. He is present in your pain and offers healing and comfort that go beyond what anyone else can provide.

Trusting God to heal the wounds caused by betrayal is not easy, but it begins with recognizing that He understands your hurt and stands ready to mend your heart. Though betrayal can make you feel alone, God's presence is constant. His love is unwavering, and He desires to replace your pain with peace. Healing from betrayal is a process, but when you allow God to take control, He can turn your brokenness into wholeness.

Today, bring your pain to God and trust Him with your healing process. Surrender the hurt caused by betrayal and open your heart to the restoration only He can bring.

Prayer

Lord, I bring the pain of betrayal to You. Heal my heart and comfort me in my brokenness. Help me to trust You through this healing process, knowing that You are always near, even in my darkest moments. Replace the hurt with Your peace and lead me toward forgiveness and wholeness. Amen.

Affirmation

I trust God to heal the wounds caused by betrayal. He is close to my broken heart and brings comfort and peace. I surrender my pain to Him, knowing that He will lead me toward healing and wholeness.

October 4
Breaking Free from Resentment

"Get rid of all bitterness, rage and anger, brawling and slander, along with every form of malice. Be kind and compassionate to one another, forgiving each other, just as in Christ God forgave you."

(Ephesians 4:31-32, NIV)

Devotional Reflection

Resentment is like a poison that slowly drains your joy, peace, and ability to move forward. As black women, we may carry resentment from past injustices, hurts, or disappointments—whether it stems from personal relationships, workplace challenges, or societal issues. Resentment often feels justified, but holding onto it keeps us locked in a cycle of anger and bitterness. God calls us to let go of resentment, replacing it with compassion, kindness, and forgiveness. When we release resentment, we make space for God's peace to enter and heal our hearts.

Breaking free from resentment doesn't happen overnight, but it starts with the decision to no longer let bitterness have a place in your life. It's not about forgetting the wrongs done to you but about choosing not to let them control your emotions or outlook. Letting go of resentment means trusting God to handle the justice and healing needed, and allowing Him to transform your heart. In return, you receive freedom, peace, and the ability to live fully in the present.

Today, reflect on any areas where resentment may be lingering. Ask God to help you release bitterness and open your heart to forgiveness and peace.

Prayer

Lord, I release resentment and bitterness. Help me let go of anger, trusting You to heal my heart. Fill me with peace, compassion, and guide me toward forgiveness. Amen.

Affirmation

I choose to break free from resentment, letting go of bitterness and opening my heart to peace. I trust God to heal my wounds, and I embrace compassion and forgiveness in every area of my life.

October 5
Forgiving Yourself for Past Mistakes

"As far as the east is from the west, so far has he removed our transgressions from us." (Psalm 103:12, NIV)

Devotional Reflection

Forgiving others is often encouraged, but forgiving yourself can be one of the hardest steps toward emotional healing. As black women, we often hold ourselves to high standards, and when we fall short, it's easy to dwell on past mistakes and carry the weight of guilt. However, God's grace is not just extended to others—it's extended to you as well. He has already forgiven you, and now it's time to extend that same grace to yourself. Holding on to shame and regret only keeps you stuck, but forgiving yourself allows you to experience the healing and freedom God offers.

God promises to remove our sins as far as the east is from the west, meaning He no longer holds your past against you. If God, in His infinite love, can forgive you, then you can trust that it's safe to let go of your guilt and embrace His grace. Forgiving yourself is a form of self-compassion, allowing you to move forward with a lighter heart, free from the burden of past mistakes. It's an invitation to step into the fullness of God's love and live a life of freedom and peace.

Today, take a moment to reflect on any mistakes or regrets you've been holding onto. Ask God to help you forgive yourself and receive the healing and grace that He has already made available to you.

Prayer

Lord, thank You for Your grace and forgiveness. Help me forgive myself, release guilt, and trust in Your healing love. Fill my heart with peace as I walk in freedom. Amen.

Affirmation

I forgive myself for past mistakes and embrace God's grace. I release guilt and regret, knowing that I am healed and made whole through His love. I walk forward in freedom, free from the weight of my past.

October 6
Healing Through God's Love

"The Lord your God is with you, the Mighty Warrior who saves. He will take great delight in you; in his love he will no longer rebuke you, but will rejoice over you with singing." (Zephaniah 3:17, NIV)

Devotional Reflection

God's love is the ultimate source of healing and restoration. As black women, we often bear many burdens—whether from past hurts, disappointments, or emotional wounds. The world may offer temporary comfort, but true healing comes from allowing God's unconditional love to fill the broken places in our hearts. His love goes deeper than any pain, bringing restoration, wholeness, and peace that surpasses all understanding.

God's love is not distant or conditional—it is present and active, always working to restore us. He sees every tear, hears every cry, and responds with compassion. His love rejoices over you and seeks to make you whole, no matter how deep the wound. When you allow God's love to penetrate the areas where you hurt the most, you invite Him to replace your sorrow with joy, your pain with peace, and your brokenness with wholeness. His love is transformative, and it is through this love that you can find lasting healing.

Today, open your heart to receive God's love in a fresh and powerful way. Allow His love to heal the wounds that have weighed you down, and trust Him to bring restoration and wholeness to every part of your life.

Prayer

Lord, I open my heart to Your healing love today. Restore my heart to wholeness and help me trust in Your unfailing love. Amen.

Affirmation

I embrace the healing power of God's love. His love restores my heart, brings me peace, and makes me whole. I am loved, I am healed, and I walk in the fullness of His grace.

October 7
The Journey to Emotional Healing

"He has made everything beautiful in its time."
(Ecclesiastes 3:11, NIV)

Devotional Reflection

Emotional healing is not an instant event but a journey, often requiring time, patience, and faith. As black women, we may experience emotional wounds from various life situations—whether from past relationships, personal struggles, or societal pressures. While the desire to heal quickly is natural, true emotional healing takes time and occurs in stages. God promises to be with us every step of the way, guiding and comforting us as we navigate the path toward wholeness.

Understanding that healing is a process means accepting that you may not always feel "better" right away, but that doesn't mean God isn't at work. Healing often requires trusting God's timing, as He knows when we are ready to fully let go of past hurts and embrace the new things He has in store. As you journey through this process, God works in your heart to bring peace, restoration, and eventually, a deeper understanding of His grace. While the road may be long, each step brings you closer to the freedom and joy that God desires for you.

Today, remind yourself that your emotional healing is a journey. Trust that God is with you, working behind the scenes to make everything beautiful in its time.

Prayer

Lord, I thank You for walking with me through my journey to emotional healing. Help me to be patient with the process and to trust that You are healing me in Your perfect timing. Give me the strength and faith to continue forward, knowing that You are making everything beautiful in its time. Amen.

Affirmation

I trust God through my journey of emotional healing. I am patient with the process, knowing that He is with me every step of the way, making everything beautiful in its time. My healing is unfolding in His perfect timing.

October 8
Forgiving Family Members

"Bear with each other and forgive one another if any of you has a grievance against someone. Forgive as the Lord forgave you."

(Colossians 3:13, NIV)

Devotional Reflection

Family relationships can be some of the most rewarding, yet also the most challenging, especially when hurt or misunderstanding arises. As black women, we often hold deep connections to our families, but sometimes those bonds can become strained due to past conflicts, unresolved grievances, or unmet expectations. Navigating family dynamics with grace requires intentional forgiveness, even when it's difficult. God calls us to forgive, just as He has forgiven us, knowing that forgiveness opens the door to healing and reconciliation.

Forgiving family members doesn't mean excusing hurtful behavior or forgetting the past, but it does mean choosing to release the bitterness and resentment that can weigh heavily on your heart. It's about choosing grace over grudges, allowing God's love to soften your heart and bring peace into your family relationships. By forgiving, you create space for healing and unity, giving God the room to work in your family in ways you may not have imagined.

Today, reflect on any unresolved issues you may have with family members. Ask God for the grace to forgive them, even if the wounds are deep, and trust Him to bring healing into your family.

Prayer

Lord, help me to navigate the complexities of family relationships with grace and compassion. Grant me the strength to forgive family members who have hurt me, and fill my heart with Your love and understanding. Help me to release any bitterness, and restore peace and unity in my family through Your healing power. Amen.

Affirmation

I choose to forgive my family members, releasing any hurt or bitterness. I navigate family dynamics with grace, allowing God's love to guide me toward healing and reconciliation.

October 9
Overcoming Grudges

"Do not seek revenge or bear a grudge against anyone among your people, but love your neighbor as yourself. I am the Lord."

(Leviticus 19:18, NIV)

Devotional Reflection

Grudges are heavy burdens that not only harm our relationships but also weigh down our spirits. As black women, we may face injustices or hurtful situations that tempt us to hold onto grudges as a way to protect ourselves or demand justice. However, holding onto these feelings does more harm than good. God calls us to release grudges and replace them with love and forgiveness. By doing so, we open our hearts to healing and free ourselves from the chains of bitterness.

Letting go of a grudge doesn't mean the pain never happened, nor does it mean we excuse the wrongs done to us. Instead, it means choosing to no longer let that pain control our emotions, thoughts, or actions. It's about trusting God to bring justice in His own time and way, while you focus on your emotional and spiritual freedom. Releasing a grudge is a powerful act of self-liberation that allows God to fill your heart with peace and healing.

Today, ask God for the strength to let go of any grudges you may be holding. Allow Him to work in your heart, releasing bitterness and replacing it with His peace and love.

Prayer

Lord, I ask for the strength to release any grudges I have been holding onto. Help me to let go of bitterness and choose forgiveness and love instead. Teach me to trust You with justice and healing, knowing that I will find true freedom in letting go. Amen.

Affirmation

I release all grudges and choose forgiveness. I trust God to bring justice in His time and to fill my heart with peace. I am free from bitterness and walk in the love and healing that God provides.

October 10
Healing from Toxic Relationships

"The Lord is my rock, my fortress and my deliverer; my God is my rock, in whom I take refuge, my shield and the horn of my salvation, my stronghold." (Psalm 18:2, NIV)

Devotional Reflection

Toxic relationships can leave deep emotional scars, making it difficult to trust and open your heart again. As black women, we may find ourselves in unhealthy relationships—whether in friendships, romantic partnerships, or even family connections—that drain us emotionally, mentally, and spiritually. Healing from these damaging experiences requires a process of surrendering the pain to God and allowing Him to mend the broken pieces of your heart.

God is your refuge and strength, and He wants to be your source of healing from the damage caused by toxic relationships. Whether it's letting go of manipulation, betrayal, or emotional abuse, God is ready to restore you to wholeness. Healing doesn't happen overnight, but it begins with acknowledging the hurt and seeking God's comfort and guidance to rebuild your heart. Through His love and grace, He can help you set healthy boundaries and restore your sense of worth and peace.

Today, surrender the pain of toxic relationships to God. Ask Him to guide you in the healing process and restore your heart with His love and peace.

Prayer

Lord, I bring You the pain from toxic relationships. Heal and restore my heart. Help me let go and trust Your love to rebuild my spirit. Guide me in setting healthy boundaries moving forward. Amen.

Affirmation

I release the pain of toxic relationships and trust God to heal and restore my heart. I am worthy of healthy, loving connections, and I set boundaries that honor my peace and well-being. God is my refuge, and through Him, I find healing and wholeness.

October 11
Embracing Vulnerability in Healing

"But he said to me, 'My grace is sufficient for you, for my power is made perfect in weakness.' Therefore I will boast all the more gladly about my weaknesses, so that Christ's power may rest on me."

(2 Corinthians 12:9, NIV)

Devotional Reflection

Healing often requires us to confront our wounds and fears, and one of the greatest challenges in this journey is embracing vulnerability. As black women, we may feel the pressure to always appear strong, capable, and resilient. However, true healing can only begin when we allow ourselves to be vulnerable—acknowledging the pain and trusting God to heal those wounded areas. Vulnerability isn't a sign of weakness but a courageous step toward emotional and spiritual restoration.

God's grace is sufficient for us in our moments of vulnerability. When we open ourselves up—whether through prayer, talking to trusted loved ones, or seeking help—we invite God's power to work in our lives. Healing isn't linear, and sometimes it involves sitting with the discomfort of being vulnerable. But through vulnerability, we make room for God's strength to cover us and for His love to do the deep work of healing that only He can provide.

Today, reflect on areas where you may need to embrace vulnerability. Ask God to help you trust the healing process and to surround you with the support needed to walk through this journey with courage.

Prayer

Lord, I come to You with an open heart. Help me trust the healing process and find strength in my vulnerability. Give me courage to allow Your healing power to work through me. Amen.

Affirmation

I embrace vulnerability in my healing journey, knowing that God's grace is sufficient for me. I trust Him with my wounds and lean on His strength, allowing His love to heal and restore me.

October 12
Forgiveness as a Daily Practice

"Then Peter came to Jesus and asked, 'Lord, how many times shall I forgive my brother or sister who sins against me? Up to seven times?' Jesus answered, 'I tell you, not seven times, but seventy-seven times.'"

(Matthew 18:21-22, NIV)

Devotional Reflection

Forgiveness is not a one-time event but an ongoing process. As black women, we may encounter numerous situations where the pain or offense feels too heavy to forgive in a single moment. Whether it's hurt from family, friends, or society, forgiveness often requires daily effort to release the anger and pain that accompany these wounds. Jesus teaches us that forgiveness is a continual practice—one that we must consciously choose, sometimes multiple times a day.

Forgiveness is not about excusing the wrongs done to us, but about freeing ourselves from the burden of holding onto the hurt. Each day presents opportunities to practice forgiveness—whether it's forgiving a new offense or reaffirming your choice to release an old wound. By making forgiveness a daily practice, you protect your heart from bitterness, allowing God's peace and love to fill the spaces once occupied by anger. In doing so, you align yourself with God's call to forgive as He forgives us.

Today, make a commitment to practice forgiveness daily. Ask God to help you release the weight of any unresolved hurt and to strengthen your heart with His grace.

Prayer

Lord, I thank You for Your endless forgiveness. Help me to embrace forgiveness as a daily practice, releasing any hurt or anger that weighs me down. Strengthen my heart to forgive others as You have forgiven me, and fill me with Your peace and love each day. Amen.

Affirmation

I choose to practice forgiveness daily, releasing anger and pain with each new day. I let go of past and present hurts, trusting God's grace to heal and restore my heart. I live in peace, free from bitterness.

October 13
Releasing Anger in a Healthy Way

"In your anger do not sin: Do not let the sun go down while you are still angry, and do not give the devil a foothold."

(Ephesians 4:26-27, NIV)

Devotional Reflection

Anger is a natural and valid emotion, but how we manage and release it determines whether it becomes harmful or healing. As black women, we may carry anger from experiences of injustice, personal hurt, or daily challenges. While anger itself is not a sin, allowing it to fester without healthy release can lead to bitterness, resentment, and even harm to ourselves and others. God encourages us to handle our anger in ways that do not cause destruction but instead lead to healing and peace.

Releasing anger in a healthy way involves acknowledging it rather than suppressing or denying it. God wants us to bring our anger to Him, to process it through prayer, reflection, and even physical outlets like exercise or creative expression. It's important to seek constructive ways to express anger, such as talking it through with trusted friends, writing down your feelings, or practicing deep breathing and mindfulness. Healthy release helps us let go of the negative energy anger brings, while maintaining our emotional and spiritual health.

Today, consider any anger you've been holding onto and ask God to guide you in releasing it in a way that brings peace rather than harm. Trust Him to help you manage your emotions with wisdom and grace.

Prayer

Lord, I bring my anger to You. Help me release it in healthy ways that bring healing and peace. Teach me to manage my emotions with grace and express them in ways that honor You. Amen.

Affirmation

I release my anger in healthy ways, trusting God to guide me. I find peace and healing, freeing my heart from bitterness and harm.

October 14
Healing from Rejection

"The stone the builders rejected has become the cornerstone.

(Psalm 118:22, NIV)

Devotional Reflection

Rejection can leave deep emotional wounds, making us feel unworthy, unseen, or unloved. As black women, we may face rejection in various areas of life—whether from relationships, career opportunities, or even societal prejudices. The sting of being cast aside or overlooked can be incredibly painful, causing us to question our value. Yet, just as the stone that was rejected became the cornerstone, God uses moments of rejection to position us for greater purpose.

God sees your pain and understands the weight of rejection. However, He also reminds you that your worth is not determined by the opinions or acceptance of others but by His unchanging love for you. Trusting God to heal your heart after rejection means allowing Him to remind you of your value and identity in Christ. Rejection is not the final word—God's love and purpose for your life are. Through His healing power, you can rise above rejection, restored in self-worth and ready to embrace the future He has for you.

Today, ask God to heal any wounds caused by rejection. Trust Him to restore your heart and to remind you of your worth and purpose in His eyes.

Prayer

Lord, I bring the pain of rejection to You. Heal my heart from the wounds of being cast aside, and restore my sense of worth and value in You. Help me to trust in Your plan, knowing that rejection is not the end but an opportunity for growth and new beginnings. Amen.

Affirmation

I trust God to heal the pain of rejection and to restore my sense of worth. My value is found in His love for me, and I rise above rejection, knowing that God has a greater purpose for my life.

October 15
The Gift of God's Forgiveness

"If we confess our sins, he is faithful and just and will forgive us our sins and purify us from all unrighteousness." (1 John 1:9, NIV)

Devotional Reflection

God's forgiveness is one of the most profound gifts we can receive. As black women, we often carry the weight of past mistakes, regrets, and even feelings of inadequacy, but God's forgiveness wipes away those burdens. His love is unconditional, and when we come to Him in repentance, He is faithful to forgive and restore us. The beauty of God's forgiveness is that it is freely given—not because we deserve it, but because of His grace.

Embracing God's forgiveness means accepting His grace and allowing it to transform your life. It's about understanding that no sin is too great for God's mercy and that His forgiveness cleanses us from all unrighteousness. Once we experience the freedom of being forgiven, we are also called to extend that same grace to others. Just as God forgives us, we are to forgive those who have wronged us, creating a ripple effect of love, grace, and healing.

Today, reflect on the gift of God's forgiveness in your life. Accept His grace, and ask Him to help you share that same forgiveness with others.

Prayer

Lord, thank You for the gift of Your forgiveness. I confess my sins to You and trust in Your promise to forgive and cleanse me. Help me to embrace Your grace fully and to extend that same forgiveness to others. May Your love transform my heart and bring healing where it's needed. Amen.

Affirmation

I embrace the gift of God's forgiveness, knowing that I am cleansed and made whole through His grace. I share that same forgiveness with others, walking in love, peace, and freedom.

October 16
Healing from Childhood Trauma

"He heals the brokenhearted and binds up their wounds."

(Psalm 147:3, NIV)

Devotional Reflection

Childhood trauma can leave lasting emotional scars, shaping the way we view ourselves, others, and the world. As black women, many of us may carry deep-rooted pain from experiences in our early years, whether it's from family struggles, community challenges, or personal hardships. These wounds can feel overwhelming, often resurfacing in adulthood, affecting our relationships and sense of self-worth. However, God is the ultimate healer, and He promises to mend the brokenhearted and bind up our deepest wounds.

Healing from childhood trauma requires courage and trust in God's ability to restore what has been broken. It involves acknowledging the pain, seeking support, and allowing God's love to penetrate the hurt and replace it with peace. No trauma is too deep for God's healing touch. While the process may take time, God's gentle hands are always at work, providing comfort, strength, and restoration. Through His grace, you can break free from the chains of the past and walk in the wholeness He has designed for you.

Today, ask God to guide you through the journey of healing from childhood trauma. Trust in His love to restore your heart and bring you the peace and freedom that only He can provide.

Prayer

Lord, I bring my deep-rooted pain from childhood before You. I trust in Your healing power to mend the broken parts of my heart. Guide me through the process of healing, and help me release the trauma of the past, knowing that You are able to restore my soul. Thank You for Your endless love and grace. Amen.

Affirmation

I trust God to heal the deep wounds of my childhood trauma. His love restores my heart and brings me peace, and I walk in the wholeness and freedom that only He can provide.

October 17
Letting Go of the Need for Revenge

"Do not take revenge, my dear friends, but leave room for God's wrath, for it is written: 'It is mine to avenge; I will repay,' says the Lord."

(Romans 12:19, NIV)

Devotional Reflection

When someone wrongs us deeply, the natural instinct may be to seek revenge or hold onto the desire for payback. As black women, the injustices we face—whether personal or systemic—can stir up feelings of anger and a need for retaliation. However, God calls us to release those feelings and trust Him with justice. He assures us that vengeance is His, and He will repay according to His perfect judgment. Letting go of the need for revenge is an act of faith, trusting that God sees every hurt and will deal with it in His own time and way.

Revenge may seem satisfying in the moment, but it often keeps us trapped in bitterness and anger. It prevents us from moving forward and experiencing the peace and freedom that God wants for us. By surrendering the desire for revenge, you open yourself up to God's healing power, allowing Him to bring justice in ways far better than we ever could. Trusting God's justice doesn't mean ignoring wrongs; it means allowing Him to handle them while you focus on your growth, peace, and healing.

Today, ask God to help you release any desire for revenge you may be holding onto. Trust His justice and seek peace, knowing that He is in control.

Prayer

Lord, I surrender my desire for revenge and trust in Your perfect justice. Help me release anger and find peace in You, trusting Your timing for justice. Thank You for Your love and grace. Amen.

Affirmation

I release the need for revenge and trust in God's justice. I let go of anger and bitterness, choosing peace and healing. God is my defender, and I trust Him to handle every wrong done to me.

October 18
Healing in Community

"Therefore encourage one another and build each other up, just as in fact you are doing." (1 Thessalonians 5:11, NIV)

Devotional Reflection

Healing is often seen as an individual journey, but we are not meant to go through it alone. As black women, the strength of community is deeply embedded in our culture and history, and it can be a powerful force in our healing process. Whether it's through family, friends, or faith communities, connecting with others who uplift, support, and encourage us can make all the difference. God designed us to live in community, where we can bear each other's burdens and build one another up in times of struggle.

Healing in community allows you to experience the comfort of others walking alongside you, sharing their wisdom, love, and prayers. There's a special strength in knowing that you don't have to carry your pain alone. It's in those moments of vulnerability with trusted people that true emotional healing begins to flourish. God works through the love and support of others to bring restoration and hope, reminding us that we are part of a larger family of believers who can help us heal.

Today, reflect on the community around you. Seek out those who offer support and encouragement, and be willing to open up about your healing journey. Allow God to work through others to help you find peace and restoration.

Prayer

Lord, thank You for the gift of community. Help me connect with those who support my healing journey. Surround me with people who reflect Your grace and guide me toward emotional healing. Amen.

Affirmation

I find healing in community, surrounded by those who uplift and support me. I embrace the love and encouragement of others, trusting that God is using them to guide me toward peace and restoration.

October 19
Embracing God's Grace

"But he said to me, 'My grace is sufficient for you, for my power is made perfect in weakness.' Therefore I will boast all the more gladly about my weaknesses, so that Christ's power may rest on me."

(2 Corinthians 12:9, NIV)

Devotional Reflection

God's grace is a profound gift that reaches into every broken area of our lives. As black women, we often carry the weight of multiple roles, responsibilities, and personal struggles. We may feel pressure to be strong at all times, but God's grace reminds us that His power is most evident when we acknowledge our weaknesses. His grace is sufficient to heal every wound, whether it comes from past trauma, present struggles, or internal battles. Embracing God's grace means recognizing that we don't have to have it all together—His love is enough to carry us through.

Grace doesn't just cover our mistakes; it transforms us. When we accept the fullness of God's grace, we allow His healing power to mend our brokenness. It is in our vulnerability and reliance on God that we experience the depth of His love and restoration. Grace teaches us that no wound is too deep for God to heal, and no situation is beyond His reach. By embracing His grace, we invite healing into the deepest parts of our hearts and lives.

Today, reflect on the areas in your life where you need God's grace. Trust that His grace is more than enough to bring healing, and allow Him to work in your heart in ways that only He can.

Prayer

Lord, thank You for Your abundant grace. Help me embrace it fully, trusting that it heals all my wounds. Teach me to rely on Your strength and find peace in Your transforming love. Amen.

Affirmation

I embrace God's grace, trusting that it is sufficient to heal every wound. His power is made perfect in my weakness, and I rest in His love and strength, knowing that His grace is all I need.

October 20
Finding Peace After a Broken Relationship

"The Lord is near to the brokenhearted and saves the crushed in spirit."

(Psalm 34:18, NIV)

Devotional Reflection

The pain of a broken relationship can leave a lasting impact, making it hard to move forward and find peace. Whether it's the end of a romantic relationship, a close friendship, or even a family bond, the hurt can feel overwhelming. As black women, we may feel the pressure to push through the pain and appear strong, but God invites us to bring our broken hearts to Him. He promises to be near to the brokenhearted and to save those whose spirits are crushed. In His presence, you can find the healing and peace you need to move forward.

Trusting God to mend your heart means allowing yourself to grieve, but also trusting that He is working to bring restoration. Healing after a breakup is a process, and it requires letting go of the hurt while embracing the hope and love that God provides. His peace surpasses all understanding, and even in the midst of pain, He can fill your heart with a sense of comfort and wholeness. With God by your side, you don't have to face the journey of healing alone—His love will sustain you.

Today, invite God into the areas of your heart that have been wounded by a broken relationship. Trust Him to mend your heart and lead you to a place of peace and healing.

Prayer

Lord, I come to You with my broken heart, trusting in Your healing and peace after this breakup. Help me release the hurt and lean on Your love. Fill me with comfort and guide me through healing. Amen.

Affirmation

I trust God to heal my heart after the pain of a broken relationship. His peace surrounds me, and His love restores my spirit. I move forward in faith, knowing that God's healing power is at work in my life.

October 21
Healing from Emotional Exhaustion

"Come to me, all you who are weary and burdened, and I will give you rest." (Matthew 11:28, NIV)

Devotional Reflection

Emotional exhaustion can leave you feeling drained, overwhelmed, and unable to cope with even the smallest challenges. As black women, we often carry the weight of multiple responsibilities—family, work, community, and personal struggles—leading to burnout and emotional fatigue. The constant demands on your emotional energy can leave you feeling empty, but God offers a place of rest and healing. He calls you to bring your weariness to Him, promising to restore your strength and give you peace.

Healing from emotional exhaustion requires acknowledging your limits and allowing God to replenish you. His healing power is not just for physical ailments but for the emotional and spiritual weariness that can weigh you down. By surrendering your burdens to Him, you make space for His love, peace, and renewal. God knows your heart and your struggles, and He is ready to refresh you in ways that only He can. Trust in His healing power to fill the empty spaces and restore your emotional well-being.

Today, take time to rest in God's presence. Allow Him to replenish your emotional strength and heal the areas where you feel exhausted. Trust Him to renew your spirit and bring you the peace you need.

Prayer

Lord, I come to You weary and emotionally exhausted. Restore my strength and refresh my spirit. Help me release my burdens and find rest in Your presence. Fill me with peace and renewal. Amen.

Affirmation

I find healing from emotional exhaustion in God's presence. He replenishes my strength and restores my peace. I trust in His healing power to renew my spirit and carry me through every challenge.

October 22
Forgiving Those Who Don't Apologize

"But if you do not forgive others their sins, your Father will not forgive your sins." (Matthew 6:15, NIV)

Devotional Reflection
One of the hardest acts of forgiveness is letting go of the pain caused by someone who has never acknowledged their wrongdoing. As black women, we may carry the weight of unresolved hurts and injustices, waiting for an apology that may never come. The desire for closure and acknowledgment can keep us bound in bitterness, but God calls us to forgive regardless of whether the other person seeks forgiveness. Forgiving those who don't apologize is not about excusing their actions, but about freeing your own heart from the burden of resentment.

Forgiveness is more about your peace and healing than it is about the other person. By forgiving those who don't apologize, you release the control that pain has over your life and allow God's grace to flow through you. Forgiveness is a choice you make for your own well-being, and through it, you can experience emotional freedom and peace. God sees the injustice and hurt you've endured, and He promises to bring healing and justice in His time. Your role is to trust Him and let go of the pain that holds you back.

Today, ask God for the strength to forgive those who have hurt you without apologizing. Trust that He will provide the healing and peace you need to move forward.

Prayer
Lord, give me strength to forgive those who have hurt me, even without an apology. Help me release bitterness and trust in Your healing and justice. Guide me to walk in peace and grace. Amen.

Affirmation
I choose to forgive, even when the apology never comes. I release bitterness and pain, allowing God's peace to fill my heart. I walk in freedom, trusting God to bring justice and healing in His perfect time.

October 23
Trusting God's Timing in Healing

"He has made everything beautiful in its time."
(Ecclesiastes 3:11, NIV)

Devotional Reflection

Healing is often not an instant event but a journey that unfolds over time. As black women, we may want healing—whether emotional, physical, or spiritual—to happen quickly, especially when the pain feels overwhelming. But God's healing doesn't always come on our timeline. He has a perfect plan, and His timing is intentional, designed to bring about complete restoration. Trusting God's timing in healing means surrendering the need for immediate results and believing that He is working behind the scenes in ways we cannot yet see.

The process of healing can be challenging, especially when progress feels slow or invisible. But even in the waiting, God is shaping you, teaching you patience, faith, and resilience. He makes everything beautiful in His time, including the areas of your life that are broken or wounded. Trusting His timing means releasing control, resting in His love, and knowing that He will bring healing when the time is right.

Today, ask God for the patience and faith to trust His timing in your healing journey. Know that He is working all things together for your good, even in the moments when it seems slow or difficult.

Prayer

Lord, I trust Your timing in my healing journey. Help me to be patient and to surrender my need for immediate results. Remind me that You are making all things beautiful in Your time, and that Your plan is perfect. Strengthen my faith as I wait, and guide me through this process with peace. Amen.

Affirmation

I trust God's perfect timing in my healing. Even when progress feels slow, I know that He is working behind the scenes, making everything beautiful in His time. I walk in patience and faith, trusting His plan for my life.

October 24
Moving Forward After Trauma

"Forget the former things; do not dwell on the past. See, I am doing a new thing! Now it springs up; do you not perceive it?"

(Isaiah 43:18-19, NIV)

Devotional Reflection

Trauma leaves deep emotional scars, and moving forward after such experiences can feel overwhelming. As black women, we may carry trauma from personal, relational, or even generational experiences. These wounds can make it difficult to envision a life beyond the pain. Yet God invites us to move forward, trusting that He is doing something new in our lives. Moving forward doesn't mean forgetting the past but allowing God to guide you into a future where healing, restoration, and hope are possible.

God is in the business of renewal, and He promises to walk with you as you move beyond trauma. He can transform your pain into purpose, and your scars into stories of resilience and strength. Moving forward is a process, one that requires surrendering the weight of trauma and allowing God to lead you step by step. With God's guidance, you can embrace a new chapter in your life, one that is filled with healing, peace, and the promise of brighter days ahead.

Today, invite God into the areas where trauma has held you back. Trust Him to guide you as you take steps forward, knowing that He is making something new in your life.

Prayer

Lord, I surrender my trauma to You and seek Your guidance. Help me release the pain of the past and trust in the new path You're creating. Give me strength and courage to walk into the future You have for me, knowing You are with me. Amen.

Affirmation

I trust God to guide me as I move forward from trauma. He is making all things new in my life, and I embrace His healing and restoration. My past does not define me; God's purpose and peace lead me into a brighter future.

October 25
Healing the Mind and Spirit

"You will keep in perfect peace those whose minds are steadfast, because they trust in you." (Isaiah 26:3, NIV)

Devotional Reflection

The mind and spirit are deeply connected, and when either is in turmoil, it can affect every part of our lives. As black women, we often juggle multiple responsibilities, face daily challenges, and carry emotional and mental burdens that can weigh heavily on us. Over time, this strain can lead to emotional exhaustion, anxiety, or spiritual unrest. But God offers a solution—His perfect peace, a peace that heals both the mind and the spirit.

Allowing God to bring healing to your mind and spirit means surrendering your worries, fears, and burdens to Him. It's an invitation to let go of the constant mental chatter and emotional weight, replacing them with His peace and presence. When you trust God, He calms your mind and restores your spirit, bringing balance and wholeness back into your life. Healing isn't just about the physical body; it's about letting God renew your thoughts and fill your spirit with His love and grace.

Today, take time to quiet your mind and invite God's healing into your spirit. Trust that His peace will guard your heart and mind, bringing rest and restoration where you need it most.

Prayer

Lord, I invite Your healing into my mind and spirit today. Calm the anxieties and worries that weigh me down, and fill me with Your perfect peace. Help me to trust You completely, knowing that You are the source of my healing and wholeness. Restore my spirit and renew my thoughts, so that I may walk in Your peace each day. Amen.

Affirmation

I trust God to heal my mind and spirit, filling me with His perfect peace. I release my worries and burdens, knowing that His love and grace bring restoration to every part of my life.

October 26
The Role of Prayer in Healing

"Is anyone among you in trouble? Let them pray. Is anyone happy? Let them sing songs of praise." (James 5:13, NIV)

Devotional Reflection

Prayer is a powerful tool for healing, both emotionally and spiritually. As black women, we often carry a wide range of emotions—whether it's stress, sadness, or even joy—and prayer provides a direct line to God, allowing us to bring all of our feelings before Him. In moments of emotional pain or spiritual emptiness, prayer acts as a healing balm, offering comfort, strength, and restoration. It is a safe space where you can be vulnerable with God, expressing your deepest hurts and fears, knowing that He listens and cares.

When you bring your emotions to God in prayer, you invite His healing presence into the broken places of your heart. Prayer is more than just asking for help; it's about building a deeper relationship with God, where you trust Him to heal your wounds and restore your spirit. Through prayer, you align your heart with God's will, finding peace in His presence even in the midst of pain. Whether you need healing from a recent hurt or from deep-rooted trauma, prayer is a continual source of strength and renewal.

Today, take time to bring your emotional and spiritual needs to God in prayer. Trust that He hears you and is ready to heal you through His love and grace.

Prayer

Lord, I come to You seeking emotional and spiritual healing. I trust You to heal my wounded heart. Help me find peace in Your presence and lean on You in pain. Restore my spirit with Your love. Amen.

Affirmation

I use prayer as a tool for emotional and spiritual healing. God hears my prayers, and through His love, I find strength, peace, and restoration. My heart is open to His healing power each day.

October 27
Forgiving the Unforgivable

"But if you do not forgive others their sins, your Father will not forgive your sins." (Matthew 6:15, NIV)

Devotional Reflection

Some wounds cut so deep that forgiveness feels impossible. As black women, we may face hurts that challenge our ability to forgive—whether personal betrayals, injustices, or painful experiences that leave lasting scars. The idea of forgiving the unforgivable can seem overwhelming, but God calls us to forgive, not just for the benefit of others, but for our own healing. True forgiveness is an act of faith, trusting God to handle the hurt and bring justice, while we release the burden of holding onto anger and pain.

Forgiving the unforgivable doesn't mean that what happened was okay or that the pain wasn't real. It means choosing to let go of the emotional chains that keep you bound to the hurt. By forgiving, you free yourself from the power that the past holds over you, allowing God's grace to heal and restore your heart. Finding the strength to forgive comes from leaning on God, who forgave us in Christ, even when we didn't deserve it. His strength empowers us to forgive others and move forward with peace.

Today, ask God for the strength to forgive the deepest hurts in your life. Trust Him to heal the wounds and provide the grace needed to release the pain.

Prayer

Lord, I bring to You the deep hurts that feel impossible to forgive. Give me strength to release the pain and forgive, just as You've forgiven me. Heal my heart and fill me with peace, trusting You for healing and justice. Amen.

Affirmation: I find the strength to forgive even the deepest hurts. I release the pain and choose to walk in God's grace, trusting Him to heal my heart and bring peace. I am no longer bound by the past; I am free through forgiveness.

October 28
Healing from Guilt and Shame

"Therefore, there is now no condemnation for those who are in Christ Jesus." (Romans 8:1, NIV)

Devotional Reflection

Guilt and shame can be heavy burdens that weigh down the soul, keeping you from experiencing the fullness of God's love and grace. As black women, we may carry guilt from past mistakes or shame from situations we could not control. These feelings can rob us of our joy and keep us from embracing the freedom that Christ offers. But God promises that in Him, there is no condemnation. He calls us to release the guilt and shame that hold us captive and to step into the freedom and healing that only He can provide.

Healing from guilt and shame begins with accepting God's forgiveness and understanding that His grace is greater than any mistake or failure. You are not defined by your past, and God does not hold your wrongs against you. He sees you through the lens of love and grace, and He desires for you to walk in that truth. Letting go of guilt and shame allows you to experience the peace and healing that come from knowing you are fully forgiven, fully loved, and fully accepted by God.

Today, take time to surrender any guilt or shame you've been carrying. Ask God to replace those burdens with His peace, love, and healing.

Prayer

Lord, I bring my guilt and shame to You. Give me strength to release these burdens and embrace the truth that in You, there is no condemnation. Thank You for Your forgiveness and grace. Heal my heart and fill me with peace. Amen.

Affirmation: I release the burden of guilt and shame and embrace God's healing grace. I am no longer defined by my past mistakes but by God's love and forgiveness. I walk in the freedom and peace that come from His grace.

October 29
Embracing Inner Peace Through Forgiveness

"Make every effort to live in peace with everyone and to be holy; without holiness no one will see the Lord." (Hebrews 12:14, NIV)

Devotional Reflection

True inner peace comes when we fully embrace forgiveness—not only of others, but also of ourselves. As black women, the pressures we face in life can lead to moments of hurt and frustration, but harboring unforgiveness only disturbs the peace we seek. When we choose to forgive, we are not excusing the wrongs done to us; we are making room for God's peace to take root in our hearts. Forgiveness is a pathway to inner freedom and lasting peace, allowing us to release the anger, pain, and bitterness that keep us bound.

Forgiveness brings healing to our souls. It allows us to move forward, no longer tethered to the hurts of the past. When we fully embrace forgiveness, we can walk in peace that is not dependent on our circumstances, but is rooted in God's grace. Through forgiveness, you open yourself up to the peace of Christ, who has forgiven us and calls us to do the same. This peace is deeper than just the absence of conflict—it is the quiet assurance that God is in control, and that His love covers all.

Today, reflect on any areas where forgiveness may be needed. Invite God to help you embrace forgiveness fully, so that His peace can reign in your heart.

Prayer

Lord, thank You for the gift of forgiveness. Help me release anger and bitterness, embracing peace. Fill my heart with love and grace as I forgive others and myself. Amen.

Affirmation

I embrace inner peace through the power of forgiveness. I release all bitterness and pain, allowing God's peace to fill my heart. I walk in the freedom and healing that comes from fully embracing forgiveness.

October 30
Trusting God to Restore What's Been Broken

"The Lord is close to the brokenhearted and saves those who are crushed in spirit." (Psalm 34:18, NIV)

Devotional Reflection

Life's losses and hurts can leave us feeling broken, as if pieces of our hearts and spirits have been shattered beyond repair. As black women, we may experience various forms of loss—whether in relationships, dreams, or personal setbacks—that cause deep emotional and spiritual pain. Yet God is a healer and restorer. He draws near to the brokenhearted and promises to save those whose spirits are crushed. Restoration is not just about putting the pieces back together; it's about God creating something beautiful from the brokenness.

Trusting God to restore what's been broken requires faith and patience. Healing may not happen overnight, but God is always at work, mending the wounds and bringing renewal to your heart and spirit. He sees what has been lost and knows how to restore it in ways that surpass our understanding. When you trust Him, you allow His love and grace to heal the deepest hurts and make you whole again.

Today, believe in God's ability to restore what's been broken in your life. Surrender your pain to Him and trust that He is making something new and beautiful from your loss.

Prayer

Lord, I come to You with the broken pieces of my heart and spirit. I trust in Your ability to restore what has been lost and to heal my deepest wounds. Help me to surrender my pain to You, believing that You are working all things for my good. Thank You for Your love and faithfulness as You bring restoration to my life. Amen.

Affirmation

I trust God to restore what has been broken in my life. His love heals my heart, and His grace renews my spirit. I believe that He is making something beautiful from my loss and hurt, and I walk in faith knowing that restoration is coming.

October 31
Walking in Wholeness After Healing

"I praise you because I am fearfully and wonderfully made; your works are wonderful, I know that full well." (Psalm 139:14, NIV)

Devotional Reflection

After experiencing the healing power of God, there is a call to walk in the wholeness He has provided. As black women, we may have endured seasons of hurt, brokenness, and emotional struggles, but God's healing brings us to a place of fullness and restoration. Wholeness means living beyond the wounds and embracing the freedom, peace, and joy that come from God's love. It's about knowing that you are fearfully and wonderfully made, and that every piece of your life—no matter how broken it once was—has been lovingly restored by God.

Walking in wholeness means choosing to live each day in the strength of God's healing. It's not just about surviving the pain but thriving after the healing. God has mended your heart, renewed your spirit, and restored your emotional well-being. Now, He calls you to live in the fullness of that healing, free from the burdens of the past and anchored in His grace and peace. Wholeness allows you to walk confidently in your identity as God's beloved, knowing that His healing is complete and perfect.

Today, celebrate the healing God has done in your life. Walk in the fullness of His restoration, living each day in emotional and spiritual wholeness.

Prayer

Lord, thank You for the healing in my life. Help me walk in the wholeness and freedom Your love brings. Guide me to live fully in Your grace, knowing I am wonderfully made and restored by You. Amen.

Affirmation: I walk in God's healing, living in emotional and spiritual wholeness. I am free from the past, restored by His love, and confident in my identity as His beloved. I thrive in His peace and joy.

November
Service and Giving Back

November 1
The Joy of Serving Others

"Serve the Lord with gladness; come before His presence with singing."
(Psalm 100:2, NIV)

Devotional Reflection

Serving others is a beautiful reflection of God's love, and there's a special joy that comes from helping those in need. As black women, we often find ourselves balancing multiple responsibilities, and while serving others can sometimes feel overwhelming, it also brings deep fulfillment. When we serve others, we're not only making a positive impact on their lives but also growing spiritually. Serving connects us to the heart of God, who calls us to love and care for others just as He loves us.

True joy in serving comes when we shift our mindset from viewing it as a duty to seeing it as an opportunity to reflect God's kindness. Every act of service, whether big or small, has the potential to change someone's day or even their life. The fulfillment that comes from helping others reminds us that we are part of something greater—God's plan to show His love to the world. Serving with gladness brings an unshakable sense of purpose and joy that flows from a heart aligned with God's will.

Today, look for opportunities to serve those around you with a joyful heart. Whether through kind words, a helping hand, or a generous spirit, know that your acts of service bring joy not only to others but also to your own heart.

Prayer: Lord, thank You for the privilege of serving others. Help me serve with joy and a willing heart, reflecting Your love through my actions. Fill my heart with gladness as I help those in need. Amen.

Affirmation: I serve others with joy, knowing that my acts of kindness reflect God's love. Each opportunity to help others fills my heart with fulfillment and brings me closer to the purpose God has for me.

November 2
Giving Back to Your Community

"Do not forget to do good and to share with others, for with such sacrifices God is pleased." (Hebrews 13:16, NIV)

Devotional Reflection

Giving back to your community is a powerful way to uplift those around you while creating meaningful change. As black women, we often serve as pillars within our communities, whether through leadership, family, or faith. By giving back, we strengthen the bonds that hold our communities together, providing support, encouragement, and resources to those in need. God calls us to share what we have, knowing that even the smallest acts of generosity can have a lasting impact.

Giving back doesn't always require grand gestures; sometimes it's as simple as offering your time, lending a listening ear, or sharing your talents. Each contribution helps build a stronger, more resilient community. When you invest in the well-being of others, you become a vessel of God's love, shining His light in practical ways. Through acts of service, mentoring, and giving, you can be a source of hope and inspiration, reflecting Christ's compassion and care for the people around you.

Today, consider how you can give back to your local community. Whether through volunteering, supporting local businesses, or helping a neighbor, trust that your efforts will make a difference.

Prayer: Lord, help me find ways to give back to my community and uplift those around me. Open my eyes to others' needs and provide me with the wisdom and resources to support them. May my actions reflect Your love and bring hope. Amen.

Affirmation: I give back to my community with a heart full of service and generosity. My actions uplift others, building a stronger, connected community. I trust God to guide me in making a meaningful impact.

November 3
Serving with a Humble Heart

"Whoever wants to become great among you must be your servant, and whoever wants to be first must be your slave—just as the Son of Man did not come to be served, but to serve, and to give his life as a ransom for many." (Matthew 20:26-28, NIV)

Devotional Reflection

Serving with a humble heart means putting the needs of others before our own desires for recognition or praise. In a world that often measures success by status and visibility, it can be challenging to embrace the quiet, unnoticed acts of service. But God calls us to serve with humility, just as Jesus did. His example shows us that true greatness comes not from being served, but from serving others without expecting anything in return.

As black women, we often serve in ways that may go unnoticed—whether in our families, communities, or workplaces. Yet these acts of service, done with humility, carry tremendous value in God's eyes. Serving with a humble heart isn't about seeking validation from others, but about honoring God by loving and caring for His people. When we serve with no desire for recognition, we align ourselves with Christ's heart, and our service becomes an act of worship.

Today, reflect on how you can serve others with a humble heart. Seek opportunities to help others without the need for acknowledgment, knowing that God sees and honors every act of kindness done in His name.

Prayer: Lord, help me serve with a humble heart, following Jesus' example. Teach me to care for others out of love and compassion, without seeking recognition. May my service honor You and reflect Your love. Amen.

Affirmation: I serve with humility, not seeking recognition. My service is done with love, reflecting Christ's example. I find fulfillment in serving others for God's glory.

November 4
Using Your Gifts to Bless Others

"Each of you should use whatever gift you have received to serve others, as faithful stewards of God's grace in its various forms."

(1 Peter 4:10, NIV)

Devotional Reflection

God has blessed each of us with unique talents and gifts, and these abilities are meant to be shared with those around us. As black women, we often carry multiple talents, whether in leadership, creativity, nurturing, or wisdom. These gifts are not just for our personal gain, but to serve and uplift those in our communities. When we use our gifts to bless others, we are being faithful stewards of God's grace, reflecting His love in practical and meaningful ways.

Identifying your gifts may take time, but once you understand how God has uniquely equipped you, it becomes clear how much of a blessing you can be to others. Whether it's offering encouragement, mentoring, volunteering, or using your creative skills to inspire, every talent has a purpose. Your gifts have the power to bring joy, healing, and support to those in need, and when you give freely, you are participating in God's work in the world.

Today, take time to reflect on your unique gifts and talents. Consider how you can use them to serve those around you, knowing that even small acts of kindness can have a lasting impact.

Prayer: Lord, thank You for the gifts and talents You have given me. Help me to use them to bless and serve those around me, being a faithful steward of Your grace. Guide me to opportunities where I can make a positive impact and reflect Your love through my actions. Amen.

Affirmation: I use my unique gifts and talents to bless others, serving as a reflection of God's grace. I recognize the power of my abilities and offer them freely to uplift and support those around me. My gifts are a blessing to others, and I honor God through my service.

November 5
The Power of Generosity

"A generous person will prosper; whoever refreshes others will be refreshed." (Proverbs 11:25, NIV)

Devotional Reflection

Generosity is a powerful force that can bring about transformation in both the giver and the receiver. As black women, we often give in many ways—whether through our time, resources, or emotional support. While it may seem that only big acts of generosity matter, even the smallest gestures of kindness and giving can have a lasting impact. God calls us to give generously, not just out of our abundance, but from our hearts, knowing that every act of giving can change lives.

Generosity has the power to uplift those who are struggling, offer hope in difficult times, and provide support where it's needed most. But it also has the ability to refresh and renew the giver, as God blesses those who pour into the lives of others. When we give without expectation of return, we reflect God's love and participate in His work on Earth. Whether it's offering financial help, lending a listening ear, or giving time to a cause, your generosity has the potential to inspire and uplift others.

Today, think about ways you can be generous—whether through your resources, time, or talents. Trust that even small acts of giving can create ripple effects that change lives, including your own.

Prayer: Lord, help me to be generous in all areas of my life, giving with a joyful heart. Teach me to see the needs around me and to give freely, knowing that even small acts of generosity can make a difference. Bless my efforts to refresh others, and let Your love shine through my giving. Amen.

Affirmation: I embrace the power of generosity, knowing that giving—whether big or small—can change lives. I give freely, trusting God to use my generosity to uplift others and bring transformation. Through my giving, I reflect God's love and grace.

November 6
Creating a Legacy of Service

"Let your light shine before others, that they may see your good deeds and glorify your Father in heaven." (Matthew 5:16, NIV)

Devotional Reflection

A legacy of service is built not just through single acts of kindness, but through a life consistently dedicated to loving and helping others. As black women, our lives are often full of opportunities to serve — within our families, communities, and workplaces. Each act of kindness, no matter how small, leaves a lasting impact on those we serve. When we make service a priority, we build a legacy that reflects Christ's love and shines His light in a world that so desperately needs it.

Christ calls us to be the hands and feet of His love, and serving others is a powerful way to live out that calling. Building a legacy of service means thinking beyond ourselves and investing in the well-being of those around us, knowing that our actions have the potential to influence generations to come. Whether it's through mentoring, volunteering, or simply being a source of encouragement, every time we serve, we are planting seeds of love that will grow long after we're gone.

Today, reflect on the legacy you are creating. Consider how your acts of service are making a difference and how you can continue to build a life that reflects Christ's love for others.

Prayer: Lord, help me to create a legacy of service that reflects Your love and kindness. Teach me to serve others selflessly, and guide me to opportunities where my actions can make a lasting impact. May my life be a light that shines brightly for You, and may my service inspire others to know Your love. Amen.

Affirmation: I am building a legacy of service that reflects Christ's love. Through my acts of kindness, I am leaving a lasting impact on others and glorifying God. My life shines brightly as a testament to His love, grace, and compassion.

November 7
Serving Through Your Career

"Whatever you do, work at it with all your heart, as working for the Lord, not for human masters." (Colossians 3:23, NIV)

Devotional Reflection

Your career can be more than just a means to make a living; it can be a platform for serving others and making a meaningful impact. As black women, we often bring a unique strength, perspective, and resilience to our professional roles, and with these qualities comes the opportunity to help those around us. Whether through leadership, mentorship, or daily interactions, your job can be a place where you reflect God's love and care for others.

Serving through your career means approaching your work with a heart of service, seeing your position as an opportunity to uplift, encourage, and make a difference. It's not about the title you hold but how you choose to use your role to positively impact the lives of others. By aligning your career with your faith, you can find deeper purpose in the work you do, knowing that even in the smallest tasks, you are serving God and contributing to the greater good.

Today, think about how you can serve others through your career. Whether it's offering support to a colleague, using your skills to help someone in need, or simply working with integrity and kindness, trust that God can use your professional life as a powerful tool for service.

Prayer: Lord, help me to see my career as a platform for serving others. Guide me to find purpose in the work I do, and show me how to reflect Your love through my actions at work. May my efforts uplift those around me and bring glory to Your name. Amen.

Affirmation: I use my career as a platform to serve others, working with purpose and dedication. Through my job, I reflect God's love, helping and uplifting those around me. My work is an opportunity to make a positive impact and glorify God.

November 8
Overcoming Selfishness to Serve Others

"Do nothing out of selfish ambition or vain conceit. Rather, in humility value others above yourselves." (Philippians 2:3, NIV)

Devotional Reflection

Serving others requires letting go of self-centered desires and putting the needs of others before our own. In a world that often encourages us to focus on ourselves and our own achievements, it can be challenging to live out the call to serve with humility. As black women, we may already carry heavy responsibilities, and it can be tempting to focus on our personal needs and goals. However, God calls us to shift our focus outward, prioritizing service to others over selfish desires.

True service is an act of love and humility, one that requires us to move beyond our comfort zones. When we overcome selfishness, we are able to see the people around us more clearly—their struggles, needs, and hurts. This selflessness allows us to serve with compassion and generosity, reflecting the heart of Christ. Serving others doesn't diminish us; it enriches us by deepening our connection with God and with those we help. When we let go of selfish ambitions, we discover the joy that comes from giving ourselves fully in service to others.

Today, reflect on how you can overcome selfish desires and focus on serving others with humility and love. Ask God to guide your heart toward selflessness as you seek to serve those around you.

Prayer: Lord, help me to let go of selfish ambitions and desires, and teach me to serve others with humility and love. Open my eyes to the needs of those around me, and give me a heart that seeks to prioritize their well-being over my own. May my service be a reflection of Your love and compassion. Amen.

Affirmation: I let go of selfish desires and embrace a heart of service. I prioritize the needs of others and serve with love, humility, and compassion. Through my selfless acts, I reflect God's love and make a meaningful impact on the lives of those around me.

November 9
The Beauty of Helping Without Expectation

"But when you give to the needy, do not let your left hand know what your right hand is doing, so that your giving may be in secret. Then your Father, who sees what is done in secret, will reward you."

(Matthew 6:3-4, NIV)

Devotional Reflection

There is a unique beauty in serving others without expecting anything in return. In a world where acts of kindness are often highlighted for recognition, Jesus calls us to give quietly, with pure motives. As black women, we often find ourselves in roles of caregiving and support, and while the recognition can feel validating, the true joy and peace come from helping others simply because it's the right thing to do.

When we serve others without the expectation of praise or reward, we allow God to be our focus. Our acts of service become about love and compassion, not about what we stand to gain. This kind of selfless giving frees us from the pressures of external validation and connects us more deeply with God's heart. The peace and joy that follow come from knowing that we are pleasing God, and His rewards, both seen and unseen, are greater than anything the world could offer.

Today, seek opportunities to help others with no expectation of return or recognition. Let the beauty of quiet, selfless service fill your heart with peace and joy.

Prayer: Lord, teach me to serve others with a pure heart, expecting nothing in return. Help me to find joy and peace in selfless giving, knowing that You see and reward what is done in secret. May my acts of kindness reflect Your love, and may I find fulfillment in pleasing You above all else. Amen.

Affirmation: I find joy and peace in helping others without expecting anything in return. My acts of service are a reflection of God's love, and I trust that He sees and rewards my selflessness. I serve with a heart full of love and compassion, content in knowing that I am pleasing God.

November 10
Giving When You Feel You Have Nothing to Offer

"Truly I tell you," he said, "this poor widow has put in more than all the others. All these people gave their gifts out of their wealth; but she out of her poverty put in all she had to live on." (Luke 21:3-4, NIV)

Devotional Reflection

There are moments when we feel that we have nothing left to give—whether it's time, energy, or resources. As black women, balancing numerous responsibilities can leave us feeling drained and uncertain about how we can serve or give to others. Yet, God sees the heart behind every act of kindness, no matter how small. The story of the widow's offering reminds us that even when we feel we have little to give, God honors our willingness to give what we can.

When we trust that small acts of kindness matter, we open ourselves up to God's transformative power. A simple word of encouragement, a small donation, or a few moments of your time can make an incredible impact in someone's life. God multiplies our efforts, turning what feels like a small contribution into something meaningful. Even when we feel empty or inadequate, we can still give out of love and faith, knowing that God can use even the smallest act to bless others.

Today, trust that whatever you have to offer—no matter how small—is valuable in God's eyes. Lean on Him for strength, and know that your kindness makes a big difference.

Prayer: Lord, help me to trust that even when I feel like I have little to give, my small acts of kindness can make a difference. Give me the strength and wisdom to serve others with what I have, and remind me that You can multiply my efforts to bless others in ways I cannot imagine. Amen.

Affirmation: Even when I feel like I have little to offer, I trust that my small acts of kindness make a big difference. God sees and honors my heart, and I believe that He multiplies my efforts to bless others. I give with faith, knowing that every act matters in His plan.

November 11
Serving Others During Difficult Times

"Carry each other's burdens, and in this way you will fulfill the law of Christ." (Galatians 6:2, NIV)

Devotional Reflection

It can be hard to think about serving others when you are facing your own challenges. As black women, we often carry the weight of personal struggles—whether emotional, financial, or spiritual—yet God still calls us to serve. Even in the midst of difficulty, there is power in reaching out to help someone else. Serving others during difficult times not only blesses those around you but also brings comfort and healing to your own heart.

When we choose to serve others while struggling, we are reminded that we are not alone in our hardships. God uses these moments to connect us with others who may be facing similar challenges. This shared experience can bring strength and encouragement to both you and those you serve. Serving from a place of struggle is an act of faith that says, "I trust God to meet my needs, so I will help meet the needs of others." In doing so, you fulfill the law of Christ, which is to love and carry one another's burdens.

Today, reflect on how you can serve others, even in your own difficult season. Trust that as you reach out to help others, God will provide the strength and peace you need to get through your own challenges.

Prayer: Lord, even in my struggles, help me to serve others with a heart of love and compassion. Give me the strength to carry others' burdens as You carry mine, and remind me that in serving, I am fulfilling Your call to love. Bring peace to my heart as I trust You to meet my needs while I reach out to help others. Amen.

Affirmation: I serve others, even in difficult times, trusting that God will provide for my needs. As I carry others' burdens, I find strength, peace, and healing in Christ. My struggles do not stop me from showing love and compassion to those around me.

November 12
Encouraging Someone Who Feels Alone

"Two are better than one, because they have a good return for their labor: If either of them falls down, one can help the other up."

(Ecclesiastes 4:9-10, NIV)

Devotional Reflection

Loneliness can be a heavy burden, and many people around us feel isolated and unseen. As black women, we often understand the importance of community and the strength that comes from supporting one another. When someone feels alone, a simple gesture of encouragement can provide the hope and comfort they need to move forward. God calls us to be there for one another, lifting each other up in times of need.

Encouraging someone who feels alone doesn't always require grand actions; sometimes it's as simple as offering a kind word, a listening ear, or spending time with them. Your presence, empathy, and understanding can be a reminder that they are not forgotten. By reaching out, you become a source of light in their darkness, showing them that God's love is real and present through the care of others. In these moments, you are fulfilling the biblical call to bear one another's burdens and to reflect Christ's love through action.

Today, think of someone in your life who may be feeling lonely. Reach out with words of encouragement or offer your time, letting them know they are seen and valued.

Prayer: Lord, help me to be a source of hope and encouragement for those who feel alone. Open my heart to the needs of those around me, and give me the words and actions that will bring comfort and strength. Use me to remind others of Your love and presence in their lives. Amen.

Affirmation: I am a source of hope and support for those who feel alone. Through my words and actions, I reflect God's love, bringing comfort and encouragement to others. I reach out to those in need, letting them know they are not forgotten or alone.

November 13
Honoring God Through Generosity

"Each of you should give what you have decided in your heart to give, not reluctantly or under compulsion, for God loves a cheerful giver."
                                        (2 Corinthians 9:7, NIV)

Devotional Reflection

Generosity is more than just an act of kindness—it is a reflection of God's heart for others. As black women, we may already have a natural inclination to nurture and give, but true generosity comes from a place of deep love and a desire to honor God by meeting the needs of others. When we give freely, without hesitation or expectation, we mirror God's own generosity toward us. He provides for us in countless ways, and our giving is a response to the abundant love and grace He pours out on us daily.

Honoring God through generosity doesn't always involve financial giving. It can be expressed through your time, energy, talents, and resources. Whether you are giving to someone in need, offering your skills to uplift your community, or simply sharing a kind word, every act of giving has the power to reflect God's love. When we give with a cheerful heart, we align ourselves with God's will, and our generosity becomes an act of worship. It is through this selfless giving that we bring glory to God and serve as His hands and feet in the world.

Today, ask God to show you ways to honor Him through generosity. Give with a cheerful heart, knowing that your acts of giving reflect God's heart for others and bring Him glory.

Prayer: Lord, thank You for the many blessings You've given me. Help me honor You through generosity, giving freely and cheerfully. Show me how to reflect Your love through acts of kindness, and may my generosity bring glory to Your name. Amen.

Affirmation: I honor God through my acts of generosity. I give freely, cheerfully, and from the heart, reflecting God's love and care for others. My giving is an act of worship, and I trust that each gift, whether big or small, brings glory to God.

November 14
Sharing Your Resources to Meet Others' Needs

"Do not withhold good from those to whom it is due, when it is in your power to act." (Proverbs 3:27, NIV)

Devotional Reflection

God has blessed each of us with resources—whether time, talent, or material goods—not just for our own benefit but to share with others. As black women, we may have experienced both scarcity and abundance at different points in our lives, but no matter where we are, we have something valuable to offer. Sharing what we have to meet the needs of others is a way to honor God and reflect His love in the world.

Meeting the needs of others isn't always about money; it's about being aware of what you can give and using it to bless those around you. Your time can bring comfort to someone who is lonely. Your talents can uplift a community in need. Your resources—no matter how small—can make a difference in someone's life. When we offer what we have to those in need, we become instruments of God's grace, showing His care and compassion to a world that desperately needs it.

Today, consider what resources you have to share—whether it's your time, your talents, or something material. Ask God to guide you to opportunities where you can use what you have to bless others and meet their needs.

Prayer: Lord, thank You for the resources You've blessed me with. Help me recognize opportunities to share with those in need. Teach me to give freely of my time, talents, and resources, reflecting Your love. Guide me to be a blessing to others today. Amen.

Affirmation: I use my time, talents, and resources to bless others and meet their needs. I am aware of the opportunities around me to share what I have, and I give freely, knowing that my actions reflect God's love and compassion. I am a vessel of His grace, using what I have to make a difference.

November 15
The Impact of Service on Your Spiritual Growth

"Just as the Son of Man did not come to be served, but to serve, and to give his life as a ransom for many." (Matthew 20:28, NIV)

Devotional Reflection

Service is not only a way to bless others but also a path to spiritual growth. When we serve others, we follow the example of Christ, who came to serve rather than be served. As black women, we often find ourselves in positions where we care for others—family, friends, and our communities. While this care can be demanding, it also brings us closer to God by aligning our hearts with His will. Every act of service, no matter how small, draws us deeper into our relationship with Him.

Serving others teaches humility, compassion, and sacrifice—qualities that strengthen our spiritual journey. Through service, we learn to see others through God's eyes, recognizing their needs and responding with love. As we give of ourselves, we grow in our understanding of Christ's love for us and His desire for us to reflect that love in the world. By serving, we also discover new areas where God can work in and through us, leading to greater spiritual maturity.

Today, reflect on how your acts of service bring you closer to God. Consider how serving others has deepened your faith and helped you grow spiritually. Let your service be an opportunity for continued growth in your walk with Christ.

Prayer: Lord, thank You for the opportunities to serve others. Help me to see each act of service as a way to grow closer to You and deepen my spiritual journey. Teach me to serve with a heart full of love and compassion, and may my service reflect Your character and bring me closer to Your presence. Amen.

Affirmation: I grow closer to God through my acts of service. As I serve others, my faith deepens, and I reflect Christ's love in my actions. My service strengthens my spiritual journey, drawing me nearer to God with each act of kindness and compassion.

November 16
The Blessing of Serving Family and Friends

"Above all, love each other deeply, because love covers over a multitude of sins." (1 Peter 4:8, NIV)

Devotional Reflection

Serving those closest to us—our family and friends—can often be the most rewarding and yet the most challenging form of service. As black women, we are often the pillars in our families and communities, providing love and support in many ways. It's easy to take for granted the people closest to us, but God calls us to serve them with the same love and care that we extend to others. Serving those in our inner circle is a reflection of God's love, creating stronger bonds and deeper connections.

When we serve our family and friends with intentionality and love, we bless them in ways that can transform relationships. Whether through acts of kindness, offering support during difficult times, or simply being present, these moments of service deepen the love we share and reflect God's care. Serving the ones we love helps us practice patience, forgiveness, and compassion. It's in these everyday moments of service that we create an atmosphere of grace, building a foundation of love and trust within our closest relationships.

Today, consider the ways you can serve your family and friends. Look for opportunities to bless them through small acts of kindness, and let your love for them be a reflection of God's heart.

Prayer: Lord, help me to serve my family and friends with a heart full of love and care. Show me how to bless those closest to me, and teach me to see the opportunities around me to serve them. Let my actions reflect Your love, and may my service strengthen my relationships. Amen.

Affirmation: I serve my family and friends with love and care. Each act of service strengthens my relationships and reflects God's love. I am a blessing to those closest to me, creating deeper connections through kindness, patience, and compassion.

November 17
Serving the Next Generation

"Start children off on the way they should go, and even when they are old they will not turn from it." (Proverbs 22:6, NIV)

Devotional Reflection

Serving the next generation is one of the most impactful ways we can leave a legacy of faith, wisdom, and love. As black women, we stand on the shoulders of those who came before us, and it is our responsibility to invest in the lives of younger women and children, passing down the lessons we've learned. By serving as mentors and role models, we are planting seeds of hope, strength, and resilience that will grow in the hearts and minds of those who follow us.

Mentorship isn't just about offering advice; it's about walking alongside someone, guiding them with love and patience, and sharing the experiences that have shaped your life. When we invest in the next generation, we're helping them navigate challenges, build confidence, and develop their own faith journey. Whether through formal mentorship, teaching, or simply being a positive presence in their lives, your influence can shape their future in powerful ways. By serving them, you create a lasting impact that extends beyond your own life.

Today, reflect on how you can serve and invest in the next generation. Whether it's offering guidance to a younger woman or teaching a child, know that your service will leave a lasting imprint on their lives.

Prayer: Lord, help me serve the next generation with wisdom, love, and care. Guide me to be a mentor and role model, offering encouragement and support. May my influence point them to You and help them grow in faith and confidence. Amen.

Affirmation: I invest in the next generation by serving as a mentor and role model. My actions shape the future with wisdom, love, and faith. Through my service, I leave a legacy of strength, hope, and resilience.

November 18
The Ripple Effect of Small Acts of Kindness

"Do not forget to show hospitality to strangers, for by so doing some people have shown hospitality to angels without knowing it."

(Hebrews 13:2, NIV)

Devotional Reflection

Often, we underestimate the power of small acts of kindness. A simple smile, a kind word, or a small gesture can touch someone's heart in ways we may never fully realize. As black women, we often carry the weight of many responsibilities, yet even in our busyness, we can make time for small, intentional acts of kindness that ripple through our communities, families, and friendships. These small actions, done with love, reflect God's compassion and leave a lasting impact on the lives we touch.

Kindness is contagious. One small act can inspire others to do the same, creating a chain of positive energy that spreads far beyond what we can see. Whether it's holding the door for someone, offering a word of encouragement, or helping a neighbor, these acts create ripples of love that can reach into places of hurt and bring healing. Even when we feel like we have little to offer, God can use the smallest gestures to accomplish big things.

Today, look for opportunities to practice small acts of kindness. Trust that God will use your gestures to create ripples of love and hope, touching lives in ways you may not even be aware of.

Prayer: Lord, help me to see the value in small acts of kindness. Give me opportunities to share Your love through simple gestures that can have a lasting impact. Let my actions reflect Your heart, and may they create ripples of kindness that touch the lives of those around me. Amen.

Affirmation: I understand the power of small acts of kindness. Each gesture of love and compassion creates ripples that can touch lives in meaningful ways. I trust that even my smallest actions can have a lasting, positive impact in the world.

November 19
Giving When It Feels Inconvenient

"And do not forget to do good and to share with others, for with such sacrifices God is pleased." (Hebrews 13:16, NIV)

Devotional Reflection

There are times when giving and serving feel inconvenient, whether because of busy schedules, personal struggles, or simply exhaustion. Yet, it is often in these moments of inconvenience that our acts of kindness and generosity have the greatest impact. As black women, we may already have numerous demands on our time and energy, but God calls us to push beyond our comfort zones and serve others even when it's difficult. When we give sacrificially, we show a deeper level of love and commitment, reflecting the heart of Christ.

Learning to give when it feels inconvenient teaches us to trust in God's provision. When we sacrifice our time, resources, or energy for the sake of others, we are reminded that God sees our efforts and rewards the sacrifices we make. Acts of kindness offered in times of inconvenience are powerful demonstrations of faith, showing that we prioritize God's call to love others over our personal comfort. These moments stretch us, grow us, and deepen our dependence on God.

Today, consider where you can give or serve, even if it feels inconvenient. Trust that God will provide the strength and resources you need to make a difference.

Prayer: Lord, help me to give and serve even when it feels inconvenient. Teach me to trust in Your provision, knowing that You see and honor the sacrifices I make. Let my heart be open to serve others in love, no matter the challenges, and may my actions reflect Your generosity and grace. Amen.

Affirmation: I give and serve even when it feels inconvenient. I trust God to provide the strength and resources I need, knowing that sacrificial acts of kindness bring joy to His heart. My service reflects Christ's love, no matter the challenges I face.

November 20
Service as a Reflection of Christ

"For even the Son of Man did not come to be served, but to serve, and to give his life as a ransom for many." (Mark 10:45, NIV)

Devotional Reflection

Every act of service is an opportunity to reflect Christ's love and compassion. Jesus, who came to serve and not be served, provided the ultimate example of selfless love through His life and sacrifice. As black women, we may find ourselves in roles where we are constantly giving, nurturing, and supporting those around us. Yet, when we see these acts of service as reflections of Christ's love, we recognize that our service is more than just a responsibility—it's a powerful way to share His heart with the world.

When we serve others, we embody the compassion, grace, and humility that Christ showed during His time on earth. Whether through helping a neighbor, volunteering, or simply offering a listening ear, our acts of service are expressions of God's love. These moments of kindness are not just for the benefit of those we help, but also a witness to the world of Christ's love in action. By serving others, we show them the character of Christ—His selflessness, His care, and His desire to uplift and heal.

Today, look for ways to reflect Christ's love through your service. Let your actions be a living testimony of His compassion, and trust that through your service, others will see His heart.

Prayer: Lord, help me to reflect Christ's love through my acts of service. Teach me to serve with the same compassion, grace, and humility that Jesus showed. May my service be a reflection of Your love and a testimony of Your goodness to the world. Use me to bring healing, hope, and kindness to those around me. Amen.

Affirmation: I reflect Christ's love and compassion through my acts of service. Every moment of kindness is an opportunity to show others the heart of Jesus. I serve with grace, humility, and a desire to reflect Christ's love to the world.

November 21

Finding Joy in Sacrificial Giving

"In everything I did, I showed you that by this kind of hard work we must help the weak, remembering the words the Lord Jesus himself said: 'It is more blessed to give than to receive.'" (Acts 20:35, NIV)

Devotional Reflection

Sacrificial giving—offering up something precious for the benefit of others—can often feel challenging, yet it is in these moments that we find the deepest joy. As black women, we are often called to give of ourselves in various ways, whether through our time, energy, or resources. When we embrace the idea of giving sacrificially, even when it's difficult, we experience the unique joy that comes from aligning our hearts with God's. Jesus taught that it is more blessed to give than to receive, and in doing so, He showed us that true joy comes not from holding on to what we have, but from offering it up for the sake of others.

Sacrificial giving stretches our faith and deepens our dependence on God. It teaches us to trust that God will provide for our needs even when we give out of what feels like lack. Through this kind of giving, we come to understand that joy is not tied to comfort or abundance, but to the act of loving others as Christ loved us. When we give freely and sacrificially, we experience a deeper sense of fulfillment, knowing that our sacrifices are pleasing to God and making a meaningful impact on the lives of others.

Today, embrace the joy that comes from sacrificial giving. Whether it's your time, resources, or energy, trust that God will use your sacrifice to bless others and bring joy to your heart.

Prayer: Lord, help me find joy in sacrificial giving. Teach me to give willingly, even when it's a sacrifice. Help me trust that You will meet my needs as I bless others. Amen.

Affirmation: I find joy in sacrificial giving. I trust God to provide for my needs as I give freely, even in sacrifice. My giving reflects Christ's love, and I embrace the fulfillment of serving others with a joyful heart.

November 22
How Serving Others Transforms You

"Whoever brings blessing will be enriched, and one who waters will himself be watered." (Proverbs 11:25, NIV)

Devotional Reflection

Serving others doesn't just bless those on the receiving end—it transforms you in profound ways. As black women, we often pour ourselves into our communities, families, and careers, giving out of love and compassion. In the process of giving, we may think we're only meeting the needs of others, but service has the unique ability to shape and refine our own hearts and character. Through acts of kindness, patience, and selflessness, we become more like Christ, developing the traits of humility, empathy, and gratitude.

Serving others opens your eyes to the needs of the world around you, making you more aware of the struggles people face and how much even small gestures of kindness can mean. This awareness deepens your compassion and stretches your capacity to love. Over time, serving becomes less about duty and more about the joy of making a difference in someone's life. It softens the heart, builds resilience, and gives you a greater sense of purpose as you see how your actions reflect God's love and impact the lives of others.

Today, reflect on how serving others has shaped your heart and character. Embrace the transformation that comes from serving, and let your acts of kindness continue to mold you into a vessel of God's love and grace.

Prayer: Lord, thank You for how serving others has transformed my heart. Help me grow in humility, empathy, and love as I serve those around me. Amen.

Affirmation: Serving others transforms my heart and character. Through acts of kindness, I grow in empathy, humility, and love. I embrace the joy of serving, knowing that God is shaping me into a reflection of His love and grace through my service.

November 23
Serving Those Who Can't Repay You

"But when you give to the needy, do not let your left hand know what your right hand is doing, so that your giving may be in secret. Then your Father, who sees what is done in secret, will reward you."

(*Matthew 6:3-4, NIV*)

Devotional Reflection

True service and generosity are most beautiful when they are extended to those who cannot repay us. As black women, we may often find ourselves in positions where we give without expecting anything in return—whether it's time, wisdom, or resources. This kind of selfless service reflects the heart of Christ, who gave everything for us without seeking repayment. Helping others without the expectation of reward requires a deep trust in God, knowing that He sees every act of kindness and will provide for our needs in His perfect way.

When you serve those who can't repay you, you step into a deeper form of love—one that mirrors God's grace. It is a pure and humble act, one that focuses on the needs of others rather than what you might gain from the situation. Trusting that God will be your reward frees you from the need for recognition or compensation. The satisfaction comes from knowing that you've helped someone simply because it's the right thing to do, and in doing so, you align yourself with God's heart for the vulnerable and the needy.

Today, look for opportunities to help those who cannot repay you. Trust that your reward comes from God, and know that He delights in your selfless acts of service.

Prayer: Lord, help me serve those who cannot repay me with a pure heart, expecting nothing in return. Teach me to trust that You see my acts of kindness and will be my reward. Amen.

Affirmation: I serve those who cannot repay me, trusting that God is my reward. My kindness is rooted in love, and I seek no recognition. I embrace the joy of giving freely, knowing that God sees my heart and honors my service.

November 24
Supporting Black-Owned Businesses

"Let each of you look not only to his own interests, but also to the interests of others." (Philippians 2:4, NIV)

Devotional Reflection

Supporting black-owned businesses is an impactful way to serve and uplift your community. As black women, we understand the significance of supporting one another, especially in spaces where we may face barriers or challenges in entrepreneurship. By choosing to invest in black-owned businesses, you are directly contributing to the growth, success, and sustainability of black entrepreneurs who are working to build generational wealth and create opportunities for others.

Your decision to support black-owned businesses is more than just a financial transaction—it is an act of solidarity, empowerment, and service to your community. When you invest in businesses that align with your values and uplift others, you are helping to build a stronger, more connected community. It's a way to share in the success of others and to ensure that economic opportunities flow back into your own neighborhoods. God calls us to care for one another and look out for each other's well-being, and supporting black-owned businesses is a tangible way to do that.

Today, think about how you can intentionally support black-owned businesses in your community. By doing so, you are serving not only those entrepreneurs but also the future generations they are empowering.

Prayer: Lord, thank You for the opportunity to serve my community by supporting black-owned businesses. Help me to be intentional in my decisions, seeking ways to uplift and empower others through my actions. Amen.

Affirmation: My actions contribute to the growth and success of entrepreneurs, and I am proud to play a part in building a stronger, more connected community.

November 25
The Power of Encouraging Words

"Gracious words are a honeycomb, sweet to the soul and healing to the bones." (Proverbs 16:24, NIV)

Devotional Reflection

Words hold immense power. They can either build someone up or tear them down, and as black women, we understand the importance of speaking life into those around us. Encouraging words have the ability to lift spirits, offer hope, and provide strength in moments of difficulty. When we use our words to serve others emotionally, we are reflecting God's love and offering a form of healing that can be just as impactful as any physical act of service.

Encouragement doesn't always have to be profound; sometimes, the simplest phrases like, "I believe in you," "You're doing great," or "You're not alone" can make all the difference in someone's life. When we speak with kindness, empathy, and positivity, we are offering emotional support that may help someone persevere through their challenges. Our words, when used wisely, can breathe life into those who feel weary or broken, reminding them of their worth, strength, and purpose.

Today, make it a point to use your words to encourage those around you. Whether through a kind text, a heartfelt conversation, or an uplifting note, trust that your words have the power to serve others in ways you may not fully realize.

Prayer: Lord, help me to use my words as a tool for building up those around me. Teach me to speak life and encouragement into the hearts of those who need it most. Let my words reflect Your love and grace, bringing comfort, strength, and hope to others. Amen.

Affirmation: I use the power of my words to build up, encourage, and support others. My words are a source of healing, strength, and comfort, reflecting God's love and kindness. I speak life into those around me, knowing that my words have the power to uplift and inspire.

November 26
Serving Beyond Your Comfort Zone

"I can do all this through him who gives me strength."

(Philippians 4:13, NIV)

Devotional Reflection

Serving others often comes naturally when it fits within our comfort zones. But true growth happens when we step beyond what feels safe and familiar. As black women, we are often called to be leaders, nurturers, and caregivers, but sometimes God pushes us toward new and challenging ways of serving. These opportunities stretch us, teach us, and deepen our faith. When we serve beyond our comfort zone, we rely less on our own strength and more on God's power to guide and equip us.

It may feel intimidating to take on a role that feels unfamiliar or serve in an area where you lack confidence. However, it's in these moments that God's strength shines the brightest. Serving outside of your comfort zone allows you to grow spiritually, as you learn to trust God in ways you haven't before. Whether it's leading a new ministry, volunteering in a different community, or stepping into a mentoring role, these challenges often lead to unexpected blessings—not only for those you serve but for your own personal growth.

Today, ask God to show you new ways you can serve beyond your comfort zone. Trust that He will equip you with the strength and courage needed to make a difference, even in unfamiliar or challenging situations.

Prayer: Lord, give me the courage to serve beyond my comfort zone. Help me to step into new challenges with faith, knowing that You will provide the strength and wisdom I need. Teach me to trust You more as I seek to serve others in ways that stretch me and deepen my faith. Amen.

Affirmation: I embrace the challenge of serving beyond my comfort zone. I trust God to guide and equip me as I step into new roles and opportunities. Through these challenges, I grow in faith, strength, and understanding, knowing that God's power works through me.

November 27
Giving Time to Those Who Need It Most

"Carry each other's burdens, and in this way you will fulfill the law of Christ." (Galatians 6:2, NIV)

Devotional Reflection

In today's fast-paced world, time is often our most precious resource. As black women, we juggle many responsibilities, and it can be challenging to balance everything. However, giving time to those who need it most—whether they're struggling emotionally, spiritually, or physically—is one of the most impactful ways we can serve others. Our presence can offer comfort, encouragement, and a sense of hope that words alone may not provide.

When you prioritize your time for someone in need, you're showing them that they matter. Being fully present for someone—whether it's through a phone call, a visit, or just listening without distractions—allows them to feel seen and valued. In moments of struggle, it's often the gift of time that means the most. By giving of your time, you help bear the burdens of others, fulfilling Christ's call to love one another.

Today, reflect on how you can intentionally give your time to those who may need it most. Trust that your presence, no matter how simple or small it may seem, can make a world of difference in someone's life.

Prayer: Lord, help me to prioritize my time for those who need my presence the most. Teach me to be fully present, offering support and love to those who are struggling. Guide me to see the opportunities around me to serve others by giving my time and attention, reflecting Your love through my actions. Amen.

Affirmation: I give my time to those who need it most, knowing that my presence is a powerful way to serve. I prioritize being fully present for others, offering comfort and support in their times of struggle. Through my actions, I reflect God's love and care for those around me.

November 28
Service as an Act of Worship

"And whatever you do, whether in word or deed, do it all in the name of the Lord Jesus, giving thanks to God the Father through him."

(Colossians 3:17, NIV)

Devotional Reflection

Service is more than just helping others—it's an act of worship. As black women, we often serve in our homes, communities, and workplaces, sometimes without recognizing the spiritual significance of our actions. When we serve others with love and a heart for God, we are offering our service as a form of devotion and worship. Just as we worship through prayer, singing, or reading the Word, serving others becomes a way to honor and glorify God.

When you approach service as an act of worship, it transforms how you view your role in the lives of others. It shifts the focus from the task itself to the One you are ultimately serving. Whether it's volunteering, caring for family, or lending a helping hand to a friend in need, each act of service becomes a way to express your love for God. Serving with a joyful and willing heart allows you to reflect God's compassion and goodness in the world, making every small act of kindness a sacred offering to Him.

Today, let your service be an intentional act of worship. Recognize that in serving others, you are also serving God and bringing glory to His name.

Prayer: Lord, help me to see my acts of service as a form of worship and devotion to You. Teach me to serve others with a joyful heart, knowing that in doing so, I am bringing honor to Your name. Let my service reflect Your love and compassion, and may it be a pleasing offering to You. Amen.

Affirmation: I serve others as an act of worship, knowing that every act of kindness honors God. Through my service, I reflect His love and compassion in the world. My service is a sacred offering, and I find joy in serving both others and God.

November 29
Learning from Those You Serve

"The greatest among you will be your servant." (Matthew 23:11, NIV)

Devotional Reflection

Service is not a one-way street; while we give to others, we often receive lessons and insights that deepen our own growth. As black women, we often serve in leadership and caregiving roles, giving to those around us. Yet, it's important to recognize that those we serve have much to teach us. In humility, we learn that service opens the door to personal growth, empathy, and deeper understanding.

When we serve with an open heart, we can learn about resilience, gratitude, and perseverance from the very people we seek to help. They may show us new perspectives, inspire us with their courage, or teach us patience and grace in ways we hadn't considered. God often uses these moments of service to mold us into better reflections of His love. Embracing the lessons that come from serving others helps us to grow in humility, compassion, and wisdom.

Today, approach your acts of service with a heart willing to learn. Reflect on the lessons and growth that come from serving others, and trust that God is using these experiences to shape you in meaningful ways.

Prayer: Lord, as I serve others, open my heart to the lessons You have for me. Teach me to embrace the growth that comes from each act of service and to see those I serve as vessels of Your wisdom and grace. Help me to learn and grow in humility and compassion through these experiences. Amen.

Affirmation: I embrace the lessons that come from serving others. Through service, I grow in humility, compassion, and understanding. I remain open to the wisdom and insight that God reveals through the people I serve, trusting that these experiences shape me into a reflection of His love.

November 30
Creating a Lifestyle of Service

"Each of you should use whatever gift you have received to serve others, as faithful stewards of God's grace in its various forms."

(1 Peter 4:10, NIV)

Devotional Reflection

Service is more than an occasional act—it can become a way of life. As black women, we are often in positions of leadership and care, but the true power of service comes when it is woven into the fabric of our everyday lives. When we make service and generosity a daily practice, we align our hearts with God's call to love and care for others consistently. Every day provides opportunities to serve, whether through kind words, acts of generosity, or simply being present for those who need us.

Creating a lifestyle of service means living with an awareness of others' needs and being intentional about offering help whenever possible. It requires a heart that is always ready to give, a mindset that seeks to uplift, and hands that are willing to work. This doesn't mean we have to give in grand, exhausting ways all the time, but that we commit to living in a way that reflects Christ's love through service. In doing so, we become stewards of God's grace, spreading kindness, love, and support wherever we go.

Today, think about how you can incorporate service into your daily routine. Commit to making acts of service and generosity a natural part of your life, trusting that God will use your faithfulness to bless others.

Prayer: Lord, help me to create a lifestyle of service, making generosity and kindness a natural part of my daily life. Let my service reflect Your love, and may it become a testimony of Your grace. Amen.

Affirmation: I create a lifestyle of service, making generosity and kindness part of my daily life. I am mindful of others' needs and serve with a willing heart. Through my consistent acts of service, I reflect God's love and spread His grace wherever I go.

December

Reflection and Hope

December 1
Reflecting on Your Journey This Year

"The Lord has done great things for us, and we are filled with joy."

(Psalm 126:3, NIV)

Devotional Reflection

As the year draws to a close, it's important to pause and reflect on the journey you've taken. This year may have been filled with a mix of triumphs and challenges, but through it all, you've grown and learned valuable lessons. Reflecting on your journey allows you to appreciate how far God has brought you, and it gives you the chance to acknowledge the personal and spiritual growth that has taken place.

For many black women, our journey is one of resilience, strength, and determination. We've overcome obstacles, embraced new opportunities, and learned to lean on God in times of uncertainty. As you reflect, consider the lessons you've gained—both in moments of success and in the face of hardship. Each experience, whether joyful or difficult, has shaped you into the woman you are today. Taking time to reflect not only reminds you of your own strength but also of God's faithfulness in carrying you through every season.

Today, give yourself space to reflect on the year's journey. Celebrate your growth and remember the lessons that have helped you become stronger and more faithful.

Prayer: Lord, thank You for guiding me through this year. As I reflect on my journey, I see Your hand in every triumph and every challenge. Help me to appreciate how far I've come and the lessons I've learned along the way. Fill my heart with gratitude for Your faithfulness and strength. Amen.

Affirmation: I reflect on my journey with gratitude, celebrating how far I've come. Each step has taught me valuable lessons, and I recognize God's faithfulness in every moment. My growth is a testament to His love and guidance throughout this year.

December 2
Finding Strength in Challenges

"But he said to me, 'My grace is sufficient for you, for my power is made perfect in weakness.' Therefore I will boast all the more gladly about my weaknesses, so that Christ's power may rest on me."

(2 Corinthians 12:9, NIV)

Devotional Reflection

Challenges are a part of life, but they also provide opportunities for growth and strength. As black women, we face unique difficulties that test our resilience, yet it's in these very moments of struggle that we often discover our greatest strength. Acknowledging the challenges you've faced this year can be empowering, as they have shaped you and helped you grow stronger—mentally, emotionally, and spiritually.

God's grace is present in every challenge. Though it may not always feel like it in the moment, each difficulty is an opportunity to rely on His strength rather than your own. Whether you've faced obstacles in your personal life, career, or health, God has used these experiences to develop your character and deepen your faith. Remember that true strength comes from trusting in God's power, especially in moments of weakness. Your challenges are not setbacks but setups for greater strength and reliance on Him.

Today, take time to reflect on the challenges you've faced this year and how they've made you stronger. Embrace the lessons you've learned, and thank God for being your source of strength through it all.

Prayer: Lord, thank You for being my strength in times of weakness. Help me to see the challenges I've faced as opportunities to grow and deepen my faith in You. Teach me to trust Your grace in every difficulty, knowing that You are making me stronger each day. Amen.

Affirmation: I find strength in the challenges I've faced, knowing that they have made me stronger and more resilient. I trust God's grace in every struggle and embrace the lessons learned through each difficulty. His power is perfect in my weakness.

December 3
Celebrating Personal Growth

"But grow in the grace and knowledge of our Lord and Savior Jesus Christ. To him be glory both now and forever!" (2 Peter 3:18, NIV)

Devotional Reflection

Growth doesn't happen overnight—it's a gradual process of learning, adapting, and trusting God through each season of life. As you look back on the year, take time to recognize the personal growth you've experienced, both spiritually and emotionally. For many black women, personal growth often comes through navigating challenges, balancing multiple roles, and learning to prioritize self-care while trusting in God's guidance.

Whether it's in your relationship with God, your emotional resilience, or your ability to forgive and love others, growth is worth celebrating. Perhaps you've learned to set healthier boundaries, deepened your prayer life, or become more confident in your purpose. Whatever the area of growth, know that every step forward is a reflection of God's work in you. Celebrating your growth isn't just about recognizing your progress—it's about giving God the glory for how He's transformed you through the year's ups and downs.

Today, take a moment to celebrate how far you've come. Reflect on the areas where you've grown and give thanks to God for His grace that has carried you through each stage of your journey.

Prayer: Lord, thank You for the personal growth I've experienced this year. I recognize that each step forward, both spiritually and emotionally, is because of Your grace and guidance. Help me to continue growing in Your love and wisdom, and let me always give You glory for the progress I make. Amen.

Affirmation: I celebrate my personal growth, knowing that God has been guiding me every step of the way. Spiritually and emotionally, I am stronger than I was before, and I give God all the glory for the transformation in my life.

December 4
Embracing the Lessons of Failure

"For though the righteous fall seven times, they rise again, but the wicked stumble when calamity strikes." (Proverbs 24:16, NIV)

Devotional Reflection

Failure is often seen as a setback, but in God's eyes, it's a stepping stone for growth and learning. As black women, we may feel the pressure to succeed in every area of life—whether in our careers, relationships, or personal goals. However, it's important to recognize that failure is not the end; it's an opportunity to rise again, stronger and wiser. Every failure carries valuable lessons that shape us into who God has called us to be.

Reflecting on your failures allows you to see them not as marks of defeat, but as moments of growth. Perhaps you've learned resilience, patience, or the importance of trusting God's timing through your setbacks. These experiences are necessary for your development, and they help you rely less on your own strength and more on God's grace. Failure is not something to fear or avoid but something to embrace as part of the journey. It's through these moments that God refines us and prepares us for greater things.

Today, reflect on any failures or setbacks you've faced this year. Consider the lessons you've learned and how they've contributed to your growth. Trust that God is using these experiences to prepare you for what's next.

Prayer: Lord, help me to see my failures not as defeats but as opportunities for growth and learning. Teach me to embrace the lessons You have for me in moments of struggle and to trust that You are refining me through every setback. Thank You for always giving me the strength to rise again. Amen.

Affirmation: I embrace the lessons of failure, knowing that each setback is an opportunity to grow and improve. I rise again with God's strength, wiser and stronger than before. My failures do not define me—they refine me for the future God has prepared for me.

December 5
Gratitude for God's Faithfulness

"The Lord has done great things for us, and we are filled with joy."
(Psalm 126:3, NIV)

Devotional Reflection

Reflecting on the past year, it's easy to get caught up in the challenges and struggles we've faced. However, as Black women, we also carry a rich history of resilience and faith. Looking back, we can see how God's faithfulness has been part of our lives, guiding us even in the toughest moments. Each step we took, each tear we shed, and every joy we celebrated was part of a divine plan. Remembering this helps us recognize that we are never alone.

In moments of doubt, we can see how God has been our anchor, providing strength when we felt weak. His hand has guided us, opening doors we couldn't have imagined and bringing people into our lives who have supported us. Today, let's take a moment to acknowledge His unwavering presence and the blessings He has poured into our lives.

Prayer: Lord, thank You for Your faithfulness throughout this year. Help me to see Your hand in every moment, guiding me and providing for me. I am grateful for the strength and support You've given. Amen.

Affirmation: I recognize God's faithfulness in my life. I am grateful for His guidance and the blessings I've received throughout the year.

December 6
Finding Joy in Small Victories

"The Lord is faithful to all his promises and loving toward all he has made." (Psalm 145:13, NIV)

Devotional Reflection

As the year draws to a close, it's a perfect time to look back and reflect on God's unwavering faithfulness. Through the highs and lows, God has been present, guiding you, providing for you, and strengthening you. His faithfulness is often most visible when we take a step back and consider how He's worked in the details of our lives—whether through answered prayers, unexpected blessings, or even the grace to endure difficult seasons.

For black women, who often carry the weight of many responsibilities, it's easy to get caught up in the daily grind and overlook the ways God has sustained and provided. But when you take time to reflect, you'll see His hand in every moment, big and small. Even in the challenges, God has been with you, offering His love, peace, and protection. Gratitude for God's faithfulness not only honors what He has done but also strengthens your faith for the future. It reminds you that just as He was with you through this year, He will continue to guide you in the years to come.

Today, take time to thank God for His faithfulness. Reflect on the moments where He showed up, provided for you, and carried you through, and let your heart be filled with gratitude for His steadfast love.

Prayer: Lord, I am grateful for Your faithfulness this year. Thank You for guiding me through every challenge. Help me remember Your hand in each moment and trust You to guide me in the future. Amen.

Affirmation: I am grateful for God's faithfulness in my life. He has guided me through every season, providing strength, grace, and love. I trust that just as He was with me this year, He will continue to lead me in the days ahead.

December 7
Healing from Disappointment

"The Lord is close to the brokenhearted and saves those who are crushed in spirit." (Psalm 34:18, NIV)

Devotional Reflection

Disappointment is a natural part of life, and we've all faced moments where things didn't go as planned. As Black women, we often navigate life with strength, yet disappointments can leave us feeling disheartened and questioning our path. It's vital to acknowledge these feelings and give ourselves the space to heal.

Healing from disappointment means letting go of unmet expectations and trusting that God's plans are greater than our own. Reflecting on the disappointments of this year provides an opportunity to release lingering frustration or sadness. God sees your heartache and is close to you in those moments. He has a purpose in every delay, rejection, or closed door, even when it's hard to see.

Healing comes when we surrender our unmet expectations to Him, allowing His peace to fill the void left by disappointment. Trust that He is working everything out for your good, even if it looks different from what you envisioned.

Today, take time to reflect on any disappointments you've experienced. Ask God to heal your heart, let go of what didn't happen, and open yourself to the new things He has in store for you.

Prayer: Lord, I bring my disappointments to You. Help me let go of unmet expectations and trust Your greater plans. Heal my heart and fill me with hope for the future. Thank You for guiding me through. Amen.

Affirmation: I release my disappointments and trust in God's greater plan for my life. I let go of unmet expectations, knowing that God's path for me is filled with purpose and hope. My heart is healing, and I embrace the future with faith.

December 8
Releasing What No Longer Serves You

"Therefore, if anyone is in Christ, the new creation has come: The old has gone, the new is here!" (2 Corinthians 5:17, NIV)

Devotional Reflection

Growth often requires letting go of what no longer serves us—whether it's habits, relationships, or patterns that may be holding us back. As black women, we are conditioned to be strong and resilient, sometimes holding on to things that we feel obligated to maintain, even when they no longer benefit us. However, part of spiritual growth and emotional healing is recognizing when it's time to release things that no longer align with who God is calling us to be.

Identifying what needs to be released can be difficult. Perhaps there are unhealthy relationships that drain you, habits that hinder your progress, or mindsets that no longer reflect your faith journey. Letting go of these things doesn't mean you've failed or given up—it means you're making space for the new blessings and opportunities that God wants to bring into your life. When we release what no longer serves us, we open ourselves to a renewed sense of purpose, growth, and alignment with God's will.

Today, take time to reflect on what you need to release. Ask God to give you the wisdom and courage to let go of anything that hinders your growth, and trust that He is preparing you for something greater.

Prayer: Lord, give me the wisdom to identify what no longer serves me and the courage to release it. Help me let go of unhealthy habits, relationships, and patterns that are holding me back from the growth You desire for me. Fill me with peace as I trust You to guide me into a new season of purpose and transformation. Amen.

Affirmation: I release what no longer serves me, trusting God to guide me toward growth and transformation. I let go of unhealthy habits, relationships, and patterns, making space for new blessings and opportunities in my life. I embrace God's purpose for my future.

December 9
Holding On to Hope in Uncertain Times

"Let us hold unswervingly to the hope we profess, for he who promised is faithful." (Hebrews 10:23, NIV)

Devotional Reflection

Life is full of uncertainty, and for many black women, navigating the unknown can feel especially heavy. Whether it's uncertainty in your career, family, or health, the weight of not knowing what comes next can be overwhelming. But even in the midst of uncertainty, God calls us to hold on to hope. Hope is not rooted in what we see or understand—it's anchored in God's promises and His faithfulness.

When the future feels unclear or challenging, it's easy to become anxious or fearful. However, it's in these moments that we are called to lean on God and trust that He is working behind the scenes, even when we can't see the full picture. Holding on to hope doesn't mean ignoring the realities of life's struggles; it means choosing to trust that God's plans for you are still good. He has not forgotten you, and His promises remain true, no matter how uncertain things seem.

Today, focus on holding on to hope, knowing that God is with you through every twist and turn. Let His faithfulness be your anchor, even when the path ahead is unclear.

Prayer: Lord, in times of uncertainty, help me to hold on to hope. When I can't see what the future holds, remind me that You are in control and that Your promises remain true. Strengthen my faith and help me trust in Your plan, even when life feels unclear. Thank You for being my source of hope and peace. Amen.

Affirmation: I hold on to hope, trusting in God's faithfulness even in uncertain times. No matter what the future holds, I know that God is with me, guiding and protecting me. My hope is anchored in His promises, and I trust that His plans for me are good.

December 10
Reflecting on Your Spiritual Growth

"But the path of the righteous is like the morning sun, shining ever brighter till the full light of day." (Proverbs 4:18, NIV)

Devotional Reflection

Spiritual growth is a continuous journey, one that deepens with every challenge, blessing, and moment of faith. As you reflect on this past year, consider how your relationship with God has evolved. Perhaps you've grown in your prayer life, experienced deeper trust in God during trials, or found peace in His presence. Growth isn't always about monumental changes; it can be found in the quiet moments of learning to depend on God more fully.

As black women, balancing life's demands can sometimes cause us to overlook the small ways we've grown spiritually. But each step you've taken to seek God, to listen to His voice, and to rely on His promises has contributed to your spiritual maturity. Even in moments of doubt, struggle, or uncertainty, your faith has carried you through. Reflecting on your spiritual growth helps you recognize that God has been with you every step of the way, gently guiding you closer to Him.

Today, take a moment to reflect on how your relationship with God has deepened this year. Celebrate the progress you've made, knowing that each step of faith is part of a greater journey toward spiritual wholeness.

Prayer: Lord, thank You for the ways You have deepened my faith and relationship with You this year. Help me to continue growing spiritually, trusting You more each day. As I reflect on this year's journey, I am grateful for Your presence, guidance, and love. May I keep growing closer to You in the years to come. Amen.

Affirmation: I reflect on my spiritual growth with gratitude, knowing that my relationship with God has deepened this year. Each step of faith has drawn me closer to Him, and I celebrate the progress I've made on my journey toward spiritual maturity. God's presence has guided me every step of the way.

December 11
Practicing Self-Compassion

"The Lord is compassionate and gracious, slow to anger, abounding in love." (Psalm 103:8, NIV)

Devotional Reflection

As Black women, we often set high expectations for ourselves, striving to excel in our careers, family life, and spiritual journeys. In difficult times, it's easy to be hard on ourselves, focusing on our perceived failures or shortcomings. However, just as God is compassionate and gracious, He invites us to extend that same grace to ourselves.

Practicing self-compassion means acknowledging that struggles and mistakes are part of being human. It involves embracing imperfections with kindness instead of harsh judgment. God sees your efforts, even when you feel like you've failed, and loves you deeply through it all. As you reflect on the year, give yourself credit for all you've endured, learned, and achieved, even amid adversity. Self-compassion allows you to view your journey with gentleness, recognizing that God's grace covers every step.

Today, take a moment to extend grace to yourself. Reflect on your challenges and remind yourself that it's okay not to be perfect. Embrace God's compassion and practice that same kindness toward yourself.

Prayer: Lord, help me to practice self-compassion as I reflect on this year. Teach me to show myself the same grace You show me. In moments of struggle and imperfection, remind me that Your love is constant and that I am worthy of kindness, even from myself. Thank You for Your compassion and grace that covers me always. Amen.

Affirmation: I practice self-compassion, giving myself grace as I reflect on my efforts and struggles. I embrace God's love and kindness, knowing that I am worthy of patience and understanding. I release harsh judgment and celebrate the progress I've made, trusting in God's compassion for me.

December 12
The Power of Reflection in Building Faith

"Remember the wonders he has done, his miracles, and the judgments he pronounced." (1 Chronicles 16:12, NIV)

Devotional Reflection

Looking back on our journey is a powerful tool for building faith. Reflection allows us to see where God has shown up in our lives, how He has answered prayers, and how His hand has guided us through both joyful and challenging times. For black women, who often carry the weight of many responsibilities, reflection serves as a reminder that even in our busiest or most difficult seasons, God has been with us, working on our behalf.

When you reflect on how God has been faithful in the past, it strengthens your trust in His promises for the future. Each answered prayer, each challenge you've overcome, and each moment of grace you've experienced are all reminders that God's presence is constant. Looking back with gratitude helps you build a deeper trust in God's ability to provide, protect, and guide you forward. It reassures you that just as He was with you in the past, He will continue to be with you in the days and years to come.

Today, spend time reflecting on the ways God has been faithful to you. Let that reflection build your faith and give you confidence as you look toward the future, knowing that the same God who was with you before will be with you always.

Prayer: Lord, thank You for the many ways You have been faithful to me. Help me to reflect on my journey with gratitude, seeing Your hand in every moment. As I look back on how You have guided and cared for me, build my faith for the future. Teach me to trust that You will continue to be with me in the days ahead. Amen.

Affirmation: I reflect on God's faithfulness in my past, knowing that each moment of His guidance and provision strengthens my faith for the future. I trust in His promises and look forward with confidence, knowing that God's presence is with me always.

December 13
Trusting God for the Next Season

"For I know the plans I have for you," declares the Lord, "plans to prosper you and not to harm you, plans to give you hope and a future."
(Jeremiah 29:11, NIV)

Devotional Reflection

As one season comes to an end and the next begins, trusting God for the future can feel both exciting and uncertain. Reflecting on the unknowns of the new year may bring up feelings of anticipation or anxiety, especially when you're unsure of what's ahead. However, trusting God means believing that His plans for your life are good, even when you don't know the specifics. He has guided you through this year, and He will continue to guide you in the next.

For black women, who often juggle various responsibilities and challenges, trusting God for the next season requires letting go of the need to control every detail and placing your faith in His wisdom. This act of trust is an invitation to surrender your worries and fears, knowing that God's plans for you are filled with hope and purpose. As you prepare your heart for the new year, allow yourself to rest in the knowledge that God has already gone ahead of you. His promises remain true, and His provision is unwavering.

Today, focus on preparing your heart to trust God for the season ahead. Embrace the hope and peace that comes from knowing that He holds your future in His hands.

Prayer: Lord, as I prepare for the next season, help me trust You completely with my future. Remind me that Your plans are good and You have prepared the way for me. Teach me to surrender my fears, knowing You are with me every step. Fill my heart with hope and peace as I look forward. Amen.

Affirmation: I trust God for the next season of my life, knowing that His plans are filled with hope and purpose. I release my fears and embrace the future with confidence, trusting that God is guiding me every step of the way. My heart is prepared for the blessings and challenges that lie ahead, with God by my side.

December 14
Celebrating the Faithfulness of Others

"Therefore encourage one another and build each other up, just as in fact you are doing." (1 Thessalonians 5:11, NIV)

Devotional Reflection

No journey is traveled alone. Along the way, God places people in our lives to support us and lift us when we need it most. Reflecting on the faithfulness of your family, friends, and community reminds you of the blessings found in connection and love. As Black women, we often draw strength from the support systems around us, making today a perfect opportunity to celebrate those who have stood by you through thick and thin.

Take a moment to reflect on the people who have been faithful in your life this year. Whether they provided a shoulder to lean on, offered encouraging words, or simply shared their presence, these moments of support were gifts from God. Relationships built on love and trust reflect God's love for us and provide the strength we need to move forward. Celebrating their faithfulness expresses gratitude to them and acknowledges God's work through the people He has placed in our lives.

Today, give thanks for the support you've received. Let those special individuals know how much their faithfulness means to you and how they have been a source of strength and encouragement.

Prayer: Lord, thank You for the people You've placed in my life who support and love me. Help me celebrate their presence and recognize their blessings. Teach me to show gratitude for how You work through others, and may I continue to encourage and uplift those around me. Amen.

Affirmation: I celebrate the faithfulness of others in my life, giving thanks for the support and love I've received from friends, family, and my community. I recognize their presence as a blessing, and I honor the ways they have lifted me up. I, too, strive to be a source of encouragement and love to those around me.

December 15
Embracing Hope for Your Family's Future

"But from everlasting to everlasting the Lord's love is with those who fear him, and his righteousness with their children's children."

(Psalm 103:17, NIV)

Devotional Reflection

As black women, we often carry the hopes and dreams of our families, wanting the best for those we love. Whether it's our children, partners, siblings, or extended family, our hearts are filled with prayers for their protection, growth, and success. While we may not know what the future holds, we can rest in the assurance that God's love and provision extend to our families. Trusting God with the future of our loved ones allows us to release worry and embrace hope, knowing that He is in control.

Praying for your family's future is an act of faith and love. It's recognizing that while you may not be able to shield them from every challenge, God is with them, guiding their steps. His promises are not just for you but for your family, covering generations to come. As you pray and trust God for their future, you can find peace in knowing that He has a plan and purpose for each one of your loved ones. Even in moments of uncertainty, God's hand is at work, shaping their path and bringing them closer to His will.

Today, embrace hope for your family's future by lifting them up in prayer. Trust that God's love and protection will continue to cover them, now and in the years to come.

Prayer: Lord, I lift my family and loved ones to You, trusting that You have a plan and purpose for each of them. Help me to embrace hope for their future, knowing that Your love and protection are with them always. Guide their steps and fill them with Your peace and wisdom as they walk through life. Amen.

Affirmation: I embrace hope for my family's future, trusting that God's love and protection cover them. I release worry and pray for their guidance, knowing that God's hand is on their lives. I find peace in His promises for my loved ones and their journey ahead.

December 16
Finding Peace Amidst Unanswered Prayers

"The Lord is good to those whose hope is in him, to the one who seeks him; it is good to wait quietly for the salvation of the Lord."

(Lamentations 3:25-26, NIV)

Devotional Reflection

Unanswered prayers can be one of the most challenging aspects of faith. As black women, we often carry deep hopes and desires, praying for breakthroughs in our families, careers, health, or personal lives. When those prayers go unanswered, it's easy to feel disheartened or question God's plan. However, faith calls us to trust that God's timing is always perfect, even when we don't understand why certain prayers remain unanswered.

God's silence doesn't mean He hasn't heard you, nor does it mean He's forgotten you. It may simply mean that His plans and timing are different from what you imagined. Accepting this truth allows you to find peace, even in the waiting. Trusting that God sees the bigger picture and knows what is best for you brings comfort during seasons of uncertainty. God's delays are not denials, and sometimes unanswered prayers are preparing us for something greater than we could have asked for.

Today, focus on finding peace in God's perfect timing. Surrender your unanswered prayers to Him, trusting that His plan is for your good, even when it's not yet revealed.

Prayer: Lord, help me to find peace in the midst of unanswered prayers. Remind me that Your timing is perfect, even when I can't see the full picture. Teach me to trust in Your plan and to wait with hope, knowing that You are always working for my good. Give me the strength to release my worries and rest in Your love. Amen.

Affirmation: I find peace in God's perfect timing, trusting that He knows what is best for me. Even when prayers go unanswered, I release my worries and embrace His plan. I wait with hope, knowing that God's delays are preparing me for greater things.

December 17
Reflecting on Your Role in Your Community

"Each of you should use whatever gift you have received to serve others, as faithful stewards of God's grace in its various forms."

(1 Peter 4:10, NIV)

Devotional Reflection

As a Black woman, you likely wear many hats within your community—whether as a leader, mentor, caregiver, or support system. Reflecting on your role allows you to see how God has used your gifts, talents, and time to bless others. Every act of service, no matter how small, contributes to the well-being of those around you and strengthens the bonds within your community.

Your contributions may take various forms—volunteering at church, mentoring young women, supporting a friend, or simply being an encouraging presence for those in need. Each act of service reflects God's love and grace working through you. Reflecting on these contributions helps you recognize the impact you've made and encourages you to consider how you can continue to serve in the future.

As you look ahead, think about how you can further embrace your role, continuing to be a light and blessing to those around you. Today, take time to reflect on your contributions to your community this year. Celebrate the ways you've served and ask God to guide you in discovering new opportunities to make a positive impact.

Prayer: Lord, thank You for the opportunity to serve my community. Help me to reflect on the ways I have contributed, and show me how I can continue to be a blessing to those around me. Guide me in using my gifts to make a difference, and give me the strength and wisdom to serve faithfully in the future. Amen.

Affirmation: I reflect on my role in my community with gratitude, recognizing how God has used my gifts to bless others. I am committed to continuing to serve, knowing that each act of service strengthens my community and reflects God's love. I look forward to finding new ways to contribute and make a positive impact.

December 18
Rejoicing in New Opportunities

"See, I am doing a new thing! Now it springs up; do you not perceive it? I am making a way in the wilderness and streams in the wasteland."

(Isaiah 43:19, NIV)

Devotional Reflection

This year may have brought new opportunities—some you expected, and others that surprised you. As black women, navigating change and embracing new doors that open can sometimes feel overwhelming, but each opportunity is a sign of God's provision and a step toward fulfilling His purpose for your life. New opportunities, whether in your career, relationships, or personal growth, are reasons to rejoice because they reflect God's continual work in your life.

Celebrating these opportunities is about recognizing that God is always doing something new, even in places where you may have felt stuck or uncertain. His promise to make a way in the wilderness reminds us that He is constantly providing fresh paths and possibilities, even when we don't see them at first. Take time today to rejoice in the new beginnings and chances for growth that have come your way this year, and trust that God's hand is in every one of them.

Today, reflect on the new opportunities that have come your way, and celebrate how God is using them to shape your future. Embrace each one as a gift, trusting that it's part of God's greater plan for your life.

Prayer: Lord, thank You for the new opportunities You have brought into my life this year. Help me to recognize and celebrate each one as a gift from You. Give me the courage to embrace these opportunities with faith, trusting that You are guiding my steps and using these moments to fulfill Your purpose in my life. Amen.

Affirmation: I rejoice in the new opportunities God has provided this year. I celebrate each one as a sign of His provision and purpose for my life. I embrace these opportunities with faith, trusting that God is guiding me toward greater growth and fulfillment.

December 19
Preparing Your Heart for What's Next

"Trust in the Lord with all your heart and lean not on your own understanding; in all your ways submit to him, and he will make your paths straight." (Proverbs 3:5-6, NIV)

Devotional Reflection

As the year winds down, it's natural to think about what lies ahead. Preparing your heart for the future requires both faith and intention. As black women, we often set goals and make plans, but it's important to remember that true peace comes from trusting God to lead your steps. You may have dreams, aspirations, and goals for the next season of your life, but placing them in God's hands ensures that your path aligns with His will for you.

Setting intentions for the future is a powerful act of faith. It involves being purposeful about your desires while surrendering control to God's plan. As you reflect on the upcoming year, focus on preparing your heart for what God has in store. Trust that He is guiding your steps, even in areas where the way forward seems unclear. Let your intentions be rooted in a desire to follow His lead, knowing that He sees the bigger picture and will direct you toward what's best.

Today, take time to set intentions for the future while inviting God to guide your steps. Prepare your heart for the next season with faith, trusting that God's plan is perfect.

Prayer: Lord, as I prepare for what's next, help me to set my intentions with faith and trust in You. Guide my steps and align my desires with Your will. Teach me to surrender control, knowing that Your plans are greater than my own. Fill my heart with peace and confidence as I trust You to lead me into the next season. Amen.

Affirmation: I prepare my heart for the future with faith, setting my intentions and trusting God to guide my steps. I release control and embrace God's perfect plan for my life, knowing that He will lead me in the right direction. My future is secure in His hands.

December 20
Reflecting on God's Promises

"For no matter how many promises God has made, they are 'Yes' in Christ. And so through him the 'Amen' is spoken by us to the glory of God." (2 Corinthians 1:20, NIV)

Devotional Reflection

Throughout the year, there have likely been moments when you needed to cling to God's promises for strength, comfort, and guidance. Reflecting on those promises reminds you of how faithful God has been, even when life felt uncertain. His promises are not just words in the Bible but living truths that continue to uphold us in times of joy and struggle. As black women, we often carry heavy burdens, and it's God's promises that give us the strength to keep going.

God's promises of peace, provision, protection, and purpose have sustained you through the challenges of this year. Whether you were trusting Him to make a way when there seemed to be none, or holding on to His promise of rest for your weary soul, His word has been a constant source of hope. As you reflect on these promises, be encouraged that they are still true and will continue to guide and sustain you in the days to come.

Today, take time to reflect on the promises of God that have carried you this year. Hold them close to your heart, knowing that God is faithful to fulfill everything He has spoken over your life.

Prayer: Lord, thank You for the promises You have made and kept in my life this year. As I reflect on Your faithfulness, I am reminded that Your word never fails. Help me to continue holding on to Your promises as I move forward, trusting that You will guide, protect, and provide for me in every season. Amen.

Affirmation: I hold on to the promises of God, knowing that they have sustained me throughout this year. His faithfulness has carried me, and I trust that His promises will continue to guide and protect me. I rest in the assurance that God's word is true, and His promises will never fail.

December 21
Letting Go of Regrets

"And we know that in all things God works for the good of those who love him, who have been called according to his purpose."

(Romans 8:28, NIV)

Devotional Reflection

Regret can often weigh heavily on our hearts. Whether it's missed opportunities, decisions we wish we could undo, or moments we felt we failed, regret can keep us stuck in the past. As black women, we often hold ourselves to high standards, and when things don't go as planned, regret can creep in. However, God reminds us that He is able to use every experience, including our mistakes and missteps, for His purpose.

Letting go of regret means trusting that nothing in your life is wasted. God's grace covers all, and He weaves together even the difficult or painful moments for your good and His glory. Releasing regrets allows you to focus on the present and the future rather than dwelling on what could have been. God's purpose for your life is not derailed by your past; instead, He uses everything to shape you into the person He's calling you to be. By trusting in God's purpose, you can move forward with hope, knowing that every experience, no matter how challenging, has a role in your growth.

Today, take a moment to release any lingering regrets and trust that God has a purpose for everything you've experienced. Allow His grace to heal your heart and lead you forward with peace.

Prayer: Lord, help me to let go of any regrets I'm holding on to. Teach me to trust that You are using every part of my story, even the difficult moments, for Your purpose. Fill me with peace as I release the past, and guide me as I move forward in faith. Thank You for Your grace that covers all my mistakes. Amen.

Affirmation: I release my regrets, trusting that God has a purpose for everything I've experienced. I embrace His grace and move forward with peace, knowing that nothing in my life is wasted. God is using every part of my story to shape me and fulfill His purpose for my life.

December 22
Hope in the Midst of Uncertainty

"May the God of hope fill you with all joy and peace as you trust in him, so that you may overflow with hope by the power of the Holy Spirit." (Romans 15:13, NIV)

Devotional Reflection

Uncertainty is a natural part of life, often leaving us feeling unsettled and anxious about the future. For Black women, who frequently juggle multiple roles and responsibilities, the unknown can be especially overwhelming. However, in the midst of this uncertainty, God invites us to lean on Him and place our hope in His promises. Hope isn't found in the absence of challenges or unanswered questions; it rests in the assurance that God is in control, even when we can't see the full picture.

When the future feels uncertain, it's normal to worry. Yet God reminds us that He is the source of our hope. Trusting Him brings peace and joy, even when the path ahead seems unclear. His track record of faithfulness in your life assures you that He will continue to guide you through whatever uncertainties may come. By focusing on His promises rather than your fears, you can find a sustaining hope that carries you through life's unknowns. Remember, God's plans for you are filled with purpose, even during these uncertain seasons.

Today, lean into God's hope and trust that He will carry you through difficult times. Allow His peace to fill your heart as you rest in His faithful hands.

Prayer: Lord, in moments of uncertainty, help me place my hope in You. Remind me that You are in control, even when the future feels unsure. Guide me through the unknown with faith and confidence in Your plan. Amen.

Affirmation: I find hope in God, even in the midst of uncertainty. I trust that He is guiding my steps, and His plans for me are filled with purpose. I lean on His promises and rest in His peace, knowing that He will carry me through every unknown.

December 23
Reflecting on God's Grace

"But he said to me, 'My grace is sufficient for you, for my power is made perfect in weakness.' Therefore I will boast all the more gladly about my weaknesses, so that Christ's power may rest on me."

(2 Corinthians 12:9, NIV)

Devotional Reflection

As the year comes to a close, reflecting on God's grace is essential. This year may have brought various challenges—emotional, spiritual, financial, or physical. Yet, through each obstacle, God's grace has been your anchor. His grace has been sufficient, providing strength when you felt weak and peace when the world seemed chaotic.

For Black women, who often navigate life's hurdles with resilience, it's vital to recognize that God's grace has been a constant source of support. As you reflect on moments of uncertainty, you'll see how God's grace provided exactly what you needed at the right time. Remember, grace isn't something you earn; it's freely given by a loving God who sees you and sustains you, even when the way forward feels unclear. Looking back on the year, acknowledge that it wasn't just your strength that carried you through—it was God's grace at work in every challenge.

Today, take a moment to reflect on how God's grace has seen you through this year's trials and triumphs. Let gratitude fill your heart as you consider the countless ways He has been your source of strength and peace.

Prayer: Lord, thank You for Your grace that has carried me through every challenge this year. I recognize that in moments of weakness, Your grace was sufficient and gave me the strength I needed. Help me to continue trusting in Your grace, knowing that it will sustain me in every season of life. Amen.

Affirmation: I reflect on God's grace with gratitude, knowing that His grace has carried me through every challenge this year. In my weakness, His strength has been made perfect. I trust in His grace to continue guiding me through all that lies ahead.

December 24
Embracing God's Plan for Your Future

"For I know the plans I have for you," declares the Lord, "plans to prosper you and not to harm you, plans to give you hope and a future."
                                        (Jeremiah 29:11, NIV)

Devotional Reflection

As we approach the end of the year, thoughts often turn to what lies ahead. The future may feel unclear, and the uncertainty can cause anxiety. Yet, God's promise is that He has a plan for you—a plan that is not only good but filled with hope. Even when you cannot see the details or understand the direction, God's purpose for your life is perfect. His wisdom far exceeds our understanding, and He is guiding you step by step, even in moments of doubt.

For black women who face unique challenges and pressures, trusting in God's plan is essential. Embracing His purpose for your future requires letting go of the need to control every outcome and trusting that God's plan is greater than your own. His timing is flawless, and His path for you is intentional, leading you toward growth, peace, and fulfillment. When you trust in God's plan, even when it's unclear, you are reminded that He sees the bigger picture, and His love for you ensures that His plan is always for your good.

Today, focus on surrendering your future to God's hands. Trust that He knows the best path for you, even when you can't see what lies ahead. Embrace His plan with confidence and hope.

Prayer: Lord, I surrender my future to You, trusting that Your plan for my life is perfect. Even when I can't see the way forward, I know that You are guiding me with love and wisdom. Help me to embrace Your plan for my future with faith, knowing that Your path is filled with hope and purpose. Amen.

Affirmation: I embrace God's plan for my future with faith and trust, knowing that His purpose for my life is perfect. Even when the path is unclear, I trust in His wisdom and timing, knowing that He is guiding me toward a future filled with hope.

December 25
Finding Joy in God's Promise of New Beginnings

"Therefore, if anyone is in Christ, the new creation has come: The old has gone, the new is here!" (2 Corinthians 5:17, NIV)

Devotional Reflection

On this Christmas Day, we celebrate the ultimate new beginning—the birth of Jesus Christ, our Savior. His arrival brought the promise of hope, redemption, and a fresh start for all of humanity. Through Christ, we are offered the gift of a new beginning, where the old is washed away, and we are made new. This promise of new life through Him brings immeasurable joy, especially in seasons when we are seeking renewal and transformation.

For black women, navigating life's challenges with grace and strength, the promise of new beginnings through Christ offers a powerful source of hope. No matter what has happened in the past, Christ's birth signifies that we can always start anew. His love renews us daily, giving us the opportunity to embrace new beginnings in our personal, spiritual, and emotional lives. Today, as you reflect on the significance of Christmas, celebrate the joy that comes with knowing that God's promise of renewal is yours through Christ.

Let this day be a reminder that through Christ, every day is filled with the hope of new beginnings. Embrace the joy and peace that comes with knowing that His grace has given you a fresh start, and trust in His promises for your future.

Prayer: Lord, thank You for the gift of new beginnings through Jesus Christ. As I celebrate His birth, I am filled with joy, knowing that Your promise of renewal and hope is mine through Him. Help me to embrace this new beginning with faith and gratitude, trusting in Your endless grace. Amen.

Affirmation: I find joy in God's promise of new beginnings through Christ. I celebrate the gift of hope, renewal, and transformation that He brings into my life. Each day is a fresh start, and I trust in His grace to lead me forward with joy and purpose.

December 26
Reflecting on the Power of Prayer

"The prayer of a righteous person is powerful and effective."

(James 5:16, NIV)

Devotional Reflection

As the year comes to a close, it's important to reflect on the moments when prayer has carried you through. Whether in times of joy, difficulty, or uncertainty, prayer has been your lifeline—connecting you to God's power, wisdom, and peace. For black women, whose strength is often drawn from faith, prayer is not only a source of comfort but a powerful tool for navigating life's challenges.

Looking back, you may see how prayer helped you find peace in the midst of storms, provided clarity when you were unsure, or opened doors that seemed impossible. Prayer has the ability to shift circumstances, strengthen your faith, and bring you closer to God. It has carried you through the valleys and helped you celebrate the mountaintops. Recognizing the impact of prayer reminds you that God is always near, listening and responding to the cries of your heart.

Today, reflect on the role prayer has played in your life this year. Consider the moments where you saw God's hand at work because of your prayers, and let that reflection inspire you to continue seeking Him through prayer in the year ahead.

Prayer: Lord, thank You for the power of prayer and the ways You have answered my prayers throughout this year. I reflect on Your faithfulness and the peace that prayer has brought into my life. Help me to continue seeking You in prayer, trusting that You hear me and are always working on my behalf. Amen.

Affirmation: I reflect on the power of prayer in my life, recognizing its impact throughout this year. Prayer has strengthened my faith, brought me peace, and allowed me to witness God's hand at work. I continue to trust in the power of prayer as I move forward, knowing that God hears me.

December 27
Hope for Healing

"He heals the brokenhearted and binds up their wounds."

(Psalm 147:3, NIV)

Devotional Reflection

As the year comes to an end, many of us are still holding on to hopes for healing—whether emotional, physical, or spiritual. You may have faced challenges this year that left you feeling wounded or weary, but the beauty of walking with God is knowing that healing is always within reach. God is not only capable of healing our bodies, but He also restores our hearts and spirits, bringing wholeness to every part of us.

For black women, who often carry so much on their shoulders, the need for healing may be deep. Perhaps you've been strong for others and now find yourself needing God's touch to heal areas of brokenness within you. Holding on to hope for healing is an act of faith, trusting that the same God who has brought you this far will continue to mend, restore, and rejuvenate you in the coming year.

Today, focus on holding on to that hope, knowing that God is the ultimate healer. Whether you're seeking healing from past trauma, emotional pain, physical illness, or spiritual dryness, trust that God is able to bring healing in His perfect time.

Prayer: Lord, I place my hope for healing in Your hands. Whether it's emotional, physical, or spiritual healing that I need, I trust that You are the one who can restore me fully. Thank You for being my healer and for the hope that You give me for the coming year. Help me to continue trusting in Your power to heal and make me whole. Amen.

Affirmation: I hold on to hope for healing, trusting that God is able to restore me emotionally, physically, and spiritually. I believe in His power to heal and make me whole, and I enter the new year with faith in His perfect plan for my healing.

December 28
Trusting God's Timing

"There is a time for everything, and a season for every activity under the heavens." (Ecclesiastes 3:1, NIV)

Devotional Reflection

Life often feels like a series of waiting periods—waiting for prayers to be answered, dreams to be realized, or breakthroughs to occur. As Black women, we are familiar with patience and perseverance, yet the uncertainty of timing can be one of the hardest aspects of faith to navigate. Trusting in God's timing means believing that everything will come together exactly when it's supposed to, even when it feels like things are moving too slowly or not at all.

God's timing is perfect, even when it doesn't align with our plans or desires. He sees the full picture when we can only see a part. Trusting in His timing invites us to rest in His peace, knowing that He is never late and that His plans are always for our good. Whether you're waiting for a career opportunity, healing, relationship breakthroughs, or personal growth, trust that God knows the best time to bring everything to fruition. As you reflect on this year, acknowledge the ways God's timing has been at work, even in the delays. Hold on to the assurance that everything will fall into place in His perfect time. Today, release any frustration or anxiety about timing and trust that God is working everything out according to His perfect plan for your life.

Prayer: Lord, help me trust in Your perfect timing. I believe everything will fall into place according to Your plan. Give me patience and peace as I wait for Your promises, reminding me that Your timing is always right. Amen.

Affirmation: I trust in God's perfect timing, knowing that everything will fall into place according to His plan. I release my worries about the future and rest in the assurance that God's timing is always for my good. I wait with patience and peace, confident that God's plans will come to fruition in His time.

December 29
Celebrating Your Resilience

"But the Lord stood at my side and gave me strength, so that through me the message might be fully proclaimed and all the Gentiles might hear it." (2 Timothy 4:17, NIV)

Devotional Reflection

As the year comes to a close, it's a time to look back and celebrate the resilience that has carried you through. You've faced challenges and obstacles that could have broken you, yet by God's grace, you've remained strong. Your resilience is a reflection of the strength God has provided. For Black women, who often bear many responsibilities, it's essential to pause and recognize how God has empowered you to endure and overcome.

Every hardship you've faced this year has contributed to your growth. Each trial was met with God's sustaining grace, equipping you to rise above. Even in moments of doubt or exhaustion, God stood by your side, giving you the strength you needed. Celebrating your resilience is an act of gratitude for the ways God has shown up in your life, helping you thrive in the face of adversity.

Today, take time to reflect on the resilience you've shown this year and the strength God has given you. Celebrate how far you've come, knowing it is by His power that you have persevered.

Prayer: Lord, I thank You for the resilience You have given me this year. In moments of struggle and hardship, You stood by my side and provided me with the strength to keep going. Help me to continue relying on Your strength in the future, and thank You for carrying me through every challenge. Amen.

Affirmation: I celebrate my resilience, knowing that God has given me the strength to overcome every challenge this year. I reflect on how far I've come, grateful for God's presence in my life, and I trust in His continued strength to guide me forward.

December 30
Ending the Year with Gratitude

"Give thanks in all circumstances; for this is God's will for you in Christ Jesus." (1 Thessalonians 5:18, NIV)

Devotional Reflection

As the year draws to a close, take a moment to reflect on the blessings, lessons, and growth you've experienced. Gratitude is a powerful way to wrap up the year, shifting your focus from challenges to moments of joy and breakthroughs. Although the year may have brought its share of struggles, it also offered opportunities to deepen your faith and character. For Black women, who often juggle various responsibilities, reflecting on God's goodness can provide peace and perspective.

Gratitude is an act of faith. It acknowledges that even in tough seasons, God was at work, teaching you valuable lessons and fostering growth. Whether through the support of loved ones, personal achievements, or quiet moments of peace, God's blessings have been part of your journey. As you conclude the year, let your heart be filled with gratitude—not just for the obvious blessings, but also for the growth that emerged from adversity.

Today, take time to thank God for all He has done this year. Reflect on both big and small blessings, and offer gratitude for the lessons learned along the way.

Prayer: Lord, I end this year with a heart full of gratitude. Thank You for every blessing, every lesson, and every moment of growth. Even in the challenges, I see Your hand at work in my life. Help me to carry this spirit of gratitude into the new year, always trusting in Your goodness and faithfulness. Amen.

Affirmation: I end this year with gratitude, thanking God for every blessing, lesson, and opportunity for growth. I recognize His goodness in every season and trust that His faithfulness will continue to guide me in the year to come. My heart is full of thankfulness for all that God has done.

December 31
Entering the New Year with Hope and Faith

"For I know the plans I have for you," declares the Lord, "plans to prosper you and not to harm you, plans to give you hope and a future."
(Jeremiah 29:11, NIV)

Devotional Reflection

As you stand on the threshold of a new year, the anticipation of what lies ahead can fill your heart with hope. The past year, with all its challenges and victories, has prepared you for this moment. Entering the new year with faith means trusting in God's promises—knowing that He holds your future in His hands and has great plans for you. Hope is rooted in the confidence that, no matter what the new year brings, God is already there, working everything out for your good.

For black women, the new year represents a fresh start, an opportunity to leave behind the burdens of the past and embrace the possibilities of tomorrow. It's a time to renew your faith in God's purpose for your life, trusting that He will guide you through whatever comes next. As you reflect on the past year and look ahead, let your faith grow stronger. God's promises remain true, and His love for you is constant, ensuring that the new year will bring growth, blessings, and opportunities for deeper trust in Him.

Today, enter the new year with hope and faith, believing that God's plans for you are filled with purpose and promise. Embrace the future with confidence, knowing that He is walking with you every step of the way.

Prayer: Lord, as I enter the new year, fill me with hope and faith in Your promises. Thank You for guiding me through the past year. Help me to walk in faith, trusting that Your plans for me are good. Amen.

Affirmation: I enter the new year with hope and faith, trusting in God's promises for my future. I embrace the possibilities and opportunities that the new year will bring, confident that God is guiding my path. His plans for me are good, and I walk forward with joy and expectation for what's to come.

Chapter 5
Year-End Conclusion

Final Reflection

As the year draws to a close, this is a perfect moment to pause and reflect on the journey you've taken. This year has been filled with moments of joy, growth, and perhaps even struggles, but through it all, you've made it. Each day has brought new lessons, challenges, and blessings, shaping you into the woman you are today. Looking back, you can see the hand of God guiding you, providing strength when you felt weak, and offering peace when the world around you seemed overwhelming.

Take time to acknowledge your growth—spiritually, emotionally, and mentally. Consider the moments when you leaned into your faith, trusting God even when the path was unclear. Think about the prayers answered, the strength found in difficult situations, and the grace that carried you through each day. Whether this year brought personal victories, quiet moments of reflection, or hard-won lessons, know that God has been with you every step of the way.

The challenges you've faced have not been in vain. Every trial has brought with it the opportunity to deepen your relationship with God and strengthen your faith. Maybe you've learned to trust more fully in God's timing, or perhaps you've discovered the power of prayer in new ways. Even in moments of uncertainty or pain, there have been blessings—whether through personal growth or seeing God's faithfulness at work in your life.

Celebrate the journey you've completed. This is not just the end of a year but a marker of how far you've come. You are not the same person who began this journey—your faith has grown, and you are stronger, wiser, and more connected to God. As you look ahead to the future, carry with you the lessons learned and the faith that has sustained you. Trust that the same God who has brought you through this year will continue to guide you in the days to come, leading you toward even greater spiritual growth and renewal.

Let this time of reflection remind you of the countless blessings that have come your way. From small daily mercies to life-changing moments, God's love and faithfulness have been with you. Use this reflection to fuel your hope for the future, knowing that your journey with God is far from over. Each day brings new opportunities to grow in faith, deepen your trust in Him, and continue the path He has set before you.

Encouragement for the Future

As you prepare to move forward from this devotional, know that your journey of faith is only just beginning. The time you've spent reflecting, praying, and growing spiritually has laid a strong foundation for the days and years ahead. God has worked in your heart this past year, shaping and molding you into a woman of strength, faith, and grace. Now, as you step into the future, hold on to the lessons you've learned and the truths you've discovered.

You are empowered to continue walking in faith. The moments of doubt or fear that may arise cannot diminish the power of God working within you. Whatever lies ahead—whether moments of joy or challenges yet to come—you are not alone. God is guiding your steps, just as He has done every day of your life. Trust in His plan, knowing that He has equipped you with everything you need to handle the future with confidence and courage.

Remember, your faith is a living, growing force. It is not confined to the pages of this book or the prayers you've spoken in the past year. It is with you in your everyday moments—whether you're facing a difficult decision, offering encouragement to someone else, or simply going about your daily routine. Every prayer you've prayed, every scripture you've meditated on, and every step you've taken in faith has strengthened you for the road ahead.

Let hope be your constant companion as you move forward. God's promises for your life are still unfolding, and the best is yet to come. When uncertainty or challenges arise, remember the faithfulness of God you've experienced this year. Hold on to the hope that He is working all things for your good, even when the path seems unclear. Trust in His timing, and continue to seek His guidance in every area of your life.

You are equipped to thrive, not just survive. The strength you've developed, the resilience you've built, and the faith you've deepened are all tools God has given you to face whatever the future holds. Lean on Him, and continue to grow, learn, and trust in the beautiful plans He has for you.

As you continue your journey, carry with you the truth that God's love for you is unwavering. His grace will sustain you, His peace will surround you, and His purpose for your life will guide you every step of the way. You are not only capable of handling what comes next—you are empowered by God to flourish in it.

Believe in His promises.
Walk forward in faith.

© Tiffany Barker